KURA

KURA

Design and

Tradition of the Japanese Storehouse

Teiji Itoh

adapted by
Charles S. Terry

photographs by
Kiyoshi Takai

KODANSHA INTERNATIONAL LTD. IN COOPERATION WITH **TANKŌSHA LTD.**
Tokyo, New York & San Francisco   Kyoto

Distributors:

UNITED STATES: *Harper & Row, Publishers, Inc.*
10 East 53rd Street, New York, New York 10022

CANADA: *Fitzhenry & Whiteside Limited*
150 Lesmill Road, Don Mills, Ontario

CENTRAL AND SOUTH AMERICA: *Feffer & Simons Inc.*
31 Union Square, New York, New York 10003

BRITISH COMMONWEALTH (*excluding Canada and the Far East*):
George Allen & Unwin, Ltd.
40 Museum Street, London WC1A 1LU

EUROPE: *Boxerbooks Inc.*
Limmatstrasse 111, 8031 Zurich

THAILAND: *Central Department Store Ltd.*
306 Silom Road, Bangkok

HONG KONG: *Books for Asia Ltd.*
379 Prince Edward Road, Kowloon

THE FAR EAST: *Japan Publications Trading Company*
P.O. Box 5030, Tokyo International, Tokyo

Published by Kodansha International Ltd., 2-12-21 Otowa, Bunkyo-ku, Tokyo 112, Japan and Kodansha International/USA, Ltd., 10 East 53rd Street, New York, New York 10022 and 44 Montgomery Street, San Francisco, California 94104.
Copyright © 1973 by Kodansha International Ltd.
All rights reserved. Printed in Japan.

LCC 73–81112
ISBN 0–87011–217–1
JBC 1052–784203–2361

First edition, 1973

Japanese edition, Nihon no kura, *published 1973 by Tankōsha Ltd., Kuramaguchi-agaru, Horikawa-dōri, Kita-ku, Kyoto.*

Book design of Japanese edition by Ikkō Tanaka.

Contents

Translator's Note

WHEN on the title page of a book one reads that the book has been "adapted" from the Japanese, rather than "translated" from the Japanese, it is a very safe assumption that the translator adapted because he was unable to translate. There can be many legitimate reasons. Often there is no really satisfactory English word, as in the case of the names of many fish, birds, plants, and trees. More often still, a straight translation would be unintelligible to most English speakers, and the translator must decide whether to add a few words of explanation or omit a word or two from the original.

Unfortunately, the more Japanese the subject, the more difficult to discuss it in English without becoming involved in so many peripheral explanations that the main point is obscured. In the case of the present volume, the translation problem begins at the very beginning and continues to the end, for there is no completely satisfactory word in English for the Japanese word *kura*. Nineteenth-century visitors to Japan used the term *godown*, but this word, derived from Malay, does not seem sufficiently current today. The word *barn* was suggested but rejected because so many kura were built in places other than farms. *Warehouse* is suitable for some types of kura, but not for most. I eventually fell back on *storehouse*, which is at least accurate, even though it lacks the same connotations as kura.

The reason for not simply using the Japanese word throughout was primarily that the repeated appearance of foreign words tends to make an English text unreadable. There are so many other words in this book that must be given in romanized Japanese that it seemed unwise to use the Japanese term for a word that appears in nearly every sentence. The printed page might, I feared, look like a stream of English running through a meadow of Japanese. Furthermore, kura is a word that most English speakers unfamiliar with Japanese can be counted upon to mispronounce. The *r*, which is sounded by flapping the tip of the tongue once against the alveolar ridge, does not exist in English (the nearest sound is a *d*, not an *r*), and there is a strong probability that the *ku* will be pronounced like the *cu* in cure, whereas it ought to be an abbreviated *coo*. For better or worse, I chose to use storehouse.

The reader will observe that the important word *dozō*, which signifies a storehouse with clay and plaster walls, defeated me, partly because it came to be used of many buildings that were not storehouses and was, in effect, the designation of a method of construction not employed in the Occident. In this case, fortunately, the pronunciation presents no difficulty, provided the reader will remember that the second *o* is drawn out a little longer than the first.

As hinted above, I have added to Mr. Itoh's text numerous passages explaining Japanese objects or phenomena that might not otherwise be clear to Western readers. At the same time, I have eliminated references to a number of obscure Japanese historical sources and have greatly abbreviated certain portions of the text that would require so much additional explanation as to constitute serious interruptions or digressions. These changes were made at the author's request and with his consent, but on my own judgment, and if I have either omitted or added too much or too little, the responsibility is solely mine.

CHARLES S. TERRY

July 3, 1973

Preface

KURA, storehouses like the ones shown in this book, are no longer built today. Indeed, at least one important early type, the log cabin, or *azekura*, has not been built for nearly a thousand years, and the only examples still standing are those at the Nikko shrines. Most farmers who still have wooden storehouses of any type would be happy to sell them, and the few people who still use plaster storehouses do so because they happen to have them. No one would consider building a new one, and if someone should take it upon himself to try, he would have a difficult time finding carpenters and plasterers able to do the work. Furthermore, a traditional plaster storehouse would doubtless cost far more today than one made of steel and concrete.

In a sense this book is no more than a fond farewell to the fast-disappearing kura of the past, a nostalgic tribute of interest primarily to those who have lived with storehouses and loved them. Still, it is precisely when the creations of men are perishing that people begin to give serious consideration to their true value. If Japanese storehouses had no value other than the purely functional, they could simply be discarded. I think, however, that they have a beauty that transcends function, and it is for this reason that others and I are laboring to prevent them from passing into oblivion. We see the storehouse not merely as a utilitarian form of architecture but as something wrapped in history and fable, a vestige of a now-vanished way of life and the legacy of an ancient culture. By becoming acquainted with the Japanese storehouse of the past, the reader can better understand the solidarity and continuity of human life in the Japanese Archipelago.

This book is the cooperative effort of three persons. Kiyoshi Takai had the task of portraying the Japanese storehouse and its environment in photographs, and to do so he covered the Japanese countryside with boundless energy. Shigenobu Nakayama was in charge of the architectural drawings, many of which are sectional diagrams in perspective that display not only his fine grasp of architecture but an exceptional ability as an illustrator. I myself wrote the text and determined the general composition, attempting as I did so to emphasize the historical and cultural significance of the traditional storehouse.

I am grateful to the many individuals and religious institutions who allowed us to visit, examine, and photograph their storehouses, and I extend my deepest thanks to Shirō Usui, Kōshirō Ozasa, and Sei Aoyagi of the Tankō-sha publishing company for their generous assistance.

TEIJI ITOH

March 20, 1973

5. *Sutra Repository*

The sutra case is an interesting variety of *kura* known as *rintenzō*, or "revolving kura." The entire Buddhist canon was stored in the octagonal structure, and turning the case around one time was thought to have the same religious merit as reading all the scriptures. (See plates, pages 112–13.)

Onjō-ji, Ōtsu, Shiga Prefecture

6–7. *Mishine-no-mikura in the Inner Shrine*

Like the Mike-no-mikura (shown on pages 108–9), this is one of the minor buildings of Ise Shrine. A rice storehouse, it is a smaller version of the main shrine building itself and indicates the close architectural relationship of early storehouses to religious buildings. This building lacks the veranda that surrounds the main building, but architectural historians usually consider that the veranda was a later addition, and that this small storehouse shows a purer version of the prehistoric form. (See diagram, page 31.)

Ise Shrine, Ise, Mie Prefecture

8–9. *Raised-floor storehouses*

Storehouses in the Amami Islands have floors as much as 2 meters off the ground, and the walls lean out so far from the columns that they are virtually extensions of the floor, though the latter consists only of the area within the four posts. (See diagram, pages 66–67, and plates, pages 124–27.)

Yamatohama, Amami-Ōshima, Kagoshima Prefecture

10–11. *Stone storehouse*

The storehouse is the building to the left. Though it appears to be stone, the structure is actually of wood, and the outer stone wall is a protective sheathing. (See diagram, page 78, and plates, pages 150–51.)

Watanabe family, Utsunomiya, Tochigi Prefecture

12–13. *Dozō storehouse*

This storehouse, belonging to the Saffron Sake Company, is used for household goods rather than sake. It is one of the most ornately decorated buildings of its style still standing. (See plate, page 211.)

Nagaoka, Niigata Prefecture

14–15. *Sake storehouse*

Some sake storehouses were traditionally used for storage, but others were used as breweries. There is no difference in the outward appearance. (See plate, page 202.)

Fushimi, Kyoto

16–17. *Dozō storehouses*

To protect the outer plaster walls from heavy rain or damage from other sources, many *dozō* were covered with tiles, and the seams between the tiles were covered with white plaster rounded on the top. The plaster strips sealed the joints and concealed the nails with which the tiles were affixed. Such walls are called *namako* walls. (See plate, pages 208–9.)

Yoda family, Matsuzaki, Shizuoka Prefecture

18–19. *Dozō shop*

When buildings of the *dozō* type were used as shops, the front of the first floor was usually one large opening, which could be secured at night with sliding plaster-covered doors. The shop was on the first floor, and the second floor was ordinarily used as storage space or as sleeping quarters for employees. (See plate, page 223.)

Harada Rice Store, Kawagoe, Saitama Prefecture

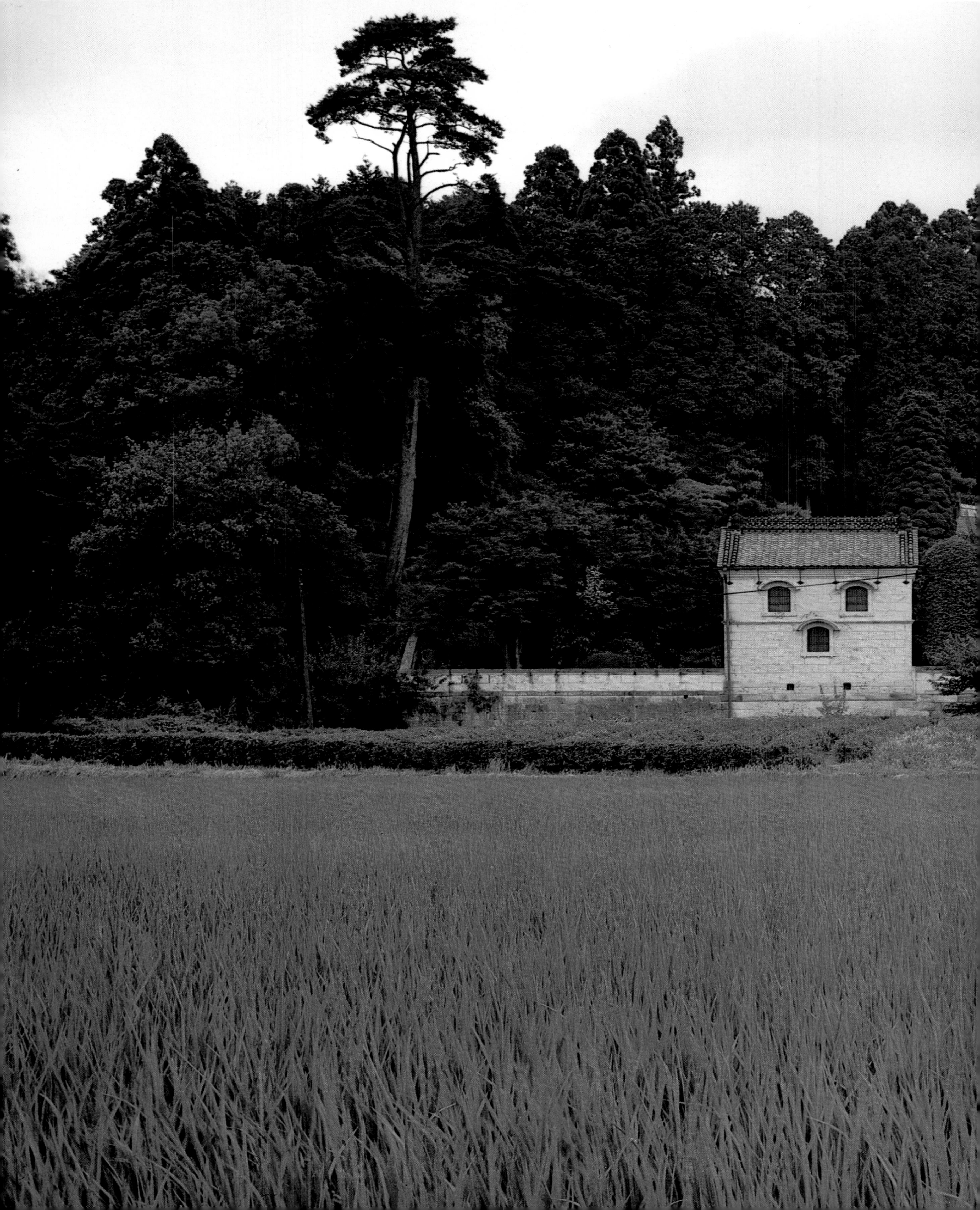

The Nature of
Japanese Storehouses

THE HISTORY of Japanese storehouses, or kura, goes back to the Jōmon period, which lasted from the seventh or eighth millenium B.C. to around the third century B.C. This was a preagricultural age, in which the people lived by hunting, fishing, and gathering wild foodstuffs, and the economy was basically hand-to-mouth, but it appears that in at least a few tribes it was the practice to build storehouses where fruits and nuts could be kept for a time. These structures were, of course, very small: they were, in effect, diminutive versions of the houses in which people lived, which usually consisted of shallow pits covered with thatched roofs. Typical examples have been found at a Late Jōmon site in Maeike, Okayama Prefecture, where, according to the findings of the archaeologist Yoshirō Kondō and his colleagues, the diameter was only from 1 meter to 1.5 meters. With a typical pit house roof, a hut of this size would be too small for a human being to enter, but it furnished ample shelter for earthenware pots containing nuts, berries, and the like. Some of the pots at Maeike contained the remains of chestnuts and acorns.

The presence of these tiny storehouses leads to one or two speculations. The end of the Jōmon period was the last stage of the hunting and gathering economy, which is to say the period in which the latent insufficiency of this mode of life was becoming apparent. Tools and methods of hunting and fishing had been improved, and the resulting increase in efficiency had made possible a growth in population. But in an age when people had to live on the natural bounty of a given area, an increase in efficiency and population constituted a threat to continued life. After the middle of the Jōmon period we find more and more clay images of an earth mother, and this means not only the beginning of earth mother worship but the spread of a sense of crisis with respect to the source of livelihood.

Still, the Jōmon people were practical enough not to rely entirely on their worship of an earth mother to keep them in food. They also built their small storehouses and stored away their nuts to tide them over in lean seasons or after natural disasters. One can argue, then, that both the worship of the earth mother and the building of storehouses reflected a desire for stability, as well as a sense of fear for the future.

To be sure, the pit house storehouses are rare among Jōmon remains, and they have been found only in the western half of Japan. This could conceivably be accidental, but the eminent archaeologist Kiyoo Yamauchi thinks not. In his opinion, the people in eastern Japan were spared the need for storehouses by the availability of salmon and other easily preserved fish. He theorizes that from the Tenryū River in Shizuoka Prefecture eastward (on the Sea of Japan side, from Tottori Prefecture eastward), salmon and sea trout swam up the rivers from the sea, but that in western Japan, where such food was rarely available, the people made up for the lack by saving up nuts in earthen vessels and storing the vessels in storehouses. The presence or absence of storehouses can consequently be taken to indicate a difference in natural environment and in the mode of life. In other words, there were two different cultures.

Around the third century B.C. Japan entered the Yayoi period, and the history of storehouses took on a new dimension. The Yayoi people knew how to make metal tools and to cultivate rice, and they constructed raised-floor storehouses as granaries. A typical example has been reconstructed at the famous Yayoi site in Toro, in the city of Shizuoka (pages 122–23). It is basically a wooden box, made of heavy boards and set on eight pillars that are planted in the ground. The roof, which is thatched, is gabled, and the boards forming the walls intersect in log-cabin style. Buildings of this type were, of course, used for storing rice.

Three important points are to be observed about the Yayoi storehouses. The first is that the raised-floor style is much more advanced technically than the style of the pit houses in which people lived. Pit houses could be, and in the Jōmon period were, built without metal tools, but metal saws, chisels, and axes were needed to prepare the wood and make the joints for the raised-floor storehouses. The raised-floor storehouse cannot therefore be regarded as merely an adjunct to the house. On the contrary, it was probably the most important building in any given community. Appropriately, it was also the loftiest.

The second point to be noted is that the raised-floor storehouse has a pronounced resemblance to the Aramatsuri Shrine in the Inner Shrine at Ise, the shrine of the Sun Goddess, Amaterasu Ōmikami. The

Aramatsuri Shrine no longer exists, but its appearance in the middle ages can be discerned with great accuracy from written sources. The shrine had certain symbolic architectural features not found in the storehouse, such as extended bargeboards (*chigi*) and cross-logs over the ridge (*katsuogi*), but the basic structure was the same. As is well known, the buildings at the Ise Shrine have been rebuilt periodically since the seventh or eighth century and are thought to retain their original form to a large degree (pages 6–7, 108–9). The Aramatsuri Shrine can therefore be considered as a developed version of the primitive Yayoi storehouse, and for this reason many architectural historians believe that the storehouse represents an archetype that developed, on the one hand, into the various types of utilitarian storehouses and granaries of later times and, on the other, into the treasure-houses and sanctuaries of Shinto shrines. This suggests that the Yayoi raised-floor storehouse, aside from serving as a place for keeping grain, had some sort of religious significance, albeit a primitive one.

The third point is that whereas from all we know the typical pit house had a hipped or a hipped and gabled roof, the raised-floor storehouse had a simple gabled roof of the inverted-V type. Since the middle ages the shape of a building's roof has had little to do with the building's prestige, but in earlier times the form of the roof indicated rank. It is no accident that the main sanctuaries of the Ise, Izumo, and Sumiyoshi shrines all had gabled roofs: clearly this was the accepted roof form for buildings of the most sacred nature. In ancient times the word *azumaya* (東屋) was used to indicate the houses of ordinary people as opposed to those of the nobility; architecturally it signified a building with a hipped roof instead of a gabled roof. Putting these various factors together, one arrives at the conclusion that the gabled raised-floor storehouse had a social significance over and above its function as a granary.

In this connection, it should be noted that in farming communities even today there is a harvest celebration that, according to ethnologists, is the last of several annual religious observances connected with rice production. It is divided into two parts, one of which involves the presentation of new rice to the gods, and the other of which commemorates the completion of the harvest. Since the seventeenth century or earlier this has been a family celebration, but in ancient times it is thought to have been a community festival. Quite possibly it goes back to the Yayoi period, and one suspects that the new rice was first offered to the gods and then placed in the storehouse, where part of it was reserved as a sacred treasure or as communal property. In the following year, some of the rice would be used as seed for a new crop.

At Tsuyama in Okayama Prefecture, archaeologists have excavated a group of five Yayoi period pit houses that are thought to have been the living and working quarters of a farming group. Located near the bottom of a hill, they are arranged in a horseshoe pattern around an open area. One of the houses is distinctly larger than the others, and it is not difficult to imagine that this was the residence of a community leader who watched over communal property and also took charge of religious matters.

Slightly up the hill from the five houses and separated from them by a ditch was a raised-floor building. By comparison with other sites, it seems certain that this was a storehouse, and the ditch probably existed for the purpose of dividing holy ground from the rest of the area.

The implication is that in the Yayoi period these raised-floor buildings were not only storehouses for grain but residences of the gods, and that their high floors and gabled roofs symbolized their religious character. They had to be practical, and they were, in the sense that their raised floors and boarded walls protected the interior from the damp climate. Some of them even had large wooden disks set between the supporting posts and the floors in order to keep out rats. Beyond practicality, however, the earlier storehouses appear to have had religious significance, and in later times the storehouse continued to be a symbol of rank or status.

The Japanese word for storehouse, *kura* (倉), is often pronounced *gura* when it is compounded with another word indicating the type of storehouse, as in *komegura* (米倉), meaning "rice storehouse," or *itagura* (板倉), meaning "board-wall storehouse." As these two examples show, there are two basic types of compounds containing *-kura* or *-gura*, one indicating what is kept in the storehouse and another telling what the storehouse is made of. Curiously enough, when the word for a type of storehouse is used as a family or place name, as is by no means rare, the *kura* pronunciation is normally used, even though it is *gura* in the common noun. For *itagura*, for example, there is the family name Itakura.

Aside from the many compound words formed from *kura*, there are many more particularized terms formed with the Sino-Japanese pronunciations of the three characters normally used to write *kura*. These are *sō* (倉), *zō* (蔵), and *ko* (庫). The characters in question had different meanings one from the other in Chinese, but they all came under the blanket term *kura* in Japanese, and the Chinese distinctions were to a large degree lost. Still, the basic meanings are reflected in quite a few terms; *sō* is apt to be a granary of some kind, *zō* a place where treasures are kept, and *ko* a place for vehicles, arms, or implements. No one has counted all the words historically used in Japan for various kinds of storehouses, but a list of fairly common ones would run to several dozen.

As to the etymology of kura, it appears in ancient times to have meant not only a place for putting things, but a place where people reside or sit. In the imperial palace, for example, the raised platform on which the emperor sits on ceremonial occasions is the *taka-mi-kura* (高御座), or "lofty sacred kura." At the Kyoto imperial palace, this is an octagonal dais resting on a 1-meter-high platform measuring 7.2 meters by 6.6 meters. The idea of kura as a residence or place to sit is also preserved in a few other compounds (in which kura is written with the character *za*, 座), but it would not be a mistake to say that nearly all words derived from kura denote some kind of storehouse.

It is important to note that storehouses were by no means confined to the farmers. Fishermen had their beach storehouses (*hamagura*, 浜蔵) and net storehouses (*amigura*, 網蔵); Shinto shrines had their sacred storehouses (*imikura*, 斎蔵) and miniature-shrine storehouses (*mikoshigura*, 御輿蔵); Buddhist temples had their scripture storehouses (*kyōzō*, 経蔵) and treasure storehouses (*hōzō*, 宝蔵). There were pawnshop storehouse (*shichigura*, 質蔵), gold storehouses (*kanagura*, 金蔵), ammunition storehouses (*enshōgura*, 焔硝蔵), bean paste storehouses (*misogura*, 味噌蔵), sake storehouses (*sakagura*, 酒蔵), and so on.

Not all of these types were used exclusively for storage. The sake storehouse, for instance, was usually also the factory in which the sake was produced, and the same was true for bean paste storehouses, soy sauce factories (*shōyugura*, 醤油蔵), yeast storehouses (*kōjigura*, 麹蔵), and indigo storehouses (*aigura*, 藍蔵). There were storehouselike buildings that were used as houses or shops or both; after the middle of the seventeenth century the storehouse-shop (*misegura*, 店蔵) was popular in Edo and other cities and towns, and a number of examples are still to be seen in the Tokyo area and northeast Japan. There was even a special storehouse-style building known as a *zashikigura* (座敷蔵), which was the part of the house used for entertaining honored guests. *Zashikigura* were built as parts of houses in cities all over the country in Tokugawa times (seventeenth-nineteenth centuries), and they have been preserved in considerable numbers in the towns and villages of Yamagata Prefecture and the Izu Peninsula.

An essay written in 1831 by Yamada Keiō lists a number of storehouse-type buildings that existed in Edo in the early nineteenth century, and they include a *tōfu* ("bean curd") shop, a barrel maker's shop, a fish store, and a hairdresser's shop. Another nineteenth-century source informs us that there were even a few Shinto shrines and Buddhist temples built in the storehouse style. Nearly all of these have disappeared, but the main building at the Yosegi Shrine in Shinagawa, Tokyo, was still standing until about 1950, as was the Sodegasaki Shrine in Shimo-Ōsaki, also in Tokyo.

It would be a mistake to consider the kura as nothing more than a place where grain or valuables were kept, for it played a much larger part in the history of Japanese culture and Japanese architecture than the word *storehouse* would suggest. It represents an aggregate of architectural forms that functioned not only as storehouses, but as factories, warehouses, shops, residences, and even temples. Indeed, the kura may be considered not only as an important cultural legacy but as an essential component in the traditional Japanese mode of living.

The Function of
Storehouses

Instruments of Government

Storehouses played a major role in the establishment of the Japanese state. Among the earliest of the important governmental institutions were the Sacred Storehouse (*imikura*, 斎蔵), where religious treasures were held; the Great Storehouse (*Ōkura*, 大蔵), which housed the possessions of the state; and the Inner Storehouse (*Naizō*, or *Uchikura*, 内蔵), where private possessions of the emperor were kept. Even today, the Ministry of Finance is known as the Ōkura-shō (大蔵省), or, literally, the "Department of the Great Storehouse." The ministry became a modern governmental agency only in 1869, but its prototypes go back to the eighth century, and the Department of the Great Storehouse was one of the eight administrative divisions provided for in the earliest legal codes. It probably goes back to prehistoric times, and it has always been the official financial branch of the government.

To judge from the name, the original department was centered around one or more large storehouses where goods submitted in taxes were collected and stored. Until A.D. 645, when the Taika Reform took place, the emperor held a number of pieces of land under his direct control, and these were called *miyake* (屯倉), a word written with characters meaning "outpost storehouse." This suggests that a storehouse was the central installation in each of the emperor's private holdings. In the *Harima fudoki* [Local history of Harima], which dates from around the seventh century, it is specifically stated that a *miyake* in the county of Shikama was a building where rice harvested from the fields was stored.

It is clear from the ancient terminology that storehouses played an important role in government, both in the capital and in the provinces. One wonders what type of structures these storehouses were. The historian Toranosuke Nishioka, quoting a passage from chapter 14 of the *Chronicles of Japan*, considers that they must have been raised-floor structures. The passage deals with Korean events and states that remnants of a Paekche army that had been defeated by Koguryo gathered together and lived "under the storehouses" at the miyake in the Japanese colony of Mimana. This, coupled with the fact that the storehouses of the Yayoi period and most of those in Shinto shrines and Buddhist temples of the early historical age were of the raised-floor type, suggests that the miyake, and perhaps other government storehouses, were of the same type. The passage quoted from the *Chronicles* is not conclusive, however, because the expression rendered here as "under the storehouses" can also be construed to mean "in the vicinity of the storehouses."

The Sacred Storehouse, *imikura* (斎蔵), existed long before the Great Storehouse. Indeed, records say that it was established in the time of Emperor Jimmu, the mythical first ruler in the imperial line. It is impossible to say just when this was, but certainly the Sacred Storehouse was the earliest of the three great government storehouses. In it were kept the articles and implements used in national religious ceremonies, but that was not all: the storehouse also contained government properties and personal properties of the emperor, for this was an age in which there was no clear differentiation between religion, government, and the imperial institution. The keepers of the Sacred Storehouse were the Imibe Clan, which also had charge of religious celebrations at the court.

During the reign of the Emperor Richū (400–405), the Inner Storehouse was divided from the Sacred Storehouse. Religious articles remained in the Sacred Storehouse, but government and imperial possessions were moved into the new storehouse, which was under the supervision of an immigrant from China named Achi-no-omi and an immigrant from the Korean kingdom of Paekche named Wani. According to the *Kogo shūi* [Gleanings from ancient writings], compiled in 807 by Imibe no Hironari, during the reign of the Emperor Yūryaku (456–79), the Great Storehouse was set up to house government properties, and from that time on the Inner Storehouse was used only for imperial goods.

In this fashion the three principal economic organs of the pre-Taika government were set up. This process reflects the gradual division of governmental functions into a religious or ceremonial branch, an imperial branch, and an administrative branch. In overall charge of the three storehouses was the Soga Clan, which used its position to such advantage that in the sixth and early seventh centuries its power exceeded that of the imperial clan.

In 701 a legal code based on that of T'ang China was promulgated, and the Great Storehouse became one of the eight great divisions of the bureaucracy. Thereafter, it may properly be spoken of as the Treasury, though, as we have seen, the name *Ōkura* was retained. During the Heian period (794–1185) the Treasury contained one block of office buildings and eight blocks of storehouses within the imperial palace grounds in Kyoto. During this age the functions of the Sacred Storehouse and Inner Storehouse were taken over by the Bureau of the Inner Storehouse (*Naizō-ryō*, 内蔵寮) in the Department of Imperial Affairs (*Nakatsukasa-shō*, 中務省). Herein were stored not only gold, silver, and precious objects belonging to the imperial household but also tribute brought from other countries and even the clothing and personal possessions of the emperor and empress.

It should be clear from the above that the storehouse was not merely a building in which sacred articles and government belongings were kept but a symbolic concept that underlay the formation and development of several important governmental institutions. We know little about the architectural form of these government storehouses, but most likely they resembled the log-cabin and board-wall types that have been preserved in temples and shrines of the eighth and ninth centuries. (See pages 105–7.)

As the bureaucracy expanded and grew more complicated, the importance of the central government's storehouses as storehouses diminished. In the Kamakura and Muromachi periods (1185–1573), the Director of Storehouses (*kura-bugyō*, 蔵奉行) had charge of such things as collecting taxes from sake stores and moneylending houses and managing government documents. He had no particular connection with storehouse facilities as such. In the Edo period (1603–1868) an office with the same title supervised the accounting for the shogun's rice storehouses and collected or disbursed rice, but its direct connection with the storehouses was slight. In effect, titles containing the term *kura* came to signify some sort of financial or economic function not necessarily involved with storehouses. This, however, should not obscure the close connection between the storehouse and the creation and development of the bureaucratic structure of government.

Storage of Grain and Treasure

Obviously, the storehouse was from the beginning a place where things were stored. It does not follow, however, that all places where things were stored were referred to as kura. In general, this term was reserved for buildings in which items of special value were stored. More ordinary things were kept in outbuildings, *naya* (納屋), or sheds, *koya* (小屋), which were normally much simpler in structure than the kura. There are rice sheds (*momigoya*, 籾小屋), woodsheds (*kinaya*, 木納屋), ash sheds (*haigoya*, 灰小屋; the ash was used for fertilizer), and many other types, and in the various Japanese dialects, there is an immense number of terms signifying storage places that are not in a class with kura.

In short, the kura was intended to house valuable goods, and it was consequently constructed more strongly than the outbuildings and sheds used for things that were considered commonplace. This was true even in the Yayoi period, for in that age rice represented the first valuable agricultural product that human beings in the Japanese Archipelago had produced. Rice not only made daily life possible but created a food surplus that made other production and cultural activity possible. Consequently, as mentioned earlier, the raised-floor storehouses in which rice was kept were of higher architectural quality than the pit houses in which people lived. It was thus not without reason that these storehouses furnished the basic style for the houses built to shelter the gods. Nor is it surprising that as a social hierarchy developed the raised-floor buildings were lofty not only in the physical sense but in social prestige as well.

In the *Utsubo monogatari* [Tales of Utsubo], written in the tenth century, Minamoto no Shitagō, a poet and scholar, in describing the luxury of the house of Tanematsu, a rich man in Kii Province, said: "The mansion is surrounded by an earthen wall eight *chō* [roughly fifteen hundred meters] long, and along each of the four sides there are 40 storehouses with cypress-bark roofs, making a total of 160 storehouses. Within these, the private possessions of the wife, such as silk twill, brocade, cotton material, raw silk, and gauzy silk, are piled to the ridgepoles." Here the number of

MISHINE-NO-MIKURA
Ise Shrine, Ise, Mie Prefecture
Plate, pages 6–7

the storehouses and the richness of the articles housed therein are clearly used as symbols of great wealth and exalted position.

Before modern times the most important source of income for the government was a tax in kind assessed on rice grown throughout the country. Over the centuries the form and structure of the tax system varied, but the principal tax was collected in the form of rice, and the rice was kept in storehouses. From ancient times on, there were storehouses throughout the country for the storage of government rice. These were called *shōsō* (正倉), or "true storehouses," from the fact that the rice tax itself was called the "true tax," *shōzei* (正税). Aside from *shōsō*, there were temporary storehouses, *shakusō* (借倉), which served the same purpose but were of less sturdy construction.

According to the *Shōsō-in monjo* [Documents of the Shōsō-in], during the Nara period (710–94) there were 208 shōsō in Suruga Province (part of the present Shizuoka Prefecture) alone. These included 7 clay storehouses and 201 wooden storehouses. In addition, there were 22 temporary storehouses. The principal contents were unhulled rice and dried cooked rice, plus a small amount of millet. Around the same time there were in the Kyushu section of Bungo Province (modern Oita Prefecture) 17 shōsō, 1 temporary storehouse, and 1 storehouse for public welfare. The difference in the number of storehouses in the two locations probably means that the rice in Suruga was for national use, while that in Bungo was for local distribution.

With the coming of Buddhism to Japan in the sixth century, there appeared in Buddhist monasteries storehouses where temple treasures were kept. These were called *hōzō* (宝蔵) or *hōko* (宝庫). An interesting variant was the sutra repository, *kyōzō* (経蔵) or *kyōko* (経庫, pages 105–7), where sutras and other Buddhist scriptures were kept. These were mostly one-story buildings, but occasionally they had two stories, in which case they were called *kyōrō* (経楼), or "sutra towers." A good example is the Sutra Tower at the Hōryū-ji, which dates from the eighth century (page 115).

The earliest Buddhist storehouses were of two types. One was a traditional raised-floor storehouse with log-cabin walls, surmounted by a Chinese-style tile roof; the other was a simple post-and-beam structure with heavy wooden walls. Occasionally a storehouse was walled with clay and plaster, as at the Kōfū-zō in the Hōryū-ji (page 114).

The log-cabin type, *azekura*, consisted of a box made from timbers of triangular section, and was set on columns. The building had either a tile or a cypress-bark roof. Excellent examples are two eighth-century storehouses that have been preserved at the Tōshōdai-ji, a monastery in Nara (pages 105–7). Each of these has a square plan, one measuring about 41.7 square meters in area, and the other about 24.1 square meters. Their floors are set at a height of about 1.7 meters, and their roofs, which are tiled, have eaves extending from 1 to 1.5 meters. Though the buildings differ somewhat in scale, in other respects they are virtually identical. In the course of repairs carried out in 1959, pieces of brocade, silk twill, banners, scriptures, mask fragments, sculpture fragments, and an incense burner were found between the ceiling and the roof. It is considered that most of these fragments were brought there by rats, but the selection indicates the type of articles that were kept in the storehouses in earlier times.

The smaller of these two buildings, which is the Sutra Storehouse, is particularly interesting. It belonged to an imperial prince who owned the land before it was turned over to the temple, and during the prince's time, the storehouse appears to have had a gabled roof, whereas it now has a hipped roof. Presumably this means that the Buddhists who built the temple and rebuilt the storehouse had no regard for the prehistoric Shinto concept of the gabled roof as a symbol of high or godly status.

An early example of the post-and-beam storehouse with thick boarded walls is the Old Sutra Storehouse of the Kasuga Shrine, which dates back to the thirteenth century. Located at Takabatake-chō in Nara, this is a square building measuring about 6 meters to the side and having a hipped roof made of thatch.

In the thirteenth century, Zen Buddhism was imported from China, accompanied by new architectural styles, and a new type of storehouse appeared in Zen monasteries. It was a variety of sutra storehouse but was different in that it had a revolving book cabinet in the center of its interior. An excellent example, built in 1407, is found at the Ankoku-ji in Gifu Prefec-

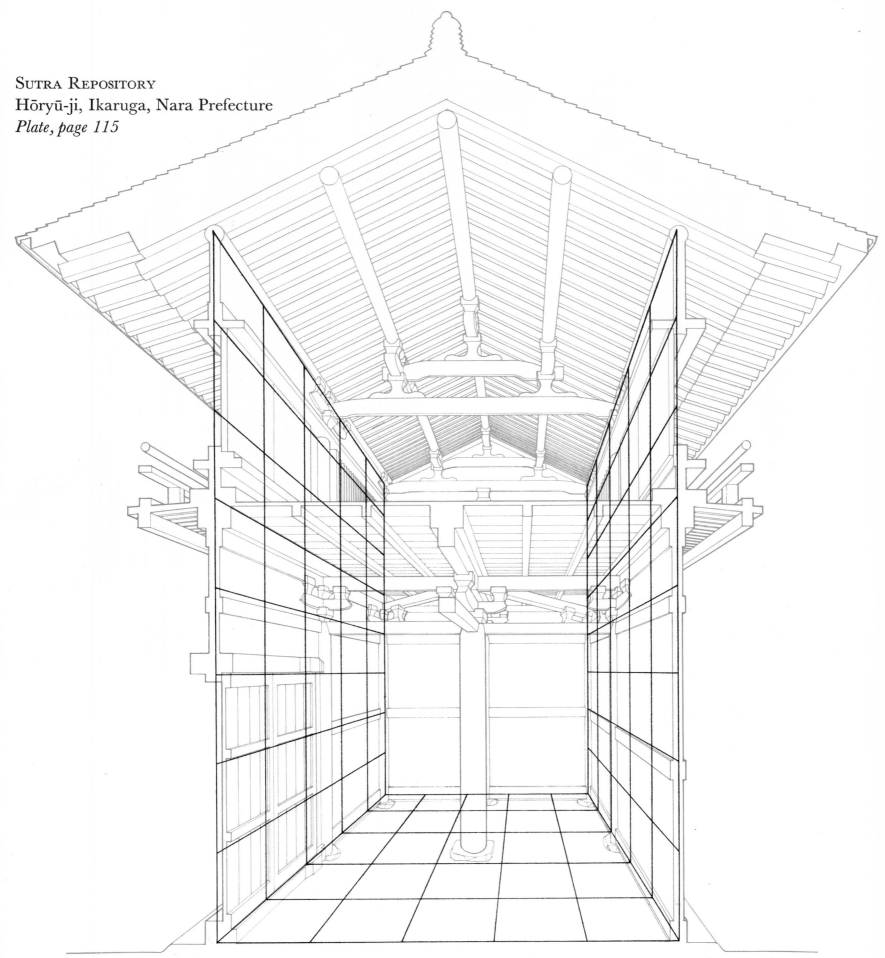

SUTRA REPOSITORY
Hōryū-ji, Ikaruga, Nara Prefecture
Plate, page 115

Each square represents an area 1 meter × 1 meter.

MINIATURE-SHRINE STOREHOUSE
Hakusan Shrine, Kamioka, Gifu Prefecture

ture. The revolving bookcase varied in size from place to place, but was invariably an octagonal structure with many boxes for the scriptures. At the center was a post with pivots at top and bottom to permit the case to be turned around.

By the Muromachi period (1333–1573), the practical value of the revolving bookcase had been recognized to the extent that it was adopted by Buddhist sects other than Zen, and one of the finest examples standing today is at the Onjō-ji, a Tendai Sect temple in Otsu, Shiga Prefecture (pages 5, 113). In the Edo period (1603–1868), the idea that turning the bookcase around once carried as much religious merit as reading all the scriptures in it (an idea that had probably inspired the creation of the device) gained currency among the common people, and revolving bookcases became even more widespread. They also doubtless appealed to the more commercial-minded members of the priesthood, who for a small sum from the worshiper could "read" through the whole Buddhist scripture for him by simply turning the bookcase around.

Smaller Buddhist temples could not afford such elaborate installations, but many of them had modest storehouses for their treasures. In a document thought to date from the early sixteenth century, for example, it is related that the village of Imabori in Ōmi Province (Shiga Prefecture) placed in the storehouse of the local temple copies of a number of sutras, a picture scroll, two drums, a jar for oil, and several other articles.

As mentioned earlier, in the course of the development of the governmental structure, the property of the emperor was separated from that of the gods and that of the government. To store the emperor's valuables, two halls, the Giyō-den and the Kyōsho-den, were built in the imperial palace in Kyoto. The buildings were quite large and were in the residential or palace style of architecture, rather than in storehouse style, but they functioned as storehouses. They were located on the east and west sides of a courtyard directly south of the main ceremonial hall of the palace, to which they were connected by covered passageways.

The Giyō-den housed the emperor's treasures, his ceremonial clothing, various accessories, and heir-looms from past emperors. These were kept in a central walled area, around which there were separate rooms used by the nobility on certain ceremonial occasions. The Kyōsho-den was a library, with a central room for books and documents and several auxiliary rooms with related functions.

The original Kyoto imperial palace burned shortly after it was built, and though it was reconstructed, it continued to be plagued in subsequent years by fires. After the eleventh century, the effort to maintain it was abandoned, and the emperor formed the habit of living with relatives in various parts of the city. Even so, the place where he lived at any given time was called the imperial palace, and a place was always provided for the Giyō-den and the Kyōsho-den.

The practice of keeping valuables in separate storehouses was nationwide, and it extended from the lowest classes to the highest. In a Jesuit report on Japan, dated September 15, 1565, it is stated that "the rich and the noble have within their compounds sturdy houses daubed with clay in which they keep their valuables." This was correct as far as it went, but the practice was by no means confined to the rich and the noble.

Cultural Repositories

Storehouses have played a vital role in the preservation of Japan's cultural heritage, particularly with regard to the arts and crafts. To be sure, many paintings have been preserved on the panels and walls of important buildings, and the most ancient examples of the crafts have been dug from the ground by archaeologists, but the great majority of the art works that have come down to us have been kept in storehouses. It would have been nearly impossible for our ancestors to pass down their art treasures from generation to generation without these places of safekeeping, and the storehouse as an institution may be regarded as one of the most important channels for the transmission of culture over the ages. It was only by building storehouses that were, insofar as possible, safe from war, fire, theft, moisture, and pollution that the men of the past preserved this channel.

In general, the cultural objects that were preserved were in the storehouses of rich people, famous families, Shinto shrines, or Buddhist temples. Very few of the cultural treasures of the past could be regarded as the property of the people as a whole. The storehouses were private strongboxes, not public museums. The first European-style museum was not established until 1871.

Still, there were institutions that functioned in some ways like museums. Buddhist temples, for example, were not only places of worship but places where people could see and admire works of art, such as Buddhist statues and their well-wrought canopies, banners and streamers, and metal pendants, as well as the wall paintings and sculptural ornaments that adorned the buildings. These were intended as aids to worship, but they were nonetheless works of art on public display.

Shinto and Buddhist institutions received gifts of paintings, calligraphy, fine swords, and other valuable objects continually, and some of the more important shrines and temples accumulated collections on what may be described as museum scale. These were housed in the storehouses known as *hōzō* or *hōko* or, in modern times, *hōmotsu-kan* (宝物館), a word similar to the usual word for museum.

The oldest and most important of the temple storehouses is the celebrated Shōsō-in in Nara. This is now a possession of the emperor and as such is under the control of the Imperial Household Agency, but originally it belonged to the Tōdai-ji, the huge monastery established by the Emperor Shōmu (701–56) toward the middle of the eighth century. The Shōsō-in was built by the Empress Kōmyō (701–60) just after the death of Shōmu to house the emperor's possessions, which had been donated to the Tōdai-ji. From the beginning it was closed with an imperial seal, and imperial permission was necessary to open it. As a result its contents have been exceedingly well preserved, as they continue to be today.

The storehouse itself is 33.1 meters long, 9.4 meters wide, and 13.2 meters high. It rests on forty posts that measure no less than 70 centimeters in diameter, and the floor is raised 2.7 meters off the ground. The building is divided into three sections, of which the two outer ones are in the log-cabin style, and the central one is in the board-wall style. The hipped roof is covered with tiles.

The original name was *narabikura* (雙倉), "double storehouse," and it seems likely that at the beginning there were two separate log-cabin structures, which were later linked by the board-wall section. However this may be, the building contains 9,020 items that date from the mid-eighth century or earlier. They include writing brushes and ink boxes, musical instruments, clothing, weapons, armor, household accessories, jewelry, ceremonial articles, Buddhist implements, tools, books, documents, and numerous other articles, many made in Japan, but many others imported from China or as far away as Persia. The collection is a unique and invaluable treasure of cultural remains from eighth-century Asia.

Many articles of historical and cultural importance were undoubtedly kept in private storehouses built by the nobility of the Heian period (794–1185). These were most often called "libraries" (*bunko*, 文庫, or *bunsō*, 文倉), and presumably they were originally built to house books, documents, records, and the like, but their contents seem also to have included paintings and calligraphy, as well as household furnishings and ornaments. In the Heian period it was even less possible to fireproof a building than it was in later times, and though the Heian nobles seem to have devoted much thought to the subject, not only the storehouses of the period but detailed records concerning them have been lost. We have only a few references in the literature of the time.

Fujiwara Yorinaga (1120–56), a high ranking court official, recorded in his diary that in 1145 he built a library, which he described as a "dirt-storehouse library" (dosō bunko). Presumably the building was daubed with clay or plaster, as were the dosō and dozō (土蔵) of later times. In this connection, it might be noted that a nobleman of a somewhat later period, Yamashina Norikoto (1328–1410) mentioned in his diary that in the eighth month of 1405 he had a library built by plasterers and coolies, which presumably means that the outer walls were made of plaster. Such fireproofing as was attempted, however, was not always effective. It is recorded that on the fifteenth day of the fourth month of 1153, the Ōe family library, which belonged to a literary family long in the emperor's service and which is thought to have contained ten thousand volumes, was destroyed by fire.

In the middle ages, the custodians of culture were the warrior class, rather than the nobility, and they too built storehouses for their valuable art objects. According to a fourteenth-century writing by a priest named Gen'e, in the Muromachi period (1333–1573) the houses of the warriors were surrounded by earthworks and moats and contained a main house, an entrance, connecting corridors, a meeting place, a study room, a kiosk, a storehouse (dozō), and a library (bunko). In the warrior lineage, presumably, was the Kanazawa library in the temple compound of the Shōmyō-ji in Musashi Province (Kanagawa Prefecture), which is recorded to have been built by Hōjō Sanetoki (1224–76), a general who was well known for his book collection. A painting showing the Shōmyō-ji and its compound in 1333 includes a sutra repository with a hipped-and-gabled wooden roof, but there is no other building that resembles a library. Perhaps the Kanezawa book collection, which is said to have been cared for by the priests, was housed in the sutra repository; or perhaps a little gabled building behind the cypress-roof building in which Sanetoki lived was the library.

After the middle of the Muromachi period, ceremonial tea drinking spread thoughout the country, and the urge to collect paintings, calligraphy, and utensils appropriate to the tea cult was felt not only by shoguns, warriors, and Zen priests but among the nobility and ordinary townspeople. Altogether, a great deal of paraphernalia was necessary for the tea ceremony. Aside from the kettle, the teabowls, and the tea caddies, it was necessary to have a variety of paintings suitable to the occasion, incense burners, ornaments for shelves, and all the dishes, trays, and so on needed for the meal that usually preceded the tea ceremony. These articles were kept in storehouses, just as they frequently are today. The Shogun Ashikaga Yoshimasa (1436–90) had a particularly fine collection of tea ceremony articles. Known as the Higashiyama collection, after the location of Yoshimasa's residence, it was very likely kept in a Higashiyama library or a storehouse of similar name.

This was not an age of great public collections but one of many small private troves, corresponding, we might say, to the age of gathering in economic history. Still, it was an age that Japan had to go through, and the gathering that was done has provided us with our cultural heritage. The storehouse, though usually a small inconspicuous building in a corner of the residential compound, was indispensable to the transmission of the various collections from age to age, and the priests, noblemen, warriors, and tea masters who collected the art objects were at great pains to build storehouses for them where they would be safe from fire and theft. It is only as a result of this effort that so many cultural treasures of the past have been preserved.

Facilities for Production and Distribution

Insofar as storehouses were used for storing raw materials intended for processing, as well as finished products waiting to be sold or consumed, they may be regarded as production and distribution facilities. It is important to try to ascertain when they began to function in this way.

Storehouses for commercial products no doubt began with the appearance of merchants and shops selling these products. In the ancient capitals of Nara and Kyoto there were officially designated market districts run by merchants known as *ichibito*. Presumably there were also government warehouses, but the *ichibito* were low-ranking public officials, rather than private merchants, and they would hardly have had need for storehouses of their own. Around the beginning of the eleventh century a number of private houses outside the official market places took up trading, and their residences came to be called "shops," *machiya*, but it is not certain that they maintained separate storehouses.

In the Kamakura period (1185–1333), however, there definitely were commercial storehouses. They were called *dosō* (土倉), or "clay storehouses," and it may be assumed that their walls were daubed with clay or plaster. The word *dosō* goes back to ancient times, and storehouses of the type in question were built not only by the government and religious institutions but by the nobility as well. It is not clear exactly how these early storehouses were constructed, but one supposes that the *dosō* belonging to the Kamakura period merchants descended directly from them.

Fortunately, we do have definite information about the *dosō* of the Kamakura period, for there is a picture of one in the sixth section of the fourteenth scroll in the famous *Kasuga gongen scroll painting*, which dates from 1309. The building is of a type later known as a "cap storehouse" (*sayakura*, 鞘倉), or "placed-roof storehouse" (*okiyane-kura*, 置屋根倉), which is to say that the storehouse proper was a clay or plaster fireproof container covered by a roof that might burn without harm to the interior. The scroll shows the storehouses

after a great fire in which the roof has been partially destroyed. The buildings has only one story and no windows. The only opening is a doorway with swinging doors on the outside, hinged at top and bottom, and a sliding grille door on the inside. This type of building seems to have been widely used by the merchants of the middle ages.

According to the diary of the poet and calligrapher Fujiwara Teika (1162–1241), on the fourth day of the eighth month of 1234 there was a great fire in Kyoto, and a large part of one of the important commercial districts was destroyed. "I do not know," says the writer, "how many storehouses were burned to the ground. Goods from all over the country, which had been stored in them, were strewn about everywhere." And among the documents of the Daitoku-ji, a great Zen temple, is one that speaks of a certain Fujiwara lady who had placed her valuables and land deeds in her own storehouse, but lost them on the night of the ninth day of the second month in 1156 in a fire that destroyed some thirty hectares of the city.

Many of the *dosō* of the middle ages belonged to usurers and pawnbrokers. The number of usurers was large; in the Muromachi period there were some 350 in Kyoto, 200 in Nara, and 30 in the relatively small community of Sakamoto, in what is now the city of Ōtsu. Actually, because of their storehouses, the pawnshops were known as *dosō*, or *dokura*, an alternative reading of the same characters.

A priest of the Seigan-ji, one Anraku-an Sakuden (1554–1642), wrote a volume of essays called *Seisuishō* [Laughter asleep and awake, 1623] in which he told a tale centered about a pawnbroker's warehouse: "A certain man pawned his clothing at a pawnbroker's in Kyoto and later went back to retrieve it. When he received it, he found that the cloth had been torn by rats. He thought this unreasonable and argued at some length with the pawnbroker, asking him at least to lower the interest somewhat. The pawnbroker was adamant. Far from lowering the interest, he brought out a dead rat and said, 'This is the culprit that ate your clothes in my storehouse, so that I had to kill him. Take him away with you.'"

The pawnbrokers also used their storehouses for purposes other than storing goods they were holding in pawn. They made a side business of storing valuables for people who were attracted by the solidity and fireproof qualities of their storehouses. In the middle Kamakura period and later, not only common people but warriors, priests, and nobles called upon them to keep their various personal treasures and their land documents, in much the same way that people employ safe-deposit boxes in banks today. The risk, to be sure, was greater than it is today: numerous records tell of storehouses that either burned down or were robbed. For instance, according to the *Tōji hyakugō monjo* [Documents of the Tōji], in 1311 a Buddhist novice living on West Seventh Avenue in Kyoto deposited the deeds to his house and lands at a storehouse on the same street but lost them when the storehouse was broken into and then burned by thieves. The same source mentions a priest named Dōken, who put his land documents in the storehouse at the Hachiman Shrine only to lose them on the fifth day of the seventh month of 1338, when the storehouse was burned down in a riot. The latter passage indicates that religious institutions also accepted valuables for safekeeping in their storehouses.

It is a well-documented fact that in the Muromachi period storehouses belonging to merchants and pawnbrokers in Kyoto grew both in number and in size. And yet neither the Sanjō version nor the Uesugi version of the famous screen painting called *Rakuchū rakugai-zu byōbu-e* [In and around the capital] shows a single storehouse. One can only conjecture the reasons.

The Sanjō version of this painting was done on commission for the noble Sanjō family, and it is quite possible that the artist deliberately avoided reminding his patrons of the pawnbrokers and usurers who were gradually taking their property away or of the merchants who threatened a whole new system of mercantilism. Similarly, the Uesugi version was a gift from the military dictator Oda Nobunaga to the head of a great warrior family, and the artist may well have considered it judicious to omit reference to the merchants and moneylenders who, in the minds of the great feudatories, were undermining the foundations of the agricultural system on which they depended for their wealth and power, not to say their livelihood.

Outside of Kyoto, there developed a network of land and sea transportation routes along which not only people but commercial goods traveled far and wide,

and warehouses were built at all strategic ports and stopover towns. In general, these belonged to distributors known as *ton'ya*, who were the wholesalers of their time. According to the *Arai monjo* [Arai documents], in 1551 a *ton'ya* named Shimizu Yasuhide, who had a storehouse in the inn town of Mishima, sold his establishment to a temple named Zuisen-an. The deed mentioned that the property contained a house, a stable, a rest house, and a storehouse. It is not hard to imagine that similar establishments existed at little towns like Mishima along all the main thoroughfares, though at the time in question the countryside was still divided into warring feudal autonomies. An outstanding example from the Edo period (1603–1868) is to be seen at the old inn town of Odai on the Nakasendō, a highway leading from Edo through the central mountains to Kyoto. Though most storehouses were behind the houses of the owners, this one opened directly onto the highway.

Among the storehouses that functioned as centers of production, the most important were the sake storehouses (*sakagura*, pages 14–15, 178–81, 202, 219). As mentioned earlier, a few of these were indeed used only for storage, but nearly all of them doubled as breweries. The origin of the sake storehouses is obscure, but they were certainly in existence in the Muromachi period (1333–1573). By this time, storehouses with thick clay and plaster walls (dozō) were widespread, and it had doubtless been recognized that such buildings were excellent places in which to ferment rice for sake because of the relatively stable temperature inside them. Until the end of the sixteenth century, the fermenting grain was usually kept in ceramic vessels, but afterwards these gave way to large wooden barrels, and in recent decades the barrels have to a large extent been replaced by enamel containers.

When storehouses figure in production, it was nearly always in connection with sake or some other fermented product, such as bean paste, soy sauce (pages 174–77), or yeast. Since all of these products are indispensable to Japanese cooking, the factory storehouse was of great importance in Japanese life. In general, the structure of the building was the same no matter what the product was; only the interior fittings differed. One interesting variation occurs, however, in storehouses where indigo dye was produced.

Indigo was made chiefly in the villages along the banks of the Yoshino River in Tokushima Prefecture (pages 168–69). The business was organized in such a way that the houses producing the indigo each held a number of shares in the house that merchandised it. Each of the producers had a storehouse of the dozō type, but with relatively small windows with double shutters. The most unusual feature of the indigo storehouse was the floor, which was made by piling up layers of gravel, sand, and rice hulls and covering them with a layer of clay from 12 to 16 centimeters thick. The fermentation of the indigo leaves requires the use of a good deal of water, and presumably this floor was devised to facilitate drainage.

The indigo leaves were stacked on the floor, and a man called the "water specialist" (mizushi) came and poured the proper amount of water on them. They were then left to ferment for about three months, after which they were usable as dye. To facilitate transportation, they were then placed in wooden mortars and pounded with mallets into hard cakes. These were then kept in storehouses in the local castle town pending sale and delivery.

Nothing that could properly be called an industrial revolution occurred in Japan until the Meiji period (1868–1912), but the beginnings of industry and commerce antedated this by several centuries. By the time of the Meiji Restoration (1868), a foundation had been laid for the remarkable industrial and commercial development that ensued, and it is certain that the factory storehouse had played an important role in the creation of the cottage industries that were so vital to the early modern Japanese economy.

Accoutrements of a Way of Life

It would not be too much to say that the storehouse was an essential component in the development of the traditional Japanese way of life, because the storehouse made feasible the traditional concept of the all-purpose living space. The Japanese house of the past did not have furniture in the ordinary Western sense of the word. Instead, people used light, movable furnishings and accessories known as chōdo, which could be kept in the storehouse and taken out as needed.

Of what did chōdo consist? The word came from China, where it meant "adjustment" or "arrangement," but in Japan it soon came to mean all sorts of personal or household articles. For example, the great miscellany contained in the Shōsō-in Repository might be referred to as the Emperor Shōmu's chōdo, or "things." To be somewhat more specific, a pre-Muromachi source in which court ceremonies of the late Heian period are described in detail indicates that chōdo were implements or appliances kept in the house to make life more livable or comfortable, such as mirror stands, mirror boxes, clothes chests, cabinets, armrests, incense burners, and clothes baskets. Objects having a more direct connection with the living space itself, such as screens, tatami mats, braziers, cushions, and standing lamps were also called shōsoku, "decorations," but as a rule chōdo included these items as well. The following is a partial list of the articles that were customarily regarded as chōdo:

Interior furnishings:

For the floor: tatami mats, straw mats, straw cushions

For partitioning: paper-covered sliding doors (shōji and fusuma), single-leaf screens, folding screens, curtain screens (kichō), bamboo blinds, draperies

For sitting: round straw cushions, stuffed cushions, chairs, stools, armrests

For sleeping: mattresses, pillows, paper pillow covers, mosquito nets

For lighting: lamp stands, candlesticks, a variety of lanterns and lamps

For heating: braziers, chest-warmers

Others: tobacco trays, teabowls, spittoons
Storage for clothing: lacquered clothes chests, oblong chests, chests of drawers, bric-a-brac boxes, covered baskets, coverless baskets, clothes racks
Books and writing: desks, bookcases, letter boxes, boxes for writing equipment and paper, lecterns, inkstones, ink boxes, brushes, paper, colored paper, strips of paper for poetry, seals
Musical instruments: lutes, mandolins, flutes, samisen
For eating:

Tables: large tables, trays, raised trays
Dishes: lacquer bowls, ceramic bowls, large bowls, rice containers, chopsticks, assorted small plates, toothpicks
For drinking: sake cups, sake jars, trays, gourds
For storing food: barrels, rice chests, bottles, urns
For carrying: lacquer boxes, baskets

In addition, in the Muromachi period and later, chōdo included the various articles used in connection with the tea ceremony.

A common feature of the various chōdo was that none was too large to be moved about easily by one or two persons. In fact, they were moved about frequently, and the furnishings that were in the house at any one time depended largely on the season of the year and on what happened to be going on in the house. Many articles were brought out only on festive occasions, and in houses of considerable means, a large proportion of the equipment was in the storehouse most of the time. Throughout Japan there has always been a sharp distinction between festive days and ordinary days, and the distinction was applied to clothing, household furnishings, eating utensils, ornaments, food and drink, and just about everything else. In larger houses, there were rooms that were not used except on festive occasions. During the Heian and Kamakura periods, for example, the southern side of the main section of a proper nobleman's mansion was reserved for ceremonial occasions, and ordinary life otherwise went on in the northern part of the building.

Festive days might be occasioned by an annual religious or political celebration, or by some personal or family celebration, such as a wedding or a coming-of-age ceremony. In any case, when a festive day occurred, that which was ordinary was banished to the storehouse, and that which was festive was brought forth, to be taken back again after life had returned to normal.

The custom of making certain changes for special occasions is, of course, not unique to Japan; housewives everywhere have their good china and their good silver, as well as their everyday utensils. And yet in the past the Japanese operation was somehow more thoroughgoing, because it involved changing the interior decoration of the house to an extent that would be impracticable in places where furniture is too big or too bulky to be moved about frequently.

Though the degree to which the shift from ordinary to festive was carried out depended upon the economic status of the family, in principle the practice was observed by the lowest classes as well as by the emperor and the nobility. It continued to be observed even after the beginning of the modern period by many middle-class people, although the architectural style of their houses had changed considerably and storehouses, which were really necessary to the preservation of this custom, were becoming rarer and rarer. It is a little difficult for anyone who has not seen a typical storehouse in an older Japanese household to imagine the immense variety of dishes, lacquer trays, hanging scroll paintings, incense burners, and the like that were kept there for use on the occasion of marriages, coming-of-age ceremonies, funerals, and seasonal celebrations.

The number of furnishings and accessories needed by Japanese households of the past was further increased by the practice of changing many elements of interior decor to coincide with the season. A few articles were changed with each of the four seasons, but in general the important distinction was between summer and winter. The period for summer decorations was from the fourth to the ninth month of the lunar year, and winter decorations were considered appropriate for the other months. To the extent that it was economically possible, each household had to have two sets of furnishings to conform with the seasonal change.

Let us take a specific example. In the *shinden* (寝殿) mansions of the Heian and Kamakura periods, an important piece of furniture was a type of movable screen called *kichō*. This consisted of a black lacquered base with two vertical poles about 1 meter in height and a cross pole at the top from which a curtain was hung. The curtain was usually of ordinary silk cloth, though at times brocade or silk twill was used. Silk of this sort was normally woven in bolts about 30 centimeters wide, and the curtain was as a rule made of five widths, with a long tassel hanging on either side of each width. The color, design, and material of the curtain varied from summer to winter. A summer curtain, for example, might be made of thin gauzy silk on which pictures of fall plants were painted with Chinese white, whereas a winter curtain might be of heavy silk and have a design of withered trees painted on it. In either case there had to be another curtain of grayish color with no design that could be used on sad or serious occasions, such as funerals or memorial services. Thus it was necessary to have four curtains in all for each *kichō*.

The practice of changing furnishings with the seasons continued in the *shoin* (書院) houses of the Muromachi and Edo periods and was not uncommonly preserved in upper middle-class houses until World War II. Indeed, despite the vast social changes that have taken place in the past three decades, the custom still exists vestigially. In particular, in houses or apartments having tokonoma where scroll paintings are hung as decorations, the scrolls are changed at least twice a year to accord with the season.

In the days before central heating and air conditioning, seasonal changes in the furnishings were intended to make the living quarters more comfortable. In premodern times, the only common devices for heating were the charcoal brazier and the *kotatsu* (a pit hearth in the center of the room, usually covered with a framework and quilting so that people can sit around the fire with their legs under the quilt). Neither the brazier nor the *kotatsu* could heat a large area, and it was for this reason that interiors were partitioned into relatively small spaces with sliding panels and screens. In the summer, when it is hot and muggy, the sliding panels could be removed completely or replaced with bamboo screens that would admit a breeze. Aside from the practical aspect, the changing of furnishings to suit the season tended to have a desirable psychological effect on the people living in the house. Summer furnishings made them feel cool, and winter furnishings made them feel warm. The mere variety enriched their lives.

Since time immemorial one of the most remarkable features of Japanese residential architecture has been the functional flexibility of its interior space. Whether in the mansions of the rich or in humble farmhouses, single rooms have usually served a variety of purposes. Indeed, in the smallest houses, one room might be living room, dining room, and bedroom. Lack of wealth may possibly be the underlying cause for this economic use of space, but it is significant that it prevailed even in the houses of the middle and upper classes. Most likely it was not a question so much of economy as of a deep cultural trait involving the fundamental concepts of architectural space.

It would appear that to the Japanese way of thinking, the interior space of a room is nothingness. Being nothingness, it has no fixed or recognizable function. Traditionally, this nothingness was converted into something and given a fixed purpose by the furnishings that were brought in from the storehouse to adorn it. In the Edo period house, for example, the interior space was split into small rooms by sliding partitions; any ordinary room could be turned into a room for entertaining guests by putting in a low table, a brazier, good cushions, a tobacco tray, and a scroll painting and flower arrangement suited to the season or the occasion. If, instead of these furnishings, one spread mattresses and quilts and installed a clothes rack, clothes baskets, and a lamp, the room became a bedroom.

It is the storehouse that made possible the development of this approach to residential architecture and of the life-style that accompanied it, for without the storehouse, it is difficult to imagine that people would ever have formed the custom of moving furniture about so frequently.

Symbols of the Mysterious

Traditional storehouses had few doors and windows, and those that they had were small. This was particularly true of dozō that were used only for storage, as opposed to those also used for manufacturing. As a consequence, the interior of the storehouses was dark and mysterious. In addition, the walls were thick, and when the openings were closed with their heavy shutters, most of the sound from without was cut off, creating a silence that added to the effect of mystery. In effect, a well-built storehouse was a secret chamber in which chill prevailed even in the summer.

This was a side effect of the functional structure of the building, rather than the result of any conscious attempt to create a dramatic atmosphere, but the atmosphere was nevertheless there, and it led people to associate storehouses with mysterious or sinister events that did not occur out in the open. In a sense, the storehouse was the haunted house of folklore.

The contemporary novelist Yasushi Inoue, in *Osanaki hi no koto* [Days of my youth], recalls the experience of having lived in a storehouse of the dozō type. "In the morning it was a wonderful feeling to wake up in the storehouse, but when I woke up in the middle of the night, I felt a sense of desolation." When he had to get up at night to go to the toilet, his grandmother, who also slept in the storehouse, led him out with a candle, undoing the screen door, the inner sliding door, and the heavy outer door. "When the doors were open, the world became a different place. In the winter, a cold wind was often raging, and in the summer, fireflies were flitting about. Sometimes there was bright moonlight, sometimes rain. The night contained a myriad of natural phenomena. Sometimes the trees were moaning and crying as though they were alive; sometimes darkness pressed down like a weight. . . . When my grandmother and I went back into the storehouse, we closed the heavy doors, threw the bolt, and climbed the stairs by the light of the candle to dive into the empty quilting."

To some, of course, the interior of the storehouse was a place of repose, shut off from the rest of the world by the heavy walls. Shut securely inside, one would not be disturbed no matter what was going on outside, and when one opened the doors and went out, somehow a new world of surprises opened up before one's eyes. Still, to the people outside, the storehouse was a thing of mystery, because they had no way of knowing what was concealed within, or what dreadful happenings might be going on. In contrast to the typical house, much of which was visible from the outside, the closed storehouse invited flights of imagination, and indeed if one were up to no good, the storehouse made a convenient hiding place.

The Zen priest Zuikei Shūhō (1391–1473) of the Shōkoku-ji in Kyoto wrote a diary in which he tells much about the capital in the years just before 1467, when it was largely destroyed in the Ōnin War. In his entry for the fifteenth day of the sixth month of 1460, he says: "On Sixth Avenue in the capital there is a widow who has a storehouse. The widow's daughter-in-law shuts herself up inside the storehouse, and the lower part of her body turns into a snake." No doubt the dark secluded interiors of storehouses led to the creation of a good deal of hearsay of this sort among the people of the capital in that age.

Katō Genki, writing around the beginning of the nineteenth century, tells the following story of events that took place one summer in the vicinity of a storehouse in Edo: "On a piece of rented property in Kon'ya-machi, just across from the back gate of the daimyo Ichihashi's mansion, there is a hairdresser's shop called Ebidoko. A rumor spread that each and every night a ghost appeared in the Ebidoko storehouse, and people began gathering every night to catch a glimpse of it. Eventually more than ten thousand people were flocking there each night, and there was barely a place to stand for blocks around. The crowds were such that merchants began coming to the area to sell melons and cool water to the sightseers. There was no fixed time for the ghost to appear, but it is said that when it did, a bluish, ghostly flame appeared in the darkness near the eaves of the storehouse, shining like a hot teakettle. So many people gathered together that the residents of the area found them a nuisance and appealed to the government. Thereupon a lot of officials came and drove the sightseers away. Some were even arrested. But the number of sightseers continued to grow by the night, and it was completely beyond the ability of five or ten officials to keep them away. Later, the local government office issued a command forbidding sightseers to come to the spot, but even that did no good. People came from as far away as Shiba and Meguro, and the fame of the ghost spread far and wide. I do not know what sort of a ghost it was, but it is said that the ghostly flame really did appear."

If, indeed, there was a "ghostly flame," it was probably the result of some natural electrical phenomenon, turned into a ghost by the presence of the storehouse, with its connotations of mystery. Storehouses had that sort of effect on the people of the time.

Storehouses were also the scenes of sinister murders such as occur in the mystery novels of our time. Ōta Gyūichi, a secretary to the Oda family, wrote in his *Nobunaga-kō-ki* [Record of Lord Nobunaga, about 1600] of an unusual murder that had taken place in the capital. The time was the fourth month of 1579, which was just before Oda Nobunaga moved from the capital to his new castle at Azuchi. Having learned of the incident on the twenty-fifth day of that month, Ōta wrote: "In a thread shop on a small street off Fourth Avenue in the Shimogyō district in Kyoto, there lived an old widow of seventy who had one daughter living with her. On the night of the twenty-fourth day of the fourth month, the daughter gave her mother a lot of good sake to drink, and when the old lady was drunk, the daughter took her into the storehouse to sleep. After it grew late, and the mother was sleeping peacefully, the daughter stabbed her to death and with her own hands put the body into a large leather basket, which she bound up securely. Being a member of the Hokke sect of Buddhism, she called a priest of the Seigan-ji, and the two went quietly and buried the basket in the temple grounds, making sure that no one saw them." Many other stories from the past show that the storehouse was considered an ideal place for committing a crime.

In the eighteenth century, a number of secret religions spread in Edo and other parts of the country, and the storehouse figured largely in their initiation rites. Indeed, the sects were referred to by such names as "Dozō Religion" or "Storehouse Religion." An initiation rite is described in some detail in *Kuri Hōmon-ki* [Record of the kura faith] by the Confucian scholar Tatematsu Kaishi. The ceremony was held in 1766 in a dozō storehouse in Edo. Great secrecy and mystery prevailed. A sacred lantern shone dimly in the dark interior of the building, and on the wall was hung a picture of the leader of the cult. The leader himself, surrounded by his leading disciples, sat on a straw mat before the picture, and the supplicant knelt before the group. The older members chanted "Save him, save him," and when the supplicant had been hypnotized into a state of ecstasy, the leader pronounced the one stanza, "Be at peace, you will be saved." In this way the new member received salvation and his body was cleansed, so that he became a Buddha, just as the leader was a Buddha. This sort of secret cult, along with its mysterious rites, could not have existed but for the privacy and apartness of the storehouse.

The storehouse also figured in the training of children, particularly boys. The practice is rare today, but before World War II when a boy did something bad or did not mind his parents, the punishment was often to be shut up in the storehouse. There must be quite a few adults alive today who can remember having had this experience in their childhood. The punishment was relatively effective, because aside from being restrained from going out to play, the children were exposed to the "dangers" of the dark, scary storehouse.

Some children, however, rose admirably to the occasion. A friend of the author's has written the following: "No doubt about it, I was frightened. But after I had been put in the storehouse a number of times, I discovered that it was possible to unlock the door from the inside, and the knowledge that I could get out anytime I wanted to was comforting. I did not make use of my secret, however, because I knew that if I went out of the storehouse, my father would be angrier with me than before. Instead I opened the window and passed the time reading the old books in the storehouse. I suspect this is where I acquired my interest in classical literature. Anyway, when I quieted down and stopped crying, my father would begin to worry and would open the door sooner than he had planned."

As suggested by the above, the traditional storehouse as a setting for mysterious or dramatic events is often referred to in Japanese literature, particularly in diaries. Here the storehouse has a significance that goes far beyond its utilitarian function.

Fundamental Requirements of Storehouses

Safety

The first requirement of a storehouse is that it be a place where goods can be kept safe. Safe from what? From the historical viewpoint, the answer is moisture, rats, fire, theft, and earthquakes.

The Japanese Archipelago is subject to high humidity much of the time. The soil tends to be damp, and each summer there is a period of from one to two months when the humidity is so high that almost everything else is damp too. In the early history of Japanese storehouses, two structural features resulted from the need to avoid excessive moisture in the interior. One was the use of wood as the building material, and the other was the use of raised floors. Wooden walls tended to stabilize the humidity, because they absorbed the moisture in humid seasons and released it in dry seasons. Raised floors not only offered protection against dampness from the ground but provided ventilation underneath. As we have seen, raised-floor storehouses were built as early as the Yayoi period (see reconstruction, pages 122–23), when they served as a prototype for Shinto shrines. The log-cabin storehouses in temples and shrines of the Nara period also had raised floors (pages 110–11), and a distinctive type of raised-floor storehouse (pages 8–9, 124–27) is found extensively in the Ryukyus, as well as in the islands off the Izu Peninsula.

In premodern Japanese towns and cities, however, the raised-floor structure lost much of its desirability because the cities themselves were dense agglomerations of wooden buildings, and buildings raised high off the ground were particularly hazardous when fires broke out. In the cities, therefore, the raised-floor storehouse was abandoned in favor of buildings with low floors and walls covered with clay or plaster. These buildings in turn posed the question of how to avoid excessive moisture. One solution was to use slatted floors that admitted air into the interior and to provide openings for ventilation in the part of the outer wall that was below the floor. Around 1780 Tsumura Sōan, a scholar of Japanese literature, wrote the following instructions: "The entire floor of the dozō should be a grille. In the rainy season, the tatami mats inside should be taken up so that wind can pass into the in-terior." In fact, descriptions and pictures from the past reveal no storehouses in which the entire floor was a grille, as suggested by Tsumura. Instead, only a part of the floor was made in this fashion. When there were two or three stories in the building, grilles also formed part of the second and third floors, helping incidentally to improve the lighting.

As a rule, whatever the uses to which a storehouse was put, it had few windows and doors, and these were relatively small. A result was that to secure sufficient light and air, people left their storehouses open a good deal of the time. Near the end of the Edo period, a writer named Suzuki Tōya made the following comment: "Since the dozō is apt to be humid, some idiots leave their storehouses open day and night 'to improve ventilation,' as they say. Try it and see! The moisture that enters at night will never dry out in the small amount of sunlight that enters the building in the day. It simply gets worse and worse until even the second floor is damp. Storehouses should be aired only in the daytime, and even then only when the weather is good." Whether this is correct or not is an open question, but it is clear from the statement that the problem of avoiding humidity was a very serious one to towns-people of the time.

In premodern times, rats also were a great source of damage. According to the *Fusō ryakki* [Abbreviated history of Japan], in 654 a great multitude of rats migrated from Naniwa to the province of Yamato, and in the *Chronicles of Japan*, there is an entry noting that in 666 rats from the area that was later Kyoto invaded Ōmi Province (Shiga Prefecture). According to the *Shoku-Nihongi* [Chronicles of Japan, continued], in 775 black rats devoured the roots of trees and plants over a large area in Shimotsuke Province (Tochigi Prefecture). Another official history, the *Sandai jitsuroku* [Record of the three reigns], notes that in 875 rats attacked the imperial palace nightly.

The attitude toward rats has always been somewhat ambivalent. Some people in the past regarded rats, and particularly white rats, as messengers of the god of fortune, and hence harbingers of good things to come. In 809 Yamashiro Province (Kyoto Prefecture) presented a white rat to the emperor for good luck, and in a well-known children's story a man claps his hands for joy at the sight of a white rat, which he takes as a

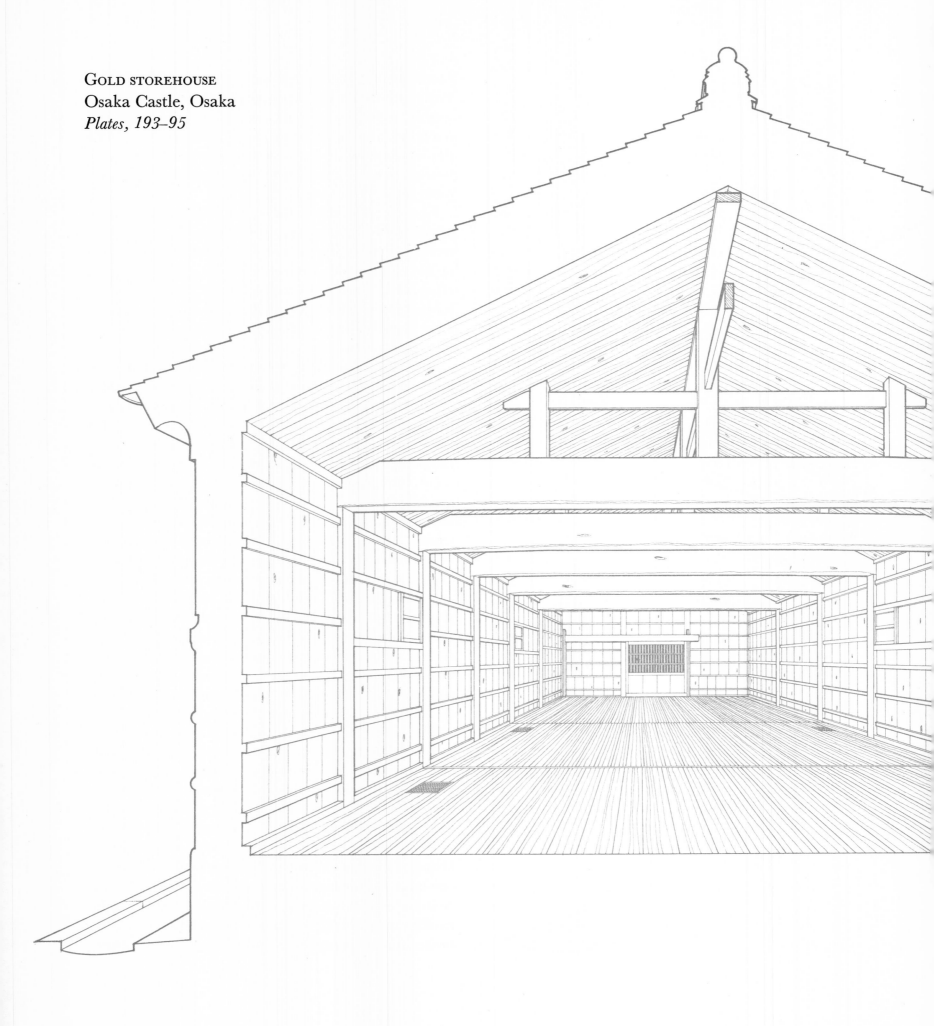

GOLD STOREHOUSE
Osaka Castle, Osaka
Plates, 193–95

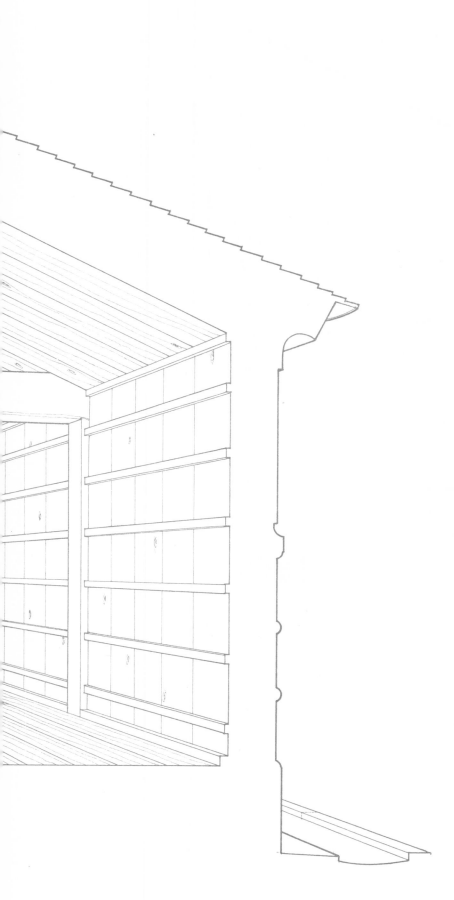

sure sign that the god of fortune has smiled on him. With a certain logic, some people welcomed rats as a sign of a rich harvest, and it was a common belief that if a house were deserted by its rats, it would soon burn down. Nobody, however, welcomed rats in the storehouse, and several devices were employed to keep them out.

Even in prehistoric times flat wooden disks were placed between the tops of the supporting columns and the floors of storehouses to turn back rats. In dozō of the Edo period, iron grilles were employed in an effort to ratproof doors and windows. Nevertheless, as we have seen in the story about the man whose clothes were torn by rats at the pawnshop, somehow rats managed to get in.

This was particularly true of storehouses that were lived in. In another passage in *Osanaki hi no koto* [Days of my youth], Yasushi Inoue wrote: "It is nothing to be particularly proud of, but one of my earliest childhood memories is of the rats that played around my pillow at night. I would awaken in the middle of the night, and there would always be a few rats running around on top of the quilt and by the side of my pillow. I was not at all afraid of them. Nearly every night when I went to bed my grandmother would put a little food in the corner for the rats. She said that if you did that, the rats would never harm people."

Storehouses also needed to be safe from thieves, particularly since they usually aimed first and foremost at the place where valuables were kept. Actually, however, since most of the storehouses were essentially wooden buildings, if a thief really tried, he could always get into one of them, and countless instances of thefts from storehouses have been recorded.

The history of the treasure-house (*hōzō*) at the Tō-ji monastery in Kyoto, for example, is virtually a chronicle of burglary. The building is a small square storehouse in log-cabin style with a tile roof. Its heavy wooden floors are said to have been made from the door panels of the famous Rashōmon gate at the southern entrance to Kyoto. According to one temple history, thieves entered this building in 1039 and stole one large mirror and a small quantity of cotton cloth. Another temple history says that on the fifth day of the twelfth month of 1216 a bandit named Kana-Tayūbō broke into the storehouse and stole silk cloth, grain, priestly robes, a relic of the Buddha, and a number of articles used in religious ceremonies. In 1328 the building was again burglarized, and the thieves took cloth, grain, and other items, including two relics of the Buddha. This time, however, a miracle occurred: as the thieves broke into the building, there was a clap of lightning, and a dragon god who resided in a pond in the temple compound arose from the water and flew off to the south. The frightened thieves discarded the relics of the Buddha and fled. In still a later history, it is recorded that in 1564 a thief burned off the lock on the south door of the storehouse, broke the lock on a chest inside, and stole a number of valuable articles. Apparently, not even the property of the Buddha or relics of his body were immune from theft.

The storehouses of noblemen and commoners alike were vulnerable. Fujiwara Teika recorded in his diary that in 1226 thieves broke a hole in the wall of his dirt-covered storehouse (dosō) and made off with a quantity of cash and gold, and sixty bolts of silk from Mino Province (Gifu Prefecture). The *Tōji hyakugō monjo* [Documents of the Tōji] records that on the fifth day of the second month of 1311 a thief broke into a storehouse belonging to the Buddhist novice Ryōa and then set it on fire.

We do not know exactly how the thieves made their way into the storehouses, but since even the best storehouses had only wooden walls covered with plaster, it should not have been difficult to break in. In the Edo period, thieves devised special saws for cutting into the walls of dozō, which had relatively thick clay or plaster walls. One type of saw appears to have been a pointed instrument with teeth on both edges. The pointed end was used to pierce the wall so that the remainder of the blade could be inserted. To make it difficult to saw through storehouse walls, people often mixed rocks or gravel into the plaster or filled the bamboo sticks that formed the lathing with sand.

In a country where nearly all buildings were constructed of wood, fire was an ever-present danger, particularly in the towns and cities. Even in the Nara period, attempts were made to fireproof government storehouses, and in the Heian period (794–1185), when there was considerable urbanization, the need for fireproofing began to exert a strong influence on the construction of storehouses in general. The problem continued to grow over the centuries, and in the Edo period (1603–1868) it would be no exaggeration to say that the development of the storehouse as an architectural form revolved almost entirely around the problem of making these wooden structures more impervious to fire. Writing in 1787, Uehara Mukyū said: "Nobody who employs twenty or thirty people in his house is without a storehouse [dozō]. The question is, for what purpose are these storehouses built? The first aim must be protection from fire." This matter will be taken up more thoroughly in a later chapter, and it is sufficient to note here that in the cities of the Edo period, the chief aim in building storehouses had come to be protection from fire.

Although numerous, earthquakes did not constitute nearly as much of a threat to storehouses as did fire. For one thing, serious earthquakes were not as frequent as fires. For another, the storehouses might suffer cracked walls or structural distortions in an earthquake, but unless the earthquake was followed by fire the damage was not usually irreparable. Traditional wooden-frame buildings, storehouses included, have a good deal of structural flexibility, and except in the most disastrous earthquakes, they rarely collapse. Normally the damage is confined to cracks in the wall. For this reason, over the centuries one observes very little conscious effort at earthquake-proofing. Rather than try to make buildings completely earthquake-proof—a task that would have been impossible in any case—people attempted to make sure that storehouses would continue to function even if they suffered a certain amount of earthquake damage.

As a rule, storehouses of the past had only one or two stories, but around the beginning of the seventeenth century, it became the fashion among the newly arisen merchant class to build three-story storehouses. These had outer walls of white plaster, and their height caused them to stand out among the surrounding buildings, thus adding to the prestige of the owners. It appears, however, that their increased height made them more vulnerable to earthquakes, and after the beginning of the eighteenth century, they rapidly went out of style. The three-story storehouses may be regarded as an example of an interesting paradox. Whenever the symbolic character of a building is strongly emphasized, there is a danger that certain structural risks will be taken. The structural risk involved in building three-story storehouses made it possible for them to serve as impressive symbols of wealth, but it also rendered them vulnerable to earthquakes, with the result that they were abandoned after only a few decades, and everybody went back to two-story storehouses.

On the second day of the seventh month of 1830, there was a great earthquake in Kyoto, so great that the government decided to change the name of the era to avoid further bad luck. A contemporary source says: "Many families' storehouses collapsed. The walls cracked or disintegrated altogether. Throughout the capital it seemed that the storehouses had been pushed over into diamond shapes, and there were none still in usable condition." The same source reports that on many storehouse walls people wrote comic inscriptions making fun of the once-proud structures. This no doubt would not have happened if such destruction from earthquakes had been a common occurrence. It is precisely because the earthquake was of unprecedented violence that people felt moved to joke about the fallen storehouses. Perhaps we may see in this an example of the Japanese attitude toward earthquakes: they are unpredictable catastrophes that must be coped with by the human spirit, not by the structure of buildings.

Status Symbols

There is a saying in the Kyoto-Osaka area that "the storehouse is the adornment of the rich man." The same statement appears in a novel by Ihara Saikaku (1642–93), and may have been originated by him. Undeniably the storehouse has been a symbol of wealth and status since ancient times, and it remains that today, insofar as private storehouses still exist. As a status symbol, it has traditionally been the pride and joy of the rich. Whether in the city or in the country, a house with a storehouse is a house with some degree of distinction and affluence. It is important to remember in this connection that we are speaking of those storehouses that are called *kura*, not the lowly sheds that go by such names as *naya*.

Since the Muromachi period (1333–1573), one popular form of worship among Zen priests, merchants, and farmers alike has been directed toward two gods of fortune called Daikoku and Ebisu, both of whom are represented in folk art as chubby, jolly little men in red clothing. The *Chirizuka monogatari* [Tale of a mound of dirt], which dates from 1552, tells of the spread of the cult of Daikoku: "Everybody makes wooden statues of Daikoku or paints pictures of him on paper, and each and every house keeps such an image and prays to it for wealth and status." Little statues of Daikoku or Daikoku and Ebisu are extremely common in ordinary houses today. They are usually kept in the living room or on a shelf in the kitchen, but in certain rural areas they are placed on the main column of the storehouse. The storehouse symbolizing wealth to begin with, no doubt it is felt that their presence will bring still more wealth.

Getsujudō, writing in 1709, tells of the storehouse of an oil merchant in Itami in Settsu Province (Hyogo Prefecture): "The ceremony of opening the family storehouse, which was held on the second day of the New Year celebration, was a particularly happy event. When the doors of the storehouse were opened and everyone went inside, they saw something that looked like a mushroom attached to the central post. As they looked closer, they found it had eyes, a nose, a mouth, and big ears (like Daikoku). Indeed, it was a little Daikoku, complete with mallet and knapsack." That a miraculous fable of this sort found its way into tales and novels intended for the common people is evidence of the strong link between the storehouse and the cult of Daikoku. At the same time it indicates that both were regarded as symbols, or even omens, of wealth.

Until some time in the Meiji period (1868–1912) strolling performers went from house to house in the Kyoto-Osaka region performing what was called the "Daikoku dance." This consisted of a dance and a good luck song, which the artists offered in exchange for rice or money. One set of words for the song went roughly as follows:

> Daikoku-san is this sort of fellow:
> One, you will stand on large sacks of rice;
> Two, you will smile and smile;
> Three, you will drink your fill of sake;
> Four, everything will go all right;
> Five, it will always be the same;
> Six, you will have no ailments or troubles;
> Seven, there will be no disturbances;
> Eight, you will enlarge your house;
> Nine, you will build a storehouse;
> Ten, everything will be the way it should be.

These simple lyrics show that, in the popular mind, to be able to enlarge the house and build a storehouse was to approach the ultimate in happiness. From the words of this song, incidentally, the clothing merchants of the Kyoto-Osaka region adopted the practice of using one of the characters for storehouse (sō, 倉) to symbolize the numeral nine in their secret price codes.

A whole branch of fortune-telling concerns itself with how houses and other buildings should be built, and particularly where certain rooms or annexes should be located. The fortune-tellers are as one in recommending that the storehouse, which represents the family's wealth, should be located in the northwest corner of the residential compound, and in the past this rule was usually followed. When there was more than one storehouse, the most important one was placed in the northwest corner. Saikaku tells the story of a rich man in Izumi Province (Osaka Prefecture) who kept in his northwest storehouse the broom, fan, dusters, and cleaning equipment that had belonged to his mother before the family became wealthy. People in general felt that such modest items invited poverty,

but this man considered his mother's humble belongings to be important treasures in his family's history, and he consequently kept them in the most honored storehouse.

Because of cramped conditions in the cities, it was not always possible to put the storehouse in the northwest corner, but whatever happened, it was never placed in the northeast corner, because that is the direction from which devils come.

The degree of a family's wealth and status was directly proportionate to the number of storehouses it had. Accordingly, writers of the past, in indicating how rich a person was, gave not only the size of his house and estate but the number of storehouses he kept. One late seventeenth-century source notes, for example, that Yodoya Tatsugorō, a rich merchant in Osaka, had "a storehouse for each of the forty-eight syllables in the Japanese syllabary," in which he had "collected all sorts of treasure." The number need not be taken to be exact, for the expression employed might well mean simply that the merchant "had everything from A to Z." The meaning is simply that Yodoya had many, many storehouses and was consequently extremely rich.

Among the rich merchant families of the Edo period was the Tomiyama of Izawa in Ise Province (Mie Prefecture), who dealt in clothing and dry goods. Aside from their main store in Izawa, they had shops in Edo, Kyoto, Osaka, and Fujioka, and each shop had a number of storehouses. In 1727 the Izawa residence of this family consisted of a main compound comprising eight buildings that had been constructed in 1688, along with a separate building with a parlor for entertaining and a house for the retired head of the family. There were three dozō-type storehouses, measuring approximately 14.9 by 9.3 meters, 13 by 5.6 meters, and 8.4 by 3.7 meters. In 1715 the Tomiyama branch at Honchō in Edo was a two-story storehouse-shop measuring approximately 10.8 by 30.6 meters. This branch had a three-story storehouse 7.2 meters square and two two-story storehouses measuring 9.0 by 3.6 meters and 5.4 by 5.4 meters.

In the Edo period, when the warrior class held absolute political power, the merchants under the warriors' control must have considered the storehouse where they kept their treasures to be their ultimate

STOREHOUSE FOR FESTIVAL FLOAT
Furukawa, Gifu Prefecture
Plate of similar storehouse, page 197

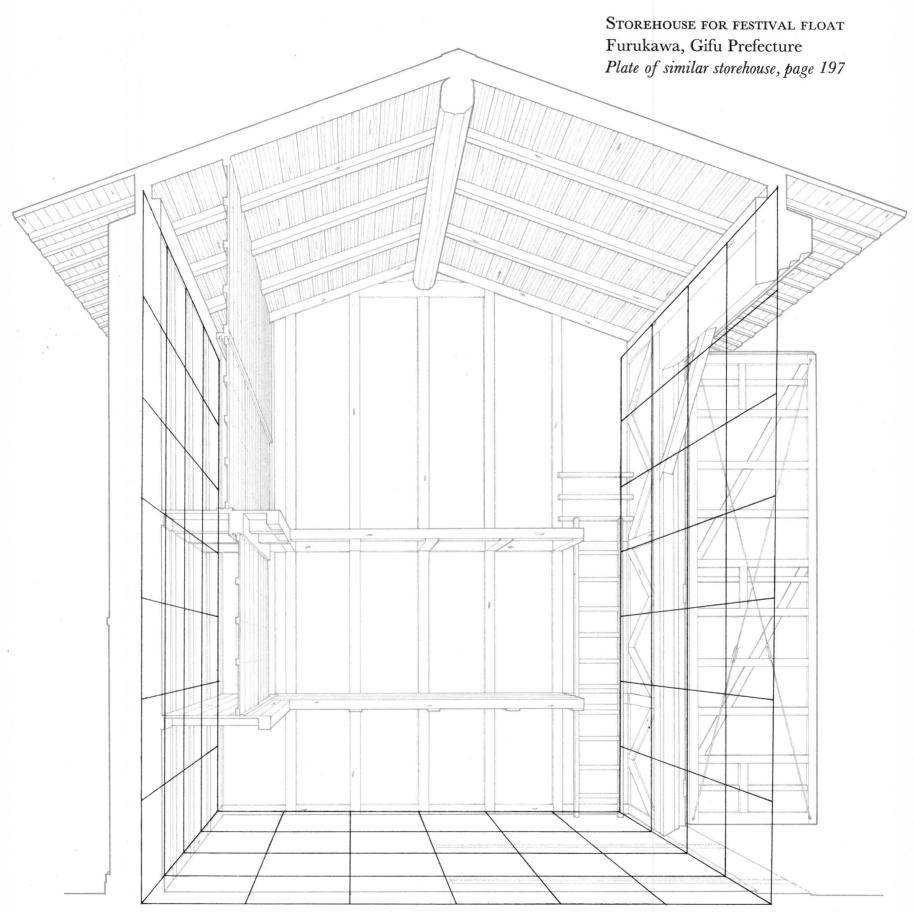

Each square represents an area 1 meter × 1 meter.

stronghold. A merchant in a novel by Saikaku says something to the following effect: "What one wants in one's house is a garden with plum trees, cherry trees, pines, maples, and the like, but what one wants even more in one's house is gold, silver, rice, and money. When I look not at the garden but at the storehouse in the garden, I wonder if even the palaces in heaven in which the Buddhas and deities live contain such pleasures." Arrogant, yes, but typical of the attitude toward well-stocked storehouses.

In the Edo period merchants kept their money in their storehouses. Money was in the form of coins, and the coins had holes in the middle so that they could be strung on strings. One important unit was a string on which there were one thousand pieces of cash. When as much as one thousand strings of money were put in the storehouse, it was the custom to keep a lantern burning in that building all night. The reason is not completely clear, but even at the beginning of the Edo period the practice was already widely observed. Saikaku speaks of a shipping agent named Amiya in Edo who contributed 8,192 strings of cash to the Buddhist temple to which he belonged, but who also had lanterns burning all night in his storehouse, indicating that there was still a large supply of money left.

Another work of Saikaku, written in 1692, tells the story of a retired merchant who took up residence with his second son in a house newly built by the latter. The old man's belongings were transferred to the son's storehouse by nine employees, and the last luggage brought was a box containing silver. Since the value of the silver exceeded one thousand strings of cash, the retainer in charge of ceremonial observances at the son's house suggested that an all-night lantern be lit in the storehouse. The son laughed and told him, in effect, "You are green at your job! The point at which a merchant puts an all-night lantern in his storehouse is when the storehouse contains one thousand strings of cash. If we took that as a measure, our household would have to have twenty-five or twenty-six all-night lanterns."

The three-story storehouses built by merchants in Edo in the seventeenth century have already been mentioned, but a word should perhaps be added about the psychological effect of these buildings. Saikaku wrote succinctly, "First, sacks of rice; second, a two-story house; third, a three-story storehouse." The meaning was simply that anyone who had accumulated a quantity of rice, built himself a fine house, and then added a white-plaster three-story storehouse was a person of some importance. These three-story storehouses appear in numerous genre paintings of the time.

It is recorded that in 1715 a merchant called Daikoku-ya, who operated at Honchō in Edo, had a three-story storehouse measuring 7.2 by 7.2 meters. A drawing, made in 1697, of the sake establishment run by Tsuboya Kichizaemon in Yamato Province (Nara Prefecture) shows a sake storehouse measuring about 16.4 by 3.9 meters, an ordinary storehouse measuring 5.9 by 3.9 meters, and a three-story storehouse measuring 5.9 by 7.8 meters. Interestingly enough, an annotation on the drawing says that the third floor of the last-named building "could be used for amusements." Presumably this third floor was a place for parties, rather than a part of the storehouse proper. A three-story storehouse owned by the Imanishi family of Imai was still in existence in the Meiji period.

Ihara Saikaku lived in the age of the three-story storehouse, and references to this type of building occur frequently in his novels. He mentions, for example, storehouses of this type in the shop of a merchant named Yorozuya in Bungo Province (Ōita Prefecture) and another in the house of Daikoku-ya in Kyoto. Getsujudō speaks of a merchant in Tamba Province (Kyoto and Hyōgo prefectures) who had three-story storehouses at each of the four corners of his property.

Endless examples could be mentioned to show that the storehouse was one of the most important status symbols in premodern Japan, if not the most important. The fact is that the wealth of a village or town, as well as the number of better-off people who lived in it, could be accurately judged by the number of white-plaster storehouses in it.

Structural Types of Storehouses

After the pit-house storehouses of the Jōmon period and the raised-floor storehouses of the Yayoi period, the tradition of the Japanese storehouse came to include a number of distinct architectural styles. With minor exceptions, however, they were alike in that their basic structures consisted of wooden posts and beams. In the main, differences in structure concerned the materials from which the walls were made and the manner in which the materials were put together.

One exception was the simple storage pit, which will be taken up later. Another exception is found only in records but is interesting enough to describe in some detail. This was a type made from large bricks. The scholar Kurihara Nobumitsu, writing in 1848, gives a description that he says he saw in a manual on carpentry from Chōshū Province (Yamaguchi Prefecture): "The danger with clay or plaster storehouses [dozō] is that rotting of the posts will cause the walls to bend out of shape and eventually to break up. The storehouse introduced here has no posts and is not subject to this kind of damage. It is a most valuable treasure. The method of making it is as follows: take wooden boxes about .9 by .3 by .6 meters in size, and fill them with clay, packing the clay tightly with a wooden pestle. Dry these in the sun, and when the clay has hardened, use the blocks to make the storehouse wall, piling them up as in a stone wall. The roof can be made of wood, covered with tiles. There are many ways of doing this, but one is to plaster the underside of the roof boards, cover the plaster on the inner side with boards, plaster the outer side of the roof boards, and cover this with tile."

Like the stone warehouses and brick warehouses copied from Western patterns in the Meiji period, the storehouse described would have had little resistance to earthquakes, but it may have been satisfactory in Yamaguchi Prefecture, where strong earthquakes are rare. In any event, it does not seem to have become popular, because no example has been preserved.

The frequency of earthquakes is no doubt one of the principal reasons why nearly all storehouses were built with a wooden post-and-beam structure. Such structures are flexible, and they may shake considerably when there is an earthquake, but they do not often collapse.

Board-wall Storehouses

Board-wall storehouses, *itagura* (板倉), are found in farming communities all over the country, and especially in mountainous areas where lumber is plentiful. Structurally, they are all very much alike (see diagram, overleaf). A grid of heavy timbers is laid to form a foundation and sleepers, and posts are placed at intervals of from 30 to 45 centimeters. The posts are linked by horizontal braces, also at intervals of from 30 to 45 centimeters, and then heavy boards are affixed on the inner side to form the walls. As a rule, the roof is a simple gable, covered with tile, but in some cases, as in the storehouses in the village of Shirakawa in Gifu Prefecture, thatched roofs, either gabled or hipped, have been employed (pages 128–29). Storehouses of the past usually had two floors, and among farmers it was the custom to store grain on the first floor and household articles on the second. In Shirakawa and the neighboring village of Shōkawa (pages 132–33), some wooden storehouses have interior walls separating the first floor into two rooms, with a wide hallway in front of them. The rooms have independent doors with locks, and one is normally used for rice and other foodstuffs, while the other is used for farm implements, tools, and the like. The stairway to the second floor is in the hallway.

Board-wall storehouses are, of course, flammable, and they have rarely been built in Japanese cities because of the danger of fire. Even in farming villages, they have usually been built at a considerable distance from the house. Indeed, in some places, such as the village of Tsushima in Hinoemata, Tochigi Prefecture, all the storehouses are grouped together in a single location outside the community proper.

It is most likely that the board-wall storehouse and the log-cabin storehouse were the most common types in the ancient period, in temples, shrines and government installations, as well as in ordinary households. The Shōsō-in in Nara, as we have seen, was an example of both types used in the same building. In the nearby Kasuga Shrine there is a sutra repository of the board-wall type, with thatched roof, that dates back to very early times.

There are frequent references even in the historical

WOODEN STOREHOUSE
Osawa family, Shōkawa, Gifu Prefecture
Plate, pages 132–33

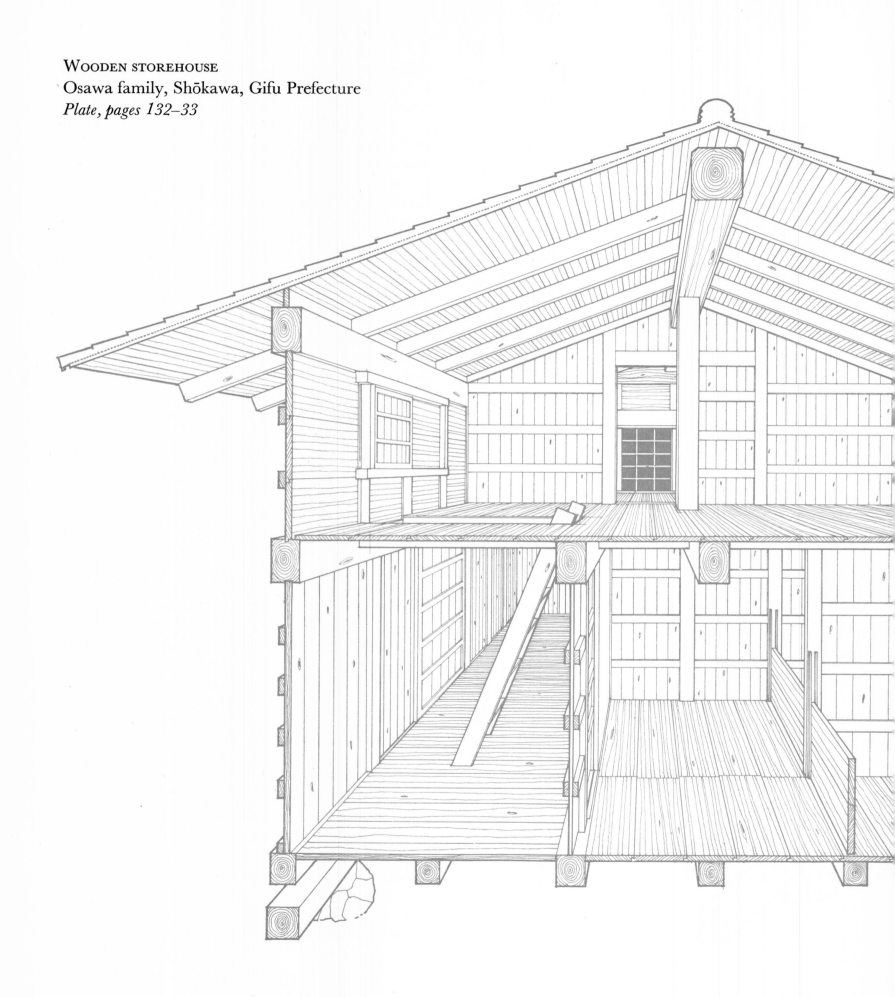

documents of the Nara period (710–94) to board-wall storehouses. In the *Shōsō-in monjo* [Documents of the Shōsō-in], for example, there is mention of one Owarita-no-Ason Fujimaro who had, in addition to a house in Nara, a relatively large tract of farmland outside Nara. The record says that in Fujimaro's household there were one cypress-roofed house, four thatched buildings, one building with a board roof, two buildings the name of which is not clear, and seven board-wall storehouses. The largest of the storehouses was 6.3 by 6.6 meters, and the smallest was 3.6 by 3.9 meters. These figures suggest that the board-wall storehouses of this period were comparatively small.

In the farmlands held by the aristocracy in the villages around Nara, as well as in their great estates in the distant provinces, board-wall storehouses were commonly used for the storage of grain. We know, for instance, that one Mabito Hironaga, who lived on Seventh Avenue in the capital, had three "board houses" (*itaya*) and one board-wall storehouse (*itagura*) on the rice farm he owned about fifteen kilometers south of the capital. Also in the eighth century, at the Kuwabara estate owned by the Tōdai-ji in Echizen Province (Fukui Prefecture) there were three board-wall storehouses with areas of 10.8 by 8.4 meters, 6 by 5.4 meters, and 5.4 by 4.8 meters. In *Heian ibun* [Writings of the Heian period] there is a statement that on one piece of property, measuring a little less than a hectare, in Settsu Province (Hyogo Prefecture) there was a log-cabin and two board-wall storehouses with areas of 6 by 5.1 meters and 5.4 by 4.5 meters. The same source mentions another piece of farmland in the same province that measured about 1.5 hectares and had eleven log-cabin storehouses, along with two board-wall storehouses. In this last example, the heights of the buildings are given. For a storehouse with an area of 10.2 by 6.6 meters, the height was 4.5 meters, and for a storehouse of 5.6 by 4.8 meters, the height was 3.3 meters. An examination of documented board-wall storehouses of the Nara and Heian periods shows that the smallest had an area of about 10 square meters, and the largest, an area of about 80 square meters. This is on the whole small in comparison with similar storehouses of later periods.

In the Heian period, there were buildings called "storehouse substitutes" (*kurashiro*, 倉代), which were

BOARD-WALL STOREHOUSE
Wada family, Shirakawa, Gifu Prefecture
Plate, page 129

either simplified storehouses or substitute storehouses. The *Konjaku monogatari* [Tales of past and present], which dates from the eleventh century, mentions building a storehouse substitute with thick wooden boards, and it consequently appears that these buildings were also of the board-wall type. One source says that in 1161 the household of Takamuku no Yorishige contained a storehouse substitute that had a thatched roof and measured 3 column spans (probably about 5.4 meters) across the front. Another source mentions the existence in 996 of a storehouse substitute in an ordinary household in which six long straw mats and twenty quires of paper were kept. Presumably these buildings were also board-wall storehouses.

Log-cabin Storehouses

The history of log-cabin storehouses, *azekura* (校倉), goes back to ancient times, when such buildings were also referred to as "armor storehouses," *yoroigura* (甲倉). According to a well-known Japanese dictionary, *Daigenkai* [Great sea of words], the *aze* in *azekura* is related to the word *azanau*, which means "to weave or interwine," and to *azenawa*, which means a "plaited rope." *Aze*, in short, means "intersecting," and the name *azekura* signifies that the boards or timbers used for the walls intersected at the corners of the building; hence, the use here of the English term *log-cabin style*, which is not completely precise, but which conveys the idea of the crisscross effect at the corners of these buildings. The term *armor storehouses* was used not because the buildings contained armor but because the walls resembled the woven breastplates of Japanese armor.

In most parts of the world buildings of this general structure were made with round logs, but in Japan the only known buildings in which this was the case are storehouses of the Ainu. Most likely, in the early stages, the Yayoi people also used round logs, but in the examples that remain, the timbers are of truncated triangular section, about 15 centimeters to the side. These timbers were stacked in such a way that the peaks of the triangles extended on the exterior, and the interior walls were smooth (see diagram, overleaf). The historical storehouses of the log-cabin type that have been preserved are all in the compounds of Buddhist temples or Shinto shrines. The most famous of all is the Shōsō-in Repository, which has been described above, but other examples are to be found at the Hombō of the Tōdai-ji, the Tōshōdai-ji (pages 105–7), the Tamukeyama Shrine in Nara, the Itsukushima Shrine in Hiroshima (pages 110–11), and the Tōshōgū Shrine at Nikko (pages 118, 120–21). In ancient times similar storehouses were also built by aristocrats and provincial leaders. As mentioned above, the eighth-century sutra repository at the Tōshōdai-ji, a square log-cabin storehouse with a tiled roof, originally belonged to an imperial prince named Nitabe, whose land was donated for the construction of the monastery. In the famous scroll painting entitled *Shigi-san engi emaki* [A history of Mount Shigi], the storehouse of a rich man in Yamazaki, which figures prominently in one of the stories depicted, was a log-cabin storehouse in which sacks of rice were kept.

The Shōsō-in Repository and other early log-cabin storehouses were used for storing assorted valuables and treasures, but in still earlier times this type of storehouse seems to have been used ordinarily for storing rice and other grains. The *Wamyō ruijū-shō*, a tenth-century lexicon, says simply that the azekura was a "place where grain was kept." As for construction, the remaining ancient examples all have tiled roofs, but it would appear that log-cabin storehouses on farm-lands and official estates usually had thatched roofs or cypress-bark roofs. It is doubtful that tiles for roofing were available in rural farming communities in the eighth and ninth centuries, and it is certain that if they were, they were extremely expensive.

As to the advantages of the log-cabin storehouse, it has often been said that in rainy weather the logs expanded so that the gaps between them closed, and the moisture was kept out, whereas in dry weather the logs shrank, opening the gaps slightly and letting in air. The interior was thus protected from changes in the humidity outside. In fact, however, this is an old-wive's tale, for the gaps between the logs are uneven, and expansion of the timbers would not close them.

A late-eighteenth century source entitled *Kōko shō-roku* [A small antiquarian record] says that in the hot sun the log-cabin storehouse does not admit moisture from the ground, and during rain it does not admit moisture from the air, so that the items inside the building can be kept "for hundreds of years without becoming worm-eaten." At the time when this was written, most storehouses had plaster walls, and since the plaster contained moisture from the beginning, these storehouses tended to be damper than wooden storehouses. Consequently, it is not surprising that a writer of this age would remark upon the relative dryness in log-cabin storehouses. At the same time, it is doubtful whether log-cabin buildings were very much superior in this respect to any other wooden storehouses. The main difference was that the timbers used were of thicker section than the boards used in other wooden storehouses and as a result the log-cabin form must have been stronger.

Like the board-wall storehouses, the log-cabin store-

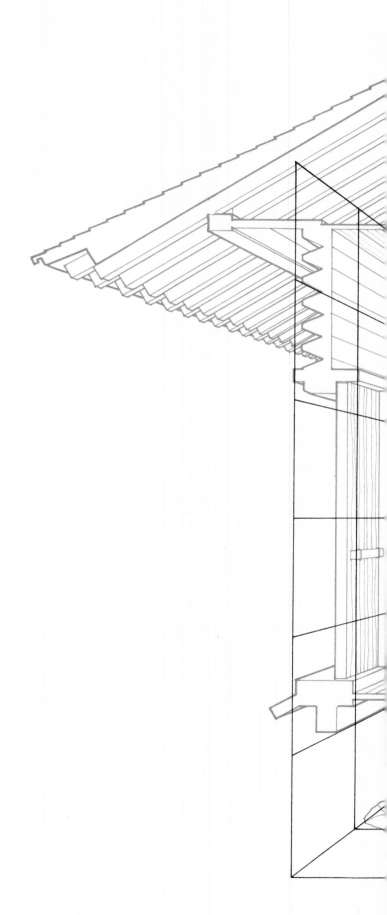

TREASURE STOREHOUSE
Tōshōdai-ji, Nara
Plate, pages 106–7

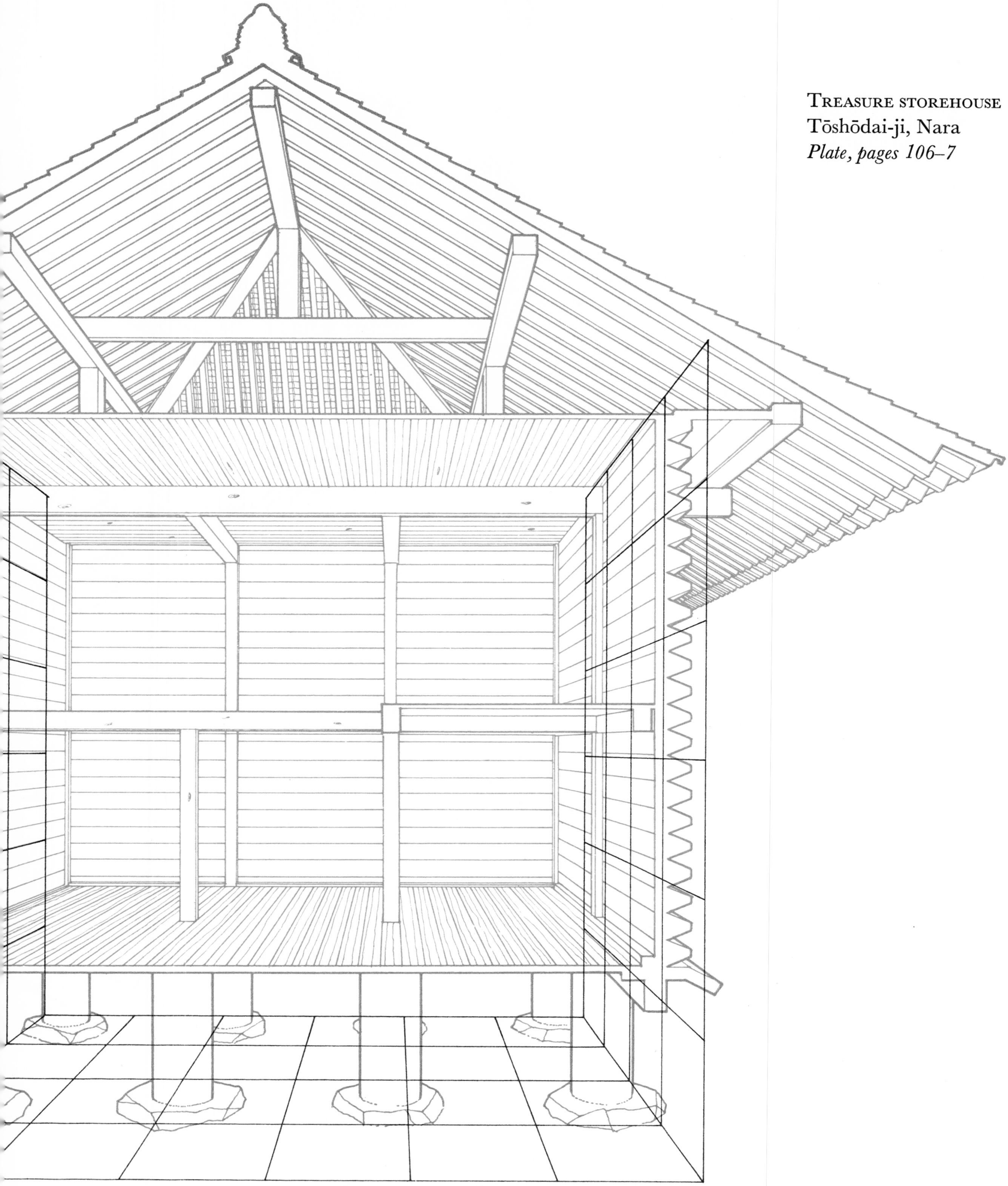

Each square represents an area 1 meter × 1 meter.

houses were very vulnerable to fire, and they were not suited to urban centers. After the early middle ages, they were built only in shrines and temples, where ancient forms of architecture were frequently preserved simply because they were ancient.

Intersecting-board Storehouses

An offshoot of the log-cabin storehouse was a type called *seirōgura* (井籠倉), which was built in the same fashion as the log-cabin buildings, but with flat, heavy planks instead of logs or triangular timbers. *Seirō*, the word from which the name of this type of storehouse is derived, means a square wooden rice steamer whose sides are put together in interlocking fashion at the corners. As in the case of the log-cabin type, the most distinctive structural feature is that the building requires no posts to support the roof. It may well be, as mentioned above, that the raised-floor storehouses of the Yayoi period, as well as the Aramatsuri Shrine at Ise, were of this type, and a Yayoi storehouse at the Toro site in Shizuoka has been reconstructed along these lines (pages 122–23), although in this case auxiliary posts have been added at the corners. Today, however, the seirō storehouse is found primarily in farming villages, most notably in the Saku and Suwa regions of Nagano Prefecture and, to a lesser extent, in the Chichibu region of Saitama Prefecture and the upper reaches of the Tone River in Gumma Prefecture.

In the examples in Nagano Prefecture, a grid of timbers forms the foundation, and the roof, which is gabled, is either of wood or of wood covered with tile. In some cases, the walls are covered with clay to help protect them from fire. The lathing for the clay walls is made by inserting pegs in the wooden walls and stringing ropes between them. The best examples of clay-covered seirō storehouses are found in the village of Katashina in Gumma Prefecture. At a glance, they look like dozō.

Clay Storehouses

The clay storehouse, *tsuchiya-gura* (土屋倉), is mentioned in historical sources of the Heian and Kamakura periods (794–1333). It is referred to, for instance, in the *Yamato monogatari* [Tales of Yamato], which dates from the tenth century, as well as in a report, dated 996, of a government inspection of the house of Mukai no Kuniaki, a local official in Harima Province (Hyogo Prefecture). In the latter document, the clay storehouses were said to contain 110 *koku* (about 2 kiloliters) of rice, 160 baskets of charcoal, and eight long straw mats.

The name *tsuchiya-gura* was often abbreviated to *tsuchiya* (土屋), "clay building" or "dirt building." Just how the earlier buildings referred to by these names were constructed is not very clear. About the only evidence is found in a regulation dated the seventh day of the eighth month of 786, in which provision is made for building clay storehouses (tsuchiya) to protect government rice in the provinces from fire. We know from this that the purpose of the clay storehouses was fire protection, and that they were used as granaries. The same regulation informs us that the wooden roofs of the buildings were covered with clay, and we can surmise that this layer of clay was in turn covered by a second wooden roof, for otherwise the clay covering would have been washed away by rain.

The regulation tells us nothing about the structure of the walls, but it seems only logical to suppose that, like the roof, they were made with wood and covered with clay. The tsuchiya-gura seems, in effect, to have been a board-wall storehouse covered with clay. Very likely the "library" (*bunsō*) built by Fujiwara Yorinaga in 1145 was a tsuchiya-gura, although in describing the building in his diary Yorinaga does not use this term. The library was 6.9 meters on the east-west axis, 3.6 meters on the north-south axis, and 3.3 meters high. It had a tile roof and heavy wooden walls, on the outside of which there was a coat of lime. There were entrances on the north and south sides, and the diary says that to keep the lime on the doors from coming off, a coating of "oyster shells" was applied.

From the above, it appears that the clay storehouses of the Heian and Kamakura periods looked on the outside like the dozō of later times, but they were different in two important respects. In the first place, whereas the structure of the dozō consisted of posts, beams, and horizontal braces, that of the clay storehouses had posts, beams, and wooden walls. In the second place, whereas the dozō had thick clay or plaster walls between the columns on the inside and around the entire structure on the outside, the clay storehouses had only a thin coat of clay, lime, or plaster over their wooden walls on the outside. One suspects that this coating was prone to fall off, and in any event it did not furnish very adequate protection against fire. No doubt it was for this reason that Fujiwara Yorinaga surrounded his library with a hedge fence, a moat, and a dirt wall.

RAISED-FLOOR STOREHOUSE
Amami-Ōshima, Kagoshima Prefecture
Plates, pages 8–9 and 124–27

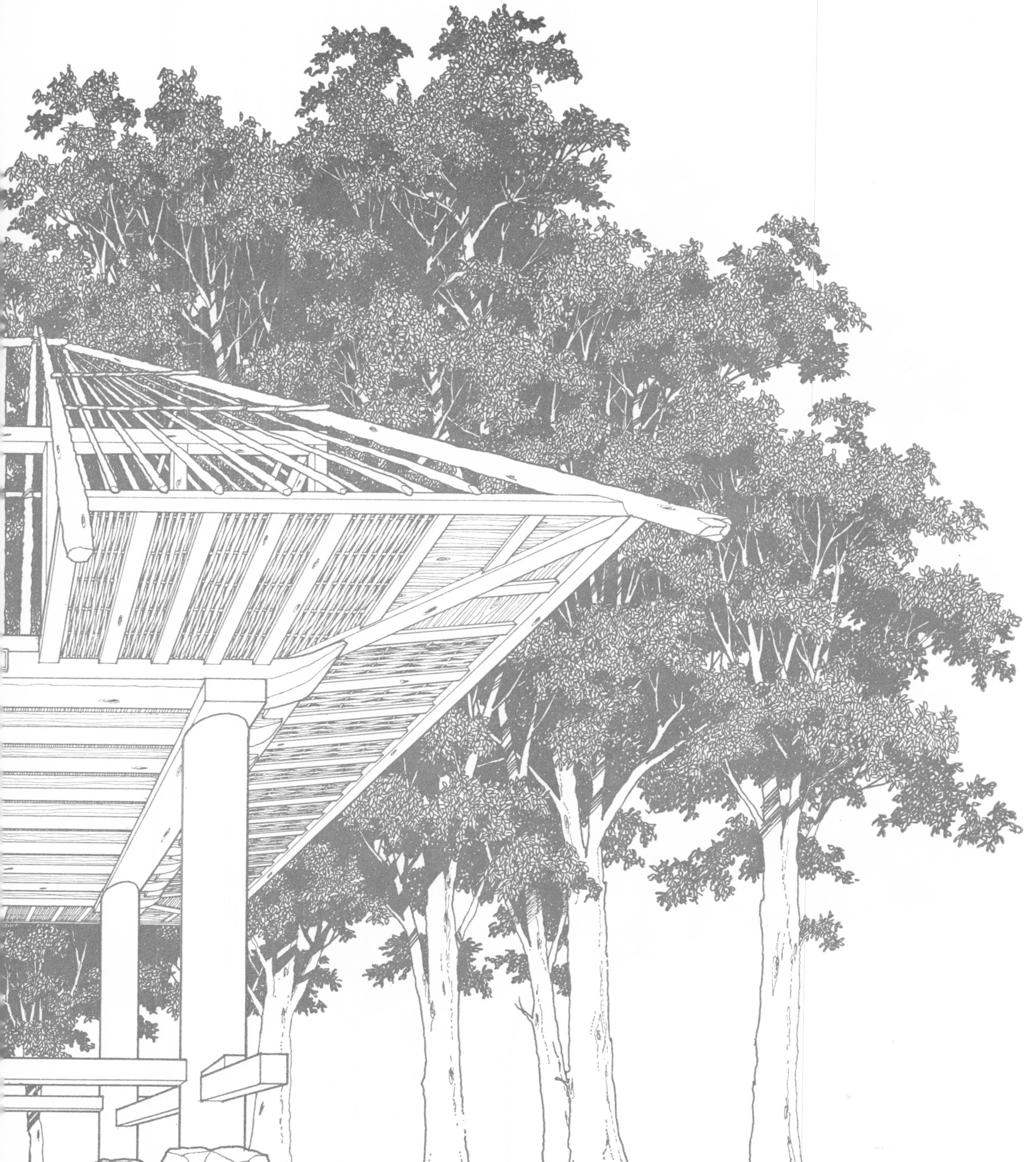

Raised-floor Storehouses

The class of storehouses known as *takakura* (高倉) (literally "high storehouses") had floors that were raised to a considerable height above ground level, and the space underneath the floors was open to the outside. Examples from the Yayoi period have been discovered at the sites of Yamaki and Toro in Shizuoka Prefecture, but after the sixteenth or seventeenth century this type was employed only in the islands off the Izu Peninsula, the islands southwest of Kyushu (including the Ryukyus), and Hokkaido. Wherever and whenever such buildings were constructed, the main purpose was to protect the grain that they held from undue moisture and, secondarily, from rats. In the Izu Islands, the takakura are found principally in Hachijō-jima and Aogashima, where they are known by names ranging from simply *kura* to *ashiage-kura* ("long-legged storehouses"). They were used for storing millet, fodder, or rice, and usually they belonged to individual families, but occasionally they were community property functioning as grain banks.

Their size is spoken of locally in terms of the number of supporting columns. Private storehouses usually have four columns or six columns, but a community storehouse might have as many as twelve columns. The height of the floor off the ground is usually around one meter, and most storehouses have rat barriers between the tops of the posts and the floor girders. These barriers are wooden plates about 80 centimeters across and are usually rectangular with rounded or truncated corners. When the floor girders are wide, the barriers are sometimes replaced by planks attached to the girders. The storehouses have hipped roofs made of thatch, and the ridgepoles are held up by straight studs or by an inverted V-shaped support. The outer walls are set about 60 centimeters outside the plane of the posts and are formed of vertically set cryptomeria planks. Sometimes the ground underneath is hollowed out to provide a sheltered work area.

Southwest of the principal Japanese islands, raised-floor storehouses are found in the Tokara, Amami, Okinawa, and Yaeyama archipelagos. In appearance and function, the storehouses in these areas are similar to those of the Izu Islands, but there are certain differences in structure and building materials. In addition to grain, these storehouses are often used for tools and dried fish. It would seem that communal storehouses were formerly numerous, but examples still standing usually belong to individuals, most often farmers of above average means. Sometimes the storehouses are located within individual farms, but occasionally they are grouped together in an area on the outskirts of the community, as at Yamatohama in Amami-Ōshima (pages 8–9, 124–27) and in Hateruma Island in the Yaeyama Archipelago. The storehouses in this area go by a wide variety of names, ranging from the standard *takakura* to dialect terms that would not be understood in most other parts of Japan. Many of the terms used indicate the number of posts in the storehouse, for as in Hachijō-jima, the size of the buildings is customarily indicated in this fashion. In Okinawa, smaller storehouses have four columns, middle-sized storehouses six or seven columns, and large storehouses eight or nine columns. The columns may be round or square, and they are usually about 20 centimeters thick.

Structurally, the storehouses fall into three types: (1) those of Hateruma Island, (2) those of Okinawa proper and Yoron Island, and (3) those of the Amami Islands north of Okinoerabu Island. The storehouses of Hateruma Island, which are raised from 1.5 to 2 meters off the ground, are basically of the board-wall type, but with grass roofs. Research by the architectual historian Takabumi Nomura has revealed that storehouses of the same structure are to be found also in Yunnan Province in China, in the Chiang Mai district of Thailand, and among the Menangkabau tribes of Sumatra. It can be assumed, therefore, that the Hateruma storehouses are of Southeast Asian lineage.

The second and third types are of the same basic structure but differ in the treatment of the walls. In Okinawa, the walls lean outward at an angle of from 50 to 70 degrees to the horizontal and are usually made of bamboo wicker. In the Amami Islands, the slant of the walls is much greater—only 10 to 20 degrees from the horizontal and sometimes even less—so that the walls become virtually a continuation of the floor (see diagram, previous page). The walls are made either of bamboo stripping or of wooden planks.

All of these storehouses have hipped roofs thatched with grass, miscanthus, bamboo, or bamboo grass. The floors are raised from 2 to 2.5 meters off the ground so that in rainy weather the space underneath can be used as a work area, for temporary storage of farm implements or lumber, or as a place for hanging out wash. Occasionally this area doubles as a stable for a horse or a cow. From time to time one encounters a storehouse of similar type that is set only 35 to 80 centimeters off the ground. This is called in this area a "ground storehouse" (*jigura*, 地倉) to distinguish it from the higher buildings.

The raised-floor storehouse has a long history in Okinawa. Just how long would be difficult to say, since little is known of Okinawa before the sixteenth or seventeenth century. There exists, however, a collection from about that time of 1244 ancient songs, which had been passed down orally over the centuries, and several of the songs are about storehouses that were obviously of this type.

The raised-floor storehouses in Hokkaido belong to the Ainu and are called *pu*, a word apparently unrelated to Japanese. Customarily these buildings are located in the southeast corner of the residential area. They rest on columns about 1.5 meters high that are sunk directly into the ground and are known as *pukema*. Small *pu* have four columns; ordinary ones, six; and large ones, eight or nine. The posts, which are surmounted by rat barriers, support a wooden floor or platform upon which rests a miniature version of a traditional Ainu house. In some cases both the roof and the walls are of miscanthus or reeds; in others the walls are in log-cabin style. The storehouse is approached by a stairway consisting of a log in which steps have been carved. The *pu* is used for storing not only grain but dried fish and other foodstuffs.

Dozō

There is no good word in English for the Japanese term *dozō* (土蔵), not only because the type of building to which it refers does not exist in Europe or America but because the kind of storehouse referred to has changed over the centuries. In the Edo period and afterward, dozō has indicated a storehouse with thick clay and plaster walls (clay on the inner side and plaster on the outside), rather than wooden walls, but such has not always been the case. Since dozō brings to the Japanese mind a storehouse with heavy plaster walls, the temptation is to call it a "plastered storehouse," but in the past the word has also been used to signify buildings with wooden walls and a daubing of dirt, lime, or plaster.

The situation is complicated by the fact that in the early stages the words *dozō* (土蔵) and *dosō* (土倉) seem to have been used synonymously, and both indicated buildings described above as "clay storehouses," *tsuchiya-gura* (土屋倉), in which a wooden wall was covered with clay or some other protective material.

Both dozō and dosō appear in historical sources of the Kamakura period (1185–1333), and both had two meanings. They referred, on the one hand, to storehouses as such and, on the other, to the moneylending establishments of Kyoto, Nara, Ōtsu, and other cities in the vicinity, which kept their own possessions, as well as goods received in security or in trust, in such clay-covered storehouses. Since some sake manufacturers doubled as moneylenders, the two words were also occasionally used to mean a sake shop or factory. In written sources of the middle ages, it is sometimes difficult to discern whether the words refer to buildings or to the moneylenders who owned the buildings. It is nevertheless true, however, that temples and shrines, as well as aristocrats and priests, sometimes owned dozō or dosō.

The earliest occurrence of the word dozō is in the *Tōdaiji monjo* [Documents of the Tōdai-ji]. It is found not only in a deed, dated 1290, for a house being sold by the priest Zenkyō but also in a document dated 1294 describing a house and land being donated by the priest Shinsei. Both documents list among the properties "one dozō," and since the dozō are listed directly

STOREHOUSE FORTIFICATION
Hikone Castle, Hikone, Shiga Prefecture

after the main houses, the implication is that the dozō were secondary in importance only to the residences themselves.

In the fourteenth century the word *dozō* appears more often. Sometimes it clearly refers to the buildings themselves: one source, for example, mentions a dozō in the residential compound of a warrior family, and the *Taiheiki* [Record of the great peace] tells of an incident in which the storehouses (dozō) of Kyoto were torn down and looted. In other sources, dozō clearly refers to pawnbrokers or moneylenders. A contemporary diary, for instance, mentions that a tax of eleven thousand strings of cash was levied in 1430 against the dozō in the capital, and other sources mention uprisings of farmers against dozō in 1447 and 1485. No doubt in these uprisings the downtrodden farmers attacked not only the moneylenders themselves but their storehouses as well.

The word *dosō* appears only shortly after dozō, also in the "Documents of the Tōdai-ji," where there is mention under the year 1313 of a Buddhist nun named Ninsai who had one house, two small separate houses, and one dosō. The same source mentions the sale in 1309 of 528 square meters of land in Kyoto on which there was a dosō. In both instances, the word obviously refers to buildings.

On the other hand, records of the Hie Shrine, near Kyoto, mention that in 1315 dosō in and around Kyoto were subjected to a tax for rebuilding a miniature shrine at Hie and that in 1394 the thirty-nine dosō of Sakamoto were required to pay for the expenses of a trip by the Shogun Ashikaga Yoshimitsu to the Hie Shrine. Here the word clearly refers to pawnbrokers and moneylenders, rather than to their storehouses.

Architecturally, dozō and dosō were indistinguishable and their uses were the same. Their contents could probably be divided into two classes: goods held in pawn and goods held in trust. The *Genkei-kyō nikki* [Diary of Lord Kototsugu] states that in order to borrow some money, Kototsugu pawned a side arm, a large sword, a lance, a musical instrument, and several articles of clothing. Other sources mention the pawning of such items as scroll paintings, screens, ink boxes, books, and deeds to property. It is recorded that in the eleventh month of 1420 thieves broke into the storehouse of a well-known pawnshop named Hōsen-bō

ENCLOSED STOREHOUSE
Masuki family, Chino, Nagano Prefecture

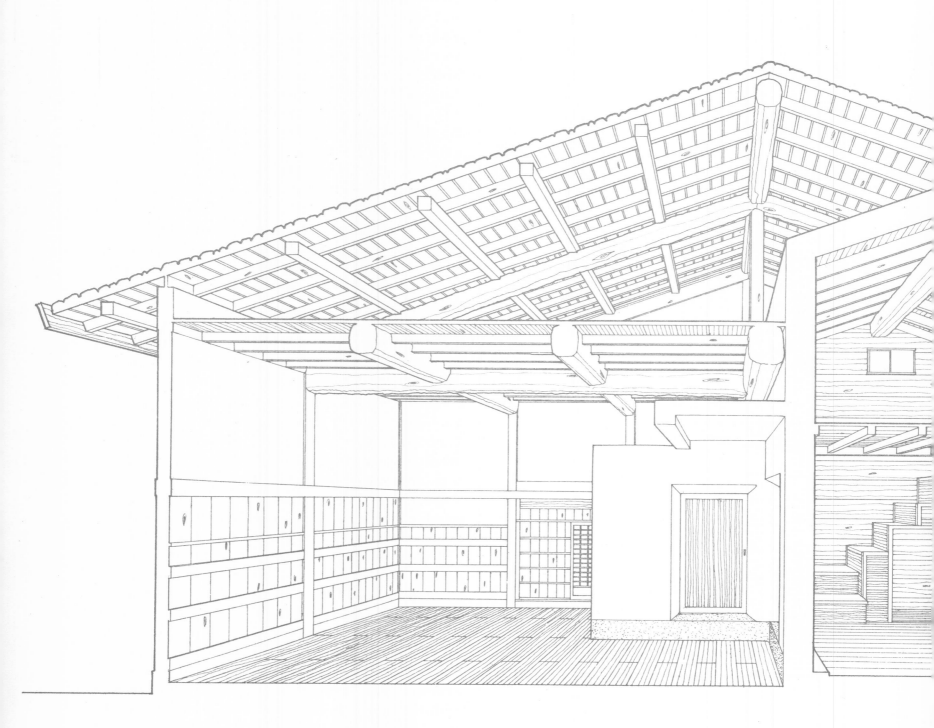

and set fire to it, burning three hundred kimonos that were in pawn at the time.

Because of the appeal of their semifireproof storehouses, the moneylenders also attracted people who merely wanted to store valuables in a safe place. This was a very common practice in the Muromachi period, not only among the common people but among warriors, priests, and aristocrats, who stored such articles as land deeds, strongboxes, and even cash. The emperor himself availed himself of such services: in 1443, when it was rumored that Prince Ogura of the Southern Court was going to attack Kyoto, the emperor entrusted two large boxes of valuables to Prince Fushimi, who in turn placed them in the care of a pawnbroker called Rinsen. In the *Sanetaka-kō-ki* [Record of Lord Sanetaka] it is recorded that on the twenty-ninth day of the seventh month of 1505, the storehouse of a moneylender named Shōjitsu-bō was looted and burned by thieves, and that ten thousand pieces of cash being held for the imperial household disappeared.

For some reason, after the Muromachi period the word *dosō* fell out of use, and from the Momoyama period (1573–1603) on we hear almost exclusively of dozō. One can only conjecture why.

The two words seem to have been completely interchangeable, but it appears that dosō was the more commonly used in reference to pawnbrokers and moneylenders. When the military government exacted a tax from these financiers, for example, it was called a *dosō* tax, and the *sō* element of *dosō* was used in the words referring to moneylenders who had special connections with the military and imperial governments.

It seems likely that when people other than moneylenders and pawnbrokers—ordinary merchants, temples, shrines, and the like—built storehouses of the dozō type, they avoided the term dosō because it had become connected with the image of usurers. In any event, in the Momoyama period, the word *dosō* fell largely into disuse, and at the same time there is ample evidence that more and more people not connected with the money business constructed storehouses. In the eighth chapter of *Seisuishō* [Laughter awake and asleep] by Anraku-an Sakuden, which was written in 1623, there is mention of a street-side salesman in Kyoto who built a storehouse (kura, written with the zō of dozō) for his goods. Also, in *Maebashi kyūzō monjo* [Documents formerly held by Maebashi], in 1614, at the time of the Siege of Osaka, the defenders of Osaka Castle dismantled storehouses (dozō) belonging to merchants outside the castle walls and brought them to the castle to be rebuilt as fortifications (*yagura*, 矢倉). It would appear from this that quite a few ordinary merchants in this area had dozō-style storehouses. One also finds references to numerous storehouses built by shrines and temples in the Momoyama period.

As to the form and structure of the dozō of these times, one example can be seen in the sixth section of the fourteenth scroll of the *Kasuga gongen scroll painting*, which dates from 1309. As mentioned above, this building was of a type that came to be known in the Edo period as *sayanegura* (鞘屋根蔵), or *okiyane-gura* (置屋根倉), both of which terms indicate a semifireproof boxlike building sheathed in clay or plaster, but having a flammable roof. When a fire occurred, the roof might be destroyed, but the contents of the storehouse would be relatively safe. During this age, tile roofs were rare, and most of the houses in the cities were covered with thatched or boarded roofs, which were quite flammable. It is consequently not surprising that the storehouses, too, would have flammable roofs. Had tiles been readily available, the situation might have been different, but they were not, and since the outer covering of the roofs was made of flammable material, there was little point in attempting to fireproof the understructures of the roofs. Storehouses of this type were common in farming villages and provincial cities in the Edo period, and many still stand today.

An interesting feature of the dozō in the *Kasuga gongen scroll painting* is that the entrance protrudes from the building about 1 meter and is sheltered by eaves covered with clay. There are double swinging doors, covered with plaster, and inside there is another slatted door that appears to have been of the sliding type. In a slightly later period, double swinging doors of dozō were as much as 30 centimeters in thickness and had recessed edges, like modern safe doors. In early examples, however, the doors are no more than 10 centimeters thick, and there are no recessed edges. It might also be noted that in a later age, the inner slatted door was often replaced by a combination of an iron grid, to keep out rats, and a plastered sliding door,

which could be left open when the storehouse was being aired.

According to *Kōgei shiryō* [A compendium of the crafts], written in 1888 by Professor Mayori Kurokawa, double swinging doors first came into use in storehouses between 1615 and 1625, before which time people had used mud-covered doors called "Osaka doors." This statement, which probably represents a theory prevalent around the end of the Edo period or the beginning of the Meiji, is very difficult to interpret because of the vagueness of the wording. It is patently untrue that double swinging doors were not used before 1615, because they are seen in the example from the *Kasuga gongen* scroll. It seems likely that the meaning intended is that until around 1615 storehouse doors were relatively thin and had no recessed edges, whereas after that time they began to be thicker and had recessed edges.

In one source, the *Yasutomi-ki* [Record of Yasutomi], in an entry for the year 1454, there is mention of a sake shop and storehouse in Kyoto that is described as an "earth-filled wooden storehouse." One supposes that this was a building having double wooden walls with a layer of earth between them. The mention of this storehouse in the source cited suggests that it was a very unusual type, rather than one encountered frequently.

It is not certain when people began trying to fireproof the roofs of their storehouses as well as the walls and ceilings. It is a safe assumption, however, that this did not occur until after tiles became plentiful enough to be used in ordinary houses. In the Kyoto region, this happened after the Battle of Sekigahara, which occurred in 1600. Genre paintings of this period show castle turrets and three-story storehouses with tile roofs, and it seems likely that, in the cities at least, storehouses with fireproof roofs were relatively common by this time.

Stone Storehouses

The word for stone storehouses, *ishigura* (石倉), is used to refer to two distinct types. The first was not actually a separate storehouse, but rather a sort of cellar within the stone foundations of castle towers. The area between the foundation walls of these buildings was dark, and the space was broken up by large columns here and there, so that the area was better suited for storage than for anything else. An early example was in the Azuchi Castle of Oda Nobunaga (1534–82). The *Nobunaga-kō-ki* [Record of Lord Nobunaga] refers to the cellar as the "first floor," probably because the entrance to the building was through the cellar. We do not know the measurements of this cellar, but the second floor of the building, which was really the first floor from the functional viewpoint, measured 36 by 42 meters, and subtracting the thickness of the stone foundation walls, one can assume that the interior measurements of the cellar were about 31.5 by 38 meters.

The second type of ishigura was a separate storehouse, but here again two subtypes are found. One had structural bearing walls made by piling up stone blocks. The other was a wooden structure around which stone walls were placed for fire protection and finishing. The *Fusō ryakki* [Abbreviated history of Japan], in an entry for 896, mentions a storehouse with stone bearing walls in the residential compound of Kaya no Yoshifuji in Bichū Province (Okayama Prefecture). According to this source, "there were no columns, but only beams above the walls, which had been made by piling up stones." The roof, it may be surmised, was made of wood. There is virtually no other mention of storehouses with stone bearing walls until the Edo period (1603–1868).

By the Edo period, firearms and cannons were in common use, and stone storehouses were occasionally built as arsenals. In the only remaining example from the period, which is in Osaka Castle, the walls, the floors, and the ceiling are all of stone (pages 143–45 and diagram, overleaf). Dirt was piled on the ceiling to form the support for a tile roof. The interior measurements of this building are 2.7 by 15.6 meters. Records relate that there was formerly another similar store-house in the same castle, placed on a stone foundation that measured 27.3 by 9.8 meters. The outer measurements of this arsenal were 6.6 by 21.5 meters, and the inner measurements were 2.7 by 15.6 meters, so that the thickness of the stone walls was approximately 1.9 meters. There also appears to have been still another stone arsenal at Osaka Castle with an outer measurement of 5.9 by 19.5 meters.

The architectual historian Yoshikuni Ōkuma, in his *Meiji izen Nihon kenchiku gijutsu-shi* [History of architectural techniques in Japan before the Meiji period], tells of an ammunition storehouse built in 1702 at the castle of Zeze (Shiga Prefecture). This was also a stone building, but it was somewhat smaller than the storehouses at Osaka Castle. The interior measurements were 1.8 by 9 meters, with a ceiling height of 2.1 meters. The stone walls were about 90 centimeters thick, and the stone slabs that formed the ceiling were about 24 centimeters thick. Unlike the arsenals at Osaka Castle, the stone structure in this case was encircled by an outer earthen wall 45 centimeters thick and a tile roof. There was a space of about 45 centimeters between the stone walls and the outer walls. The roof, which was tiled, was supported by sand and earth piled on top of the ceiling. Outside the building, at a distance of about 3.6 meters from the wall, there was another earthen wall about 2.3 meters high, and outside of this, at a distance of 1.8 meters, there was a moat 1.5 meters wide.

During the Edo period at least, no storehouses other than those used for ammunition appear to have had stone bearing walls. In certain areas, Western-style storehouses with stone walls were built in the first quarter of the twentieth century, but they were soon found to be lacking in strength against earthquakes, and buildings of this type are no longer constructed today.

Storehouses in which the stone walls were an outer sheath for a wooden building were more common. In the Edo period, Dutchmen living on the island of Dejima in Nagasaki built stone storehouses that looked like European buildings, and it is commonly supposed that these had stone bearing walls, but those that are still standing have wooden frame structures and are quite Japanese in concept (pages 152–53). Even this variety of stone storehouse was relatively unusual, but a few are recorded in the Muromachi and later periods. For example, the *Hisamori-ki* [Diary of Hisamori] mentions, in an entry for the seventeenth day of the first month of 1488, the bringing of twenty logs to be used in constructing a stone storehouse at the Higashiyama Palace of Ashikaga Yoshimasa. The *Tamon-in nikki* [Diary of Tamon-in], in an entry for the eighteenth day of the fifth month of 1585, speaks of piling stones for a stone storehouse. In *Daijō-in jisha zōji-ki* [Various records concerning the shrines and temples of the Daijō-in], under the twelfth day of the sixth month of 1489, we read that "Saburōjirō, the son of the priest Myōkan in Jūza, performed so well as the carpenter who built the eastern stone storehouse (of the Daijō-in) that he was given an honorary title." It might be noted that Jūza refers to ten areas in the northern half of Nara, which in the middle ages were set aside as residences for people of the lowest classes, such as beggars, prostitutes, and coolies. One suspects from the passage quoted that work such as piling stones was done only by members of the lowest class of laborers.

Today in certain localities there are quite a few stone storehouses of the second type. Some of the best examples are found in the vicinity of Utsunomiya in Tochigi Prefecture (pages 10–11, 146–51, and diagram, overleaf), particularly in the town of Tokujirō and the village of Nishine. Other examples are to be found in the upper reaches of the Kinugawa river in the same prefecture, in the town of Kanaya, Kimitsu County, Chiba Prefecture, and in parts of the Izu Peninsula in Shizuoka Prefecture.

At Ōya, about seven kilometers northwest of the center of Utsunomiya, and at Shimotanaka, seven kilometers north of Ōya, there are stone quarries where an unusual soft rock called Ōya stone or Nikko stone is obtained. This is a kind of tufa that is gray or greenish-gray in color. Since it is inexpensive, it was considered a good material for stone storehouses. It is soft and easily abrased, but it is waterproof and does not effloresce quickly. It also has the advantage of being easy to cut or carve. Frank Lloyd Wright was very much attracted to Ōya stone and used large quantities of it in his Imperial Hotel in Tokyo (1922). It is said that the owners of the hotel objected to the use of this stone at first, apparently because they thought it was

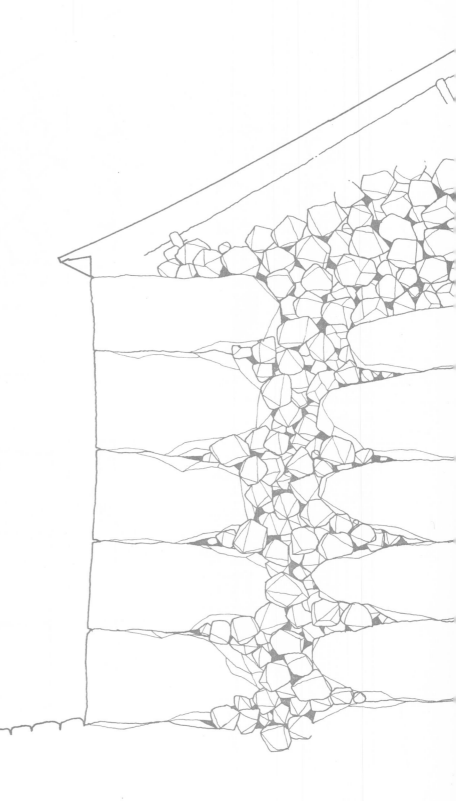

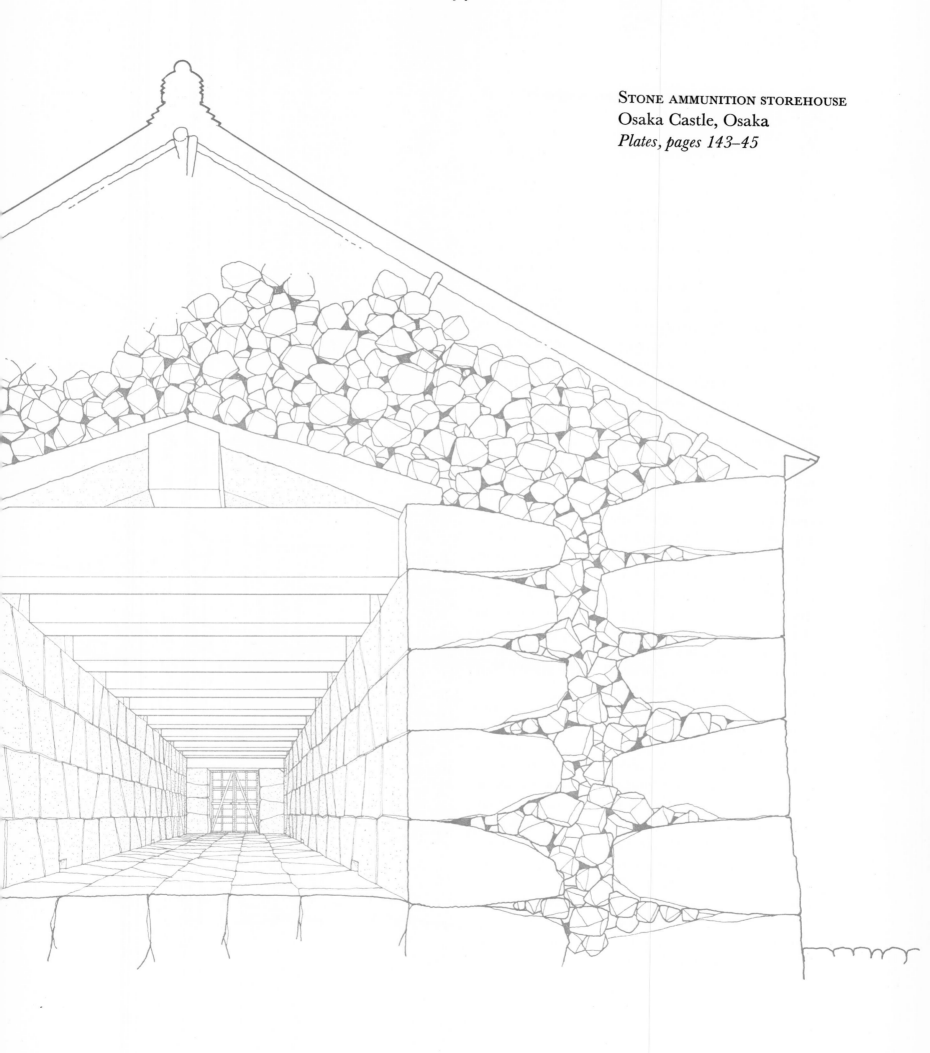

STONE AMMUNITION STOREHOUSE
Osaka Castle, Osaka
Plates, pages 143–45

STONE STOREHOUSE
Watanabe family, Utsunomiya,
Tochigi Prefecture
Plates, pages 10–11 and 150–151

too cheap a rock to be used in a magnificent luxury hotel in which even the Imperial Household Ministry was investing. Wright used the stone anyway, and it doubtless made possible much of the architectural ornamentation in the building, though its low cost does not seem to have prevented him from exceeding his original budget considerably.

Properly speaking, Nikko stone and Ōya stone are not exactly the same. The principal difference is that Nikko stone has a somewhat finer grain than Ōya stone and is consequently better for finely detailed sculpturing. The town of Tokujirō, where Nikko stone is obtained, has a number of stone storehouses with skillfully carved relief ornamentation (page 148).

Nikko stone and Ōya stone were used to make roofs for houses and storehouses before they were used for walling. These stone roofs date from the Edo period, but no example from that age has been preserved, and the oldest now in existence are from the Meiji period. A good example is the storehouse of Mr. Tokuji Ikeda in the village of Nishine, which was built in 1880. This has a stone roof, but otherwise it is a typical wooden storehouse.

These Ōya stone roofs caught the attention of Edward S. Morse (1838–1925), who came to Japan and taught zoology at Tokyo Imperial University, and who also had a keen interest in Japanese residential architecture. Morse mentions the stone roofs in his *Japanese Homes and Their Surroundings*, and his remarks suggest that in the middle part of the Meiji period, that is, in the 1880s, Ōya stone was being used principally in storehouse roofs. This book provides a drawing of the stone tiles, which apparently were very much like the tiles one sees in the Ōya region today. The only difference is that whereas today both upper and lower tiles have shallow U-shaped centers, in Morse's drawing, only the upper tiles had this shape. The stone tiles used today, it might be noted, are quite large. The upper tiles are usually about 90 centimeters long, 33 centimeters wide, and 10 centimeters thick. The lower tiles are about the same, except that they are somewhat thinner. One upper stone usually weighs around 40 kilograms.

After the middle of the Meiji period, it became the practice in the Utsunomiya area to add stone walls to what had formerly been simple board-wall storehouses (itagura). The purpose of the stone walls, of course, was to add a measure of protection against fire. The stones were stacked in customary brick-wall style, and at first no mortar was used in the seams, though after around 1910 mortar and cement came into use. Iron or steel nails with large heads were driven through the seams to the inner wooden walls in order to anchor the stone walls to them (see page 150).

Although the stone storehouses in Tochigi Prefecture contained wooden structures, their exteriors were modeled on the dozō storehouses. In particular, the treatment of the window frames and the thicker section of the walls directly under the eaves were almost identical to that seen in the dozō (see page 151). Also, in place of the so-called "trowel pictures" (*kote-e*) found on the doors, windows, and gable walls of the dozō, the stone storehouses often had relief carvings of such typical subjects as family crests, arabesques, dragons, the tortoise and crane motif, the tortoise and wave motif, the crane and cloud motif, or blossoming plum trees. These carvings by nameless craftsmen are inclined to be trite, but the painstaking care with which the various propitious themes were executed attests to the solicitousness with which the workmen sought to ensure the long life of the storehouses.

Storage Pits

Storage pits are called *anagura* (穴倉), a compound of *ana*, meaning "hole" or "pit," and *kura*. Theoretically, the English translation would be "pit storehouses," but in fact the *anagura* was no more than a pit dug under the floor of a building, and the word is still another illustration of the translation-defying broadness of the word kura.

The origin of the anagura is uncertain, but it is probably identical with the *tsuchigura* (窖), literally, "clay storehouse," mentioned in the *Wamyō ruijū-sho*, the tenth-century lexicon. According to this source, the *tsuchigura* was a pit hollowed out under a house as a storage place for grain.

We know from a number of sources that such storage pits were used by noblemen during the Muromachi period (1333–1573). There is mention of one, for example, in the diary of Fujiwara Chikanaga (1424–1500), a courtier of the time of the Emperor Gotsuchimikado (reigned 1465–1500). According to this source, on the night of the twenty-fifth day of the tenth month of 1478, there was a great fire that spread toward the writer's house, and everybody rushed to put valuable possessions in the storage pit. It would appear that the storage pit at this time was a place for safekeeping articles in times of emergency, rather than on a permanent basis. This seems logical, because the dampness of a pit of this sort would militate against storing anything in it for extended periods of time.

A source from 1658 contains a New Year's haiku by a Kyoto poet that was dedicated to the safety and well-being of the storage pit in the coming year. That anyone would compose such a poem for a storage pit suggests that the latter must have been considered important, at least among the townspeople of Kyoto. There is no way of knowing how many pits of this type existed, but one suspects that they could not have been very unusual.

In the eighteenth century, the scholar Kamisawa Sadamiki mentioned in his essays entitled *Okinagusa* [Leaves of an old man], the story of a Kyoto doctor named Genshuku who had a remarkable experience with a storage pit. It seems that Genshuku, for want of business, was living a very humble life, but decided one day to set about making something of himself. First, he reasoned, he needed a fine house, and in order to buy one, he borrowed money from everyone who would lend it. Finally he acquired enough to buy a good corner house in a good area, and in preparation for moving into it, he sent workmen in to clean it. As they were washing the stone walls of the storage pit, they noticed something shiny at the bottom. Curious, they took out one of the stone blocks from the wall and discovered that it was not a stone at all, but a block of high-grade zinc from olden times, worth far more than the zinc currently in use. The doctor sold off his trove of zinc at such a high price that even after he paid back his debts, he was a wealthy man. After that, we are told, the people of Kyoto spoke of high-grade zinc as "Genshuku."

The substitution of blocks of zinc for stones in the walls of storage pits could not have been very widespread, but the casual way in which Kamisawa refers to the stone-lined pit indicates that it was commonplace in the capital. According to *Kinsei Fūzoku-shi* [Manners and customs of the Edo period] by Kitagawa Morisada, the storage pits of Kyoto were built of Mikage stone, a type of granite found in the vicinity of present-day Kobe.

Storage pits spread from the Kyoto area to Edo around 1656. At this time more than half a century had passed since the founding of the Tokugawa shogunate in Edo, and the central section of the city had come to be fairly densely populated. According to *Waga koromo* [My robe] by Katō Genki, the first storage pit was built by a clothing merchant named Izumiya Kuzaemon, whose shop was at No. 2 Honchō. Kuzaemon was a declassed samurai who had formerly been in the service of a daimyo named Fukushima, and it may well be that he had become acquainted with the storage pits of Kyoto and Osaka during his travels as a military man. In any event, the storage pit served him well, because in the first month of the following year there occurred the famous Furisode Fire, the most disastrous fire of the whole Edo period, and while most of the city was razed, Kuzaemon's storage pit came through unscathed.

After that the Tokugawa government promoted the building of storage pits. The experience of 1657 showed that property damage and loss of life could have been reduced but for the fact that many of the narrow streets had become clogged with the carts in which fleeing people had packed their valuables. These carts not only blocked passageways but helped spread the fire by becoming links between the houses on one side of the street and those on the other. The government issued a ban on carting away articles from burning or threatened buildings, and it was to compensate for this restriction that storage pits, which were much less expensive than dozō, were officially encouraged.

Six years after Izumiya built his storage pit, another clothing merchant, Daikoku-ya, built, also at No. 2 Honchō, what was for the time a very magnificent shop. The building was so grand that upon seeing it, Mitsui Takafusa, owner of the well-known store Echigoya (precursor of the modern Mitsukoshi department store) and a relative of the proprietor of the Daikoku-ya, criticized the latter for his extravagance and predicted that he would go broke if he did not mend his ways. According to *Chōnin kōkin-roku* [Record of thoughts about merchants], dated 1728, the Daikoku-ya was indeed splendid by Edo standards. It was built in the dozō style and was two stories high. With a frontage of 11.7 meters and a depth of 28.8 meters, it was the largest store in the city.

Fortunately, a floor plan of this building has been preserved. It shows that there were storage pits in five places on the first floor. All of them were small, the largest being only 60 centimeters by 120 centimeters. These measurements are for the mouths of the pits, and the open spaces underneath may have had a larger area, but when one considers that the artisans who made these pits subsequently turned their skills to the production of wooden bathtubs, it seems unlikely that the pits were very large. It is most likely that they were about the size of a wooden bathtub, 50 or 60 by 80 or 90 centimeters, and of similar construction.

In the seventeenth century, storage pits seem to have been still rare in Edo. A passage in *Jinteki mondō*, which dates from 1706, says: "These days more and more people are building storage pits. This is because these pits offer protection from fire, and because there are so many buildings and people in the city now that not much land is vacant." The implication is that it was becoming increasingly difficult to acquire enough land to build dozō, and people were consequently content-

ing themselves with storage pits under their houses.

The storage pits of Kyoto were, as we have seen, made of stone, but those of Edo were essentially wooden boxes sunk into the ground. According to the architectural historian Yoshikuni Ōkuma, the wood was usually Japanese cypress (*hinoki* or *hiba*), and the boxes were put together with boat nails and covered with pitch. No doubt the choice of this type of water-proof box was dictated by the fact that Edo was on very low ground, and the level of the rivers in the city was high, so that pits lined with stone would have been very damp. Logically enough, the first storage-pit boxes were made by shipwrights, some of whom apparently gave up boats to specialize in the boxes. One Edo period source even mentions by name a certain Koteemon, whom it describes as a "skillful storage-pit maker" (*anagura-ya*). "Manners and customs of the Edo period" mentions that at the end of the Tokugawa period, there were several storage-pit carpenters in the Kawaguchi district of Reigan-jima in Edo. Some of these carpenters remained active even in the Meiji period: the Tokyo *Asahi Newspaper* for July 10, 1888, mentions a storage-pit carpenter named Akashiya Chōhachi.

In Edo, an order was issued by the government in 1658 forbidding people to build *nuritare* (塗垂) storage pits on the river banks unless they had first obtained permission. The meaning of *nuritare* is not certain, but it would appear that the storage pits in question were built in the Kyoto manner, that is, of stone, but with plaster or mortar waterproofing at the seams.

The scholar Kitagawa Morisada, writing in the early eighteenth century, speaks of the difference between storage pits in Edo and in the Kyoto-Osaka region: "These days in the Kyoto-Osaka area, rich people build storage pits for their gold and silver. As a rule, people who are not rich do not build such pits, but small and medium-sized money changers do. Rich families in Edo also build storage pits, usually behind their houses or behind their dozō. For the most part, the pits are used for storing gold and silver. Some middle- and lower-class merchants also build pits, but not to store gold and silver. Lacking the capital to build dozō, they build pits to put their goods in when there is a fire. Dozō cost much to build, whereas storage pits do not. Also, even people who have the means to build a dozō often make do with storage pits for the lack of a place in which to build the dozō.''

This passage suggests that the storage pits built by Daikoku-ya and other Edo merchants were used for storing gold and silver coins in the event of fire. The pits, consequently, did not need to be very large.

Other Types

Storehouses of unusual structure are found here and there in various districts. An example is to be seen in the area around the village of Kuriyama, Tochigi Prefecture, where the structure and walls of the storehouse are made by lining up vertically square posts measuring from 12 to 15 centimeters to the side and covering these with a wooden gabled roof. To avoid fires, these buildings were usually placed in the fields or along the roads outside the village.

In the Musashino and Chichibu regions (Tokyo and Saitama prefectures), there was a type of wooden storehouse called a *kokubitsu* (穀櫃), or literally a "grain chest" (page 134). Typically, this was of small scale, the largest being no more than 5.4 by 3.6 meters. The walls were made by hollowing out grooves in the sides of the posts and sliding in planks about 30 centimeters across. Buildings of this type had either a board roof with stones placed on top of it or a thatched roof, and occasionally the roof support structure was independent of the building proper. The storehouses were used for grain, and some belonged to individual families, while others were community grain banks. Examples of the former are found rather frequently in the Chichibu Mountains.

This type of storehouse is an outgrowth of a grain bin that was often built in the corners of dirt floor rooms (*doma*) in South Kanto (the region around Tokyo Prefecture). These bins usually had an area of 90 by 90 or 180 centimeters and a height of 180 centimeters. Boxes of this size constituted a unit, and dependent upon the harvest, farmers might build two or three or four of them, lining them up along the wall. Ōhara Yūgaku (1797–1858), a late Tokugawa agricultural leader, incorporated a bin of this type in a model farmhouse that he designed.

One difficulty was that these rice bins, being inside the house, burned down when the house burned down. Consequently, some farmers placed them outside the house, where they became miniature kura. It might be noted that the Kodera family's main house was recently destroyed by fire, and the little storehouse shown here was preserved only because it was placed at a distance from the house.

Dozō Architecture and Fire Prevention

The Structure of Dozō Buildings

Until the development of the dozō (土蔵) in the late middle ages, and even afterward in some farming communities, the simplest and most effective way of avoiding fires in storehouses was to place them at a distance from other buildings. Even in the earliest legal code of Japan, there was a regulation saying: "Storehouses are all to be built on high and dry ground, and there should be a pond nearby. No buildings are to be constructed within 152 meters of the storehouse. These provisions are for the sake of preventing fires."

It is not known to what extent this law was carried out. In the early Heian period, it would appear that in various provinces and districts storehouses were built quite close to each other, for an order promulgated in 791 banned this practice and stipulated that there should be an interval of at least 30 meters between storehouses. An almost identical order, however, was issued only four years later, and similar regulations were put out from time to time after that, raising the suspicion that the law was being observed mostly in the breach, but the laws themselves show a consciousness of the need for providing open space between buildings as a means of preventing fires from spreading. This need was reduced by the development of the dozō storehouse, which played an important part in the physical formation of early modern Japanese towns and cities.

Though dozō are no longer built today, they were an important utilitarian architectural form for at least 650 years. During that time many changes occurred in their structure and details. Broadly speaking, the development was from a board-wall structure covered with clay, plaster, or lime to a much more fireproof building with thick clay and plaster walls and no wooden parts exposed on the outside. There were numerous variations in architectural detail, but the developed dozō of the Edo period were constructed more or less as described in the succeeding paragraphs.

Structural framework

A groundwork of two or three layers of stone (see, for example, pages 236–38) was laid, and on this was placed a grid of heavy timbers as a foundation. Upon this a wooden post-and-beam structure was erected, with columns spaced at an interval of about 90 centimeters, except where wider spaces were left for doors. The columns were linked by horizontal braces, and, as a rule, there were no transverse horizontal beams in the roof support framework, since horizontal beams tended to interfere with the work of piling up goods and at the same time to reduce the usable space. Diagonal beams ran from the girders to the ridgepole. In many cases they were supported at the center by a second timber, larger than the ridgepole and directly underneath it. (See diagram, overleaf, which does not, however, show the double ridgepole arrangement.)

Walls

The walls consisted of two layers. The inner one, which ran between the columns, was composed of a bamboo lathing covered with several coats of clay mixed with one of a variety of fibrous materials. The outer walling, which was the most important element in the fireproofing, covered the posts and any other wooden parts that would otherwise have been exposed to the exterior. A simple version of this layer was sometimes made by attaching planks to the outer sides of the columns and covering them with a 6- to 8-centimeter layer of clay finished with plaster. By far the most common method, however, was much more elaborate and much more effective. In this case, the outer walls were as much as 12 to 16 centimeters thick. A bamboo lathing was made on the outer sides of the posts, and a clay wall built up by a laborious process involving repeated applications and corrections and ending with the application of a plaster finishing. The standard number of steps in making this outer wall was eighteen, and some plasterers used as many as twenty-four. Furthermore, the procedure was very time-consuming: it is said that in the case of a black plaster finish, the final polishing of the surface alone involved so much work that it required one workman a whole day to finish a patch 90 centimeters square.

The outer plaster walls were subject to damage by heavy rain or by being accidentally struck by people or cargo, and it became the custom in many places to add, either over the whole wall or over the lower half, a protective sheathing of flat tiles. These were usually square and about 30 centimeters across, but occasionally one encounters hexagons or other variations. When square, the tiles were lined up either diagonally or horizontally, and the joints were covered with thick plaster spreading two or three centimeters on either side and rounded on the top (pages 188–89, 193, 198, 207–13). Since the rounded strips of plaster reminded people of the elongated sea cucumber, or *namako*, the walls were called *namako* walls. Such walls first appeared on houses of the warrior class in the early Edo period, but they were later used widely on houses and dozō belonging to merchants and other commoners.

Skirt wall

In the dozō of Edo and other parts of eastern Japan, additional security was often achieved by adding a skirt wall around the bottom of the buildings. This was usually from 90 to 180 centimeters high and around 15 centimeters thick, and it covered the stone underpinning. The wall was made of clay mixed with gravel and was finished with plaster. It protected the building against the ground fires that are apt to occur during large conflagrations.

Under the eaves

Since flames are apt to be particularly severe under the eaves of the roof, the walls of the dozō were made thicker in this section (see, for example, pages 202–3, 236–37).

Rain deflectors

It was not uncommon to provide a protruding horizontal strip along the walls at one or two levels to deflect rain water that dripped down from the walls above (page 203). In some locales, the strips were wide enough to resemble small eaves, and were covered with tiles (pages 204–5).

Doors

The doors of dozō were often very impressive. Typically, there were heavy double swinging doors on the outside, an inner "white door" behind this, and a grille door behind the white door. The double swinging doors were sometimes omitted, but when they were present, their leaves were usually about 105 centimeters wide by 180 centimeters high, and their thick-

LIBRARY STOREHOUSE
Kusakabe family, Takayama, Gifu Prefecture
Plates, pages 241–43

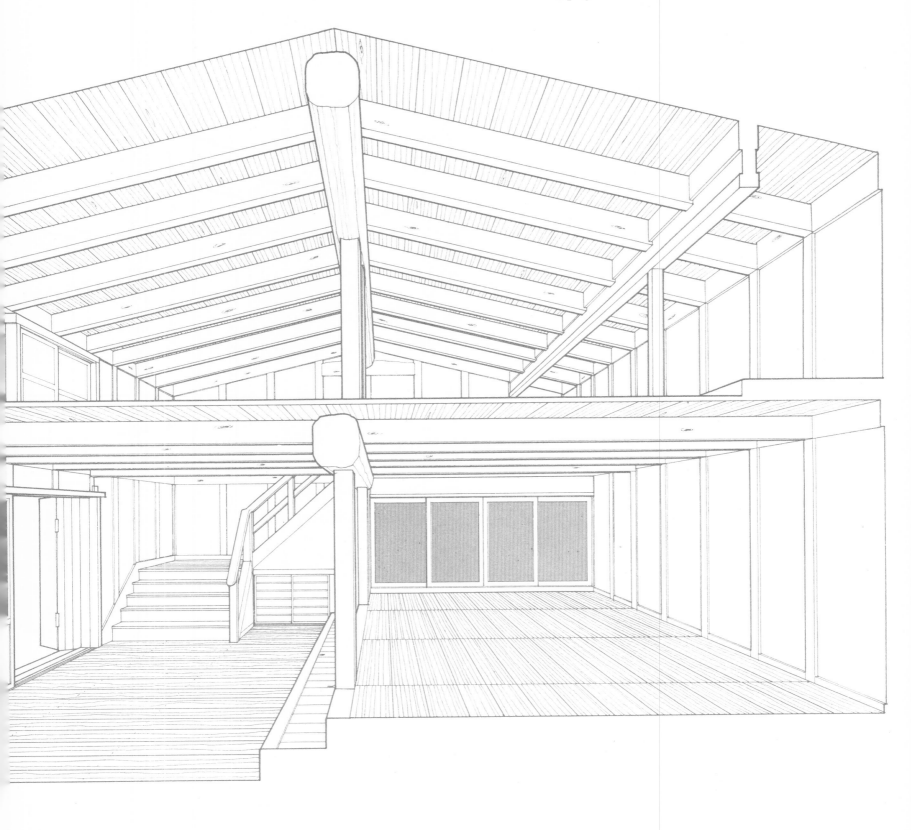

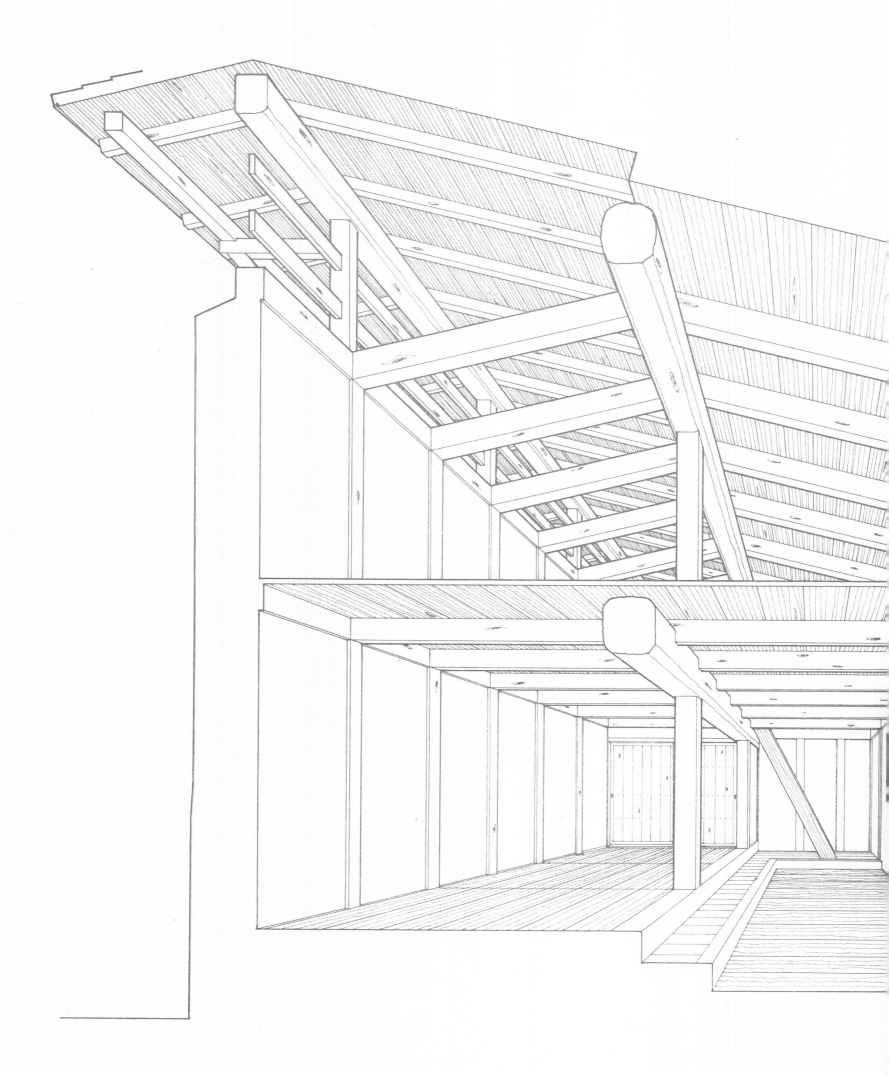

LIBRARY STOREHOUSE
Kusakabe family, Takayama, Gifu Prefecture
Plates, pages 241–43

ness was roughly the same as that of the layer of the wall outside the columns. At top, right, and left, their edges were recessed in three or four steps, so as to fit in with similar recesses on the door frame in the fashion seen on modern bank vault doors (pages 219, 230–31). The recessed edges, devised to avoid a straight gap through which fire might pass easily, were called *jabara*. It is said that one of the first lessons taught to apprentices who went to work for merchants of the Edo period was how to close the door without damaging the *jabara*. Actually, since these doors were left open most of the time, damage to the *jabara* was more likely to result from a blow of some sort on the outside, and in some places protective grilles were placed around the lower halves of the doors (page 219). As a rule, these doors had no locks other than a simple iron latch (page 215).

The inner "white door" was a sliding door made of wood planks covered on the outside with plaster. Some people left this door open most of the time; others kept it closed. The white door had no lock. The only real lock in the entranceway was usually on the innermost door (pages 214, 216), which usually had wooden paneling for its lower half and a wooden or iron grille for the upper, with a copper screen across the grille. When it was necessary in the course of putting things into or taking them out of the storehouse to leave this door open, a wooden panel 60 to 90 centimeters high was often placed temporarily in the doorway to prevent rats from entering.

Windows

In the Kyoto-Osaka region, storehouse windows were usually shuttered with single swinging panels, but in the Edo region and eastern Japan, they were miniature versions of the double panel doors at the entrance (pages 18–19, 224–25). The difference probably arose from the fact that there were more serious fires in Edo than in the Kyoto-Osaka region.

When fire broke out, the doors and windows of the dozō were closed, and the cracks at the edges were covered with clay. It was customary to keep a quantity of good clay somewhere in the neighborhood of the main entrance for use in emergencies. It is said that at the warning of fire plasterers went around to their various customers and sealed their storehouse doors and windows for them. It was also customary to keep a tub of water inside the dozō to prevent the air inside from drying out excessively because of the heat. After a fire ended, the doors and windows of the dozō were left shut for a few days until the temperature came down. This was to avoid the danger that fresh air coming into the heated building might cause a fire.

It would appear that the dozō was comparatively effective against fire. After a great fire in Edo in 1829, in which it was rumored that two thousand people lost their lives, a contemporary writer composed the following poem:

> At the break of day
> Fire and smoke dwindle and dim—
> The white walls of the storehouses
> Lingeringly appear.

Dozō *of East and West Japan*

The dozō of the Edo period were the product of a preindustrial feudal society, and they reflect the environment and mores of that society. They varied to some extent in form from district to district, but in general there were two main traditions, the dozō of Edo and eastern Japan and the dozō of the Osaka-Kyoto region. These two regions are known respectively as Kanto and Kansai and are the two most important cultural regions of Japan.

The dozō of the Kansai region have a tradition going back directly to the middle ages; those of the Kanto region developed under the influence of the great urban center that was Edo.

This is not to say that the dozō of Kanto had no historical connection with those of Kansai. On the contrary, in the early stages the two types were very much alike. A seventeenth-century screen painting of Edo (*Edo-zu byōbu*), for instance, shows dozō belonging to merchants, daimyos, and temples, and these buildings are almost indistinguishable from two- and three-story storehouses seen in a contemporary screen painting of Kyoto (*Keiraku fūzoku-zu byōbu*). In both cases, the buildings had gabled tile roofs of the *hongawara* (本瓦) type, in which slightly concave under tiles alternate with round upper tiles, as opposed to the *sangawara* (桟瓦) type in which the tiles are identical except at the edges. In both cases also, all wooden parts of the buildings were covered with a white material of some kind. These early storehouses differed in some respects from the later dozō of both Kyoto and Edo, and they seem to be related to the clay-covered storehouses (tsuchiya-gura) of the Kyoto region or to castle architecture of the Momoyama period. Unlike the later dozō, for instance, the plastering under the eaves is not solid; the wooden parts are covered, but the shapes of the rafters can be seen. Again, the windows of the buildings are grilles whose slats are covered with plaster, whereas later dozō had outside shutters.

It could be argued that the painter of the Edo screen ignored storehouses that actually existed in the city and instead copied images from other screen paintings showing views of Kyoto, of which a good number were in existence. It is far more likely, however, that in the early stages Edo had no distinct dozō tradition of its own. That was to come later, when the population rose above a million, making the city far larger than either Kyoto or Osaka. By that time Edo was a dense conglomeration of wooden buildings—a vast pile of tinder, constantly in danger of a conflagration. People had a very real motive for devising a dozō that could withstand fires better than the plastered buildings of Kyoto.

The year 1657, which was the date of the Furisode Fire, was a turning point. Curiously, however, the effect of this and other fires did not cause everybody to work for better fireproofing. There was a widespread viewpoint in which fires were held to be inevitable anyway, and resignation to that fact was the only sensible course. Sakurada Komon (1774–1839) was a government official who was a proponent of this idea. In outlining factors that must be kept in mind when building a house in Edo, he wrote: "The building is going to burn down anyway, so everything should be made as simple as possible: 10-centimeter columns rather than 14-centimeter columns; 2-centimeter roof boards rather than 3-centimeter roof boards; 4.8-meter beams rather than 5.7-meter beams; flat tiles instead of rounded tiles; modest rather than grand gates; natural rather than cut stone. . . . One can also save by using a lower grade of lumber. With the saving, the thing to do is buy lumber and make ready for building a new house after the next fire. The lumber can be kept in the suburbs." In fact, such advice was often followed in the residential sections of the mansions of the daimyos.

There was also an activist viewpoint. People no doubt found that the plaster-covered wooden storehouses of Kyoto were not adequate in the great fires of Edo. Fires spread into the interiors of these buildings, and often the interiors burned even though the walls did not. Sometimes the interior walls were turned to charcoal by the heat, even when there was little exterior damage. It was no doubt dissatisfaction with these failings that led Edo to develop its own form of dozō, with its greatly improved fireproofing. In a way, this development was symbolic, for the culture of Edo at the time of its foundation was only an offshoot of the culture of Kyoto, but as the city grew, new urban situations, not the least of them the catastrophic fires, led to cultural independence. The fireproof dozō whose structure and details are described above was an important architectural contribution, even though it was not the work of a great architect, but that of rich Edo merchants and a number of unknown plasterers.

Just when the new type of dozō came into being is uncertain, but it had undoubtedly taken form by the 1660s, for the great dozō-style stores such as the Daikoku-ya were built around that time. Still, the dozō style does not appear to have been common until after the beginning of the eighteenth century, and particularly after 1720. Even then, dozō were owned only by the relatively well-off merchants whose shops opened on the main streets.

The fireproofing developed by the plasterers of Edo was not free of charge. In ordinary buildings, which had only clay walls between the posts, the fee paid the plasterer was no more than 20 to 30 percent of the amount paid the carpenter, but in the case of the developed dozō, the fee for the plasterer was three times the fee for the carpenter. By around 1730, carpentry was considered a reasonably profitable profession, but plastering was, to borrow a modern term, a growth "industry."

The difference is reflected in the inscriptions that carpenters customarily attached to the ridgepoles of the buildings they constructed. Until around this time, these inscriptions usually contained the name of the carpenter, the sawyer, and other woodworkers, and the plasterer was never mentioned, but now the plasterer's name began to appear on the plaque. An example is found in a three-story storehouse belonging to the Kameya store in Kawagoe, built in 1863, where the inscription gives the name of the carpenter Umekichi and the plasterer Yoshirō. It appears that until around 1500 plasterers were of the lowest class of laborers, but that their status improved in the Momoyama period as a result of the importance of their work in building castles. They took several more steps up the social ladder after the development of the dozō.

The principal element in the fireproofing of the Kanto-style dozō was the thick plaster and clay wall. This type of wall spread to the Kansai region, but other fireproofing devices used in Edo, such as the 15-centimeter-thick skirt wall, were not adopted there, and still others, such as the thick plaster walling under the eaves, were adopted, but only in modified form. An interesting difference between Kanto and Kansai is that in many Kanto dozō there are are permanent hooks in the walls for scaffolding needed in times of repair, but these are not found in the Kansai region (pages 18–19, 207).

There is also a difference in roofing. The storehouses of Kansai had hongawara roofing, no doubt in imitation of Buddhist temples and the houses of rich merchants. Kyoto merchants gradually abandoned hongawara in favor of the less expensive sangawara for their houses, but continued to use hongawara for their dozō. Hongawara were thicker, heavier, and more fireproof than sangawara, but they did not find favor with the storehouse owners of Edo, who apparently felt that the desired result could be achieved by making the buildings themselves more fireproof and increasing the amount of earth underneath the sangawara tiles. Some people, however, took the added precaution of sealing the cracks between the tiles with plaster. When this was done, it was possible to reduce costs by using perfectly flat tiles, which were even less expensive than sangawara.

A feature peculiar to Kanto-style dozō is the so-called "boxed ridge," or *hakomune* (箱棟). In this arrangement, the ridgepole was surrounded by heavy boards, which were in turn covered with a tile roof of their own (pages 222–23). Ridgepoles of this type had been used in the Kansai region by wealthy merchants for the purpose of enhancing their status, but they dropped out of use there after about 1600. The *hakomune* continued to be used in Edo, however, until modern times. In an age when tiles in general were not of very high quality, it was probably felt that the extra roofing was needed to protect the ridgepole from moisture.

In Kansai the tiles at the ends of the ridgepole were made in the form of gargoyles, in the fashion of Buddhist temples. This practice was continued in the Kanto district for a time, but after 1700 the gargoyles were replaced by family crests or trademarks (page 188).

The thick walls, heavy doors, boxed ridgepoles, and ornamental crests of the dozō in Edo gave them, in comparison with other buildings, an ostentatious appearance. In the Edo period, it was generally considered that these somewhat over-ornamented dozō represented an attempt on the part of the merchants to ape the proud daimyo, whose huge residences dominated much of the city's landscape. In a way, however, the dozō of Edo symbolized the aggressive mercantilism of the merchants of the city, as contrasted to the conservative attitude of the merchants in the Kansai area. It could be argued that the Edo merchants, by building impressive dozō, were engaging in a form of advertising that emphasized the solidity of their trading houses and the quality of their goods. Here again we see the storehouse as a status symbol.

In nearly all of Japan, the walls of dozō-style storehouses were white, though in some districts sumptuary laws forbade the white finishing. Curiously, in Edo, though white walls were not banned, the merchants apparently preferred a black plaster finishing. This was by no means for the sake of economy, for the black plaster was added on top of the white plaster, and it entailed an arduous polishing job the white walls did not require. The color of the Edo dozō was called "Edo black," and it too was considered a symbol of wealth or at least of extravagance.

One can only speculate as to why the merchants of Edo preferred black walls to white. It could be, of course, that they felt it would be arrogant to build white storehouses like the ones in the residences of the feudal lords. More likely, however, it was the other way around. Since the black plaster was added over the white, it actually cost more than the latter, and to a person who knew, a black storehouse indicated greater wealth than a white one. Perhaps the rich Edo merchants were telling their social betters, the warrior class, that the warriors could keep the gleaming white walls, but the merchants would keep the money.

Dozō *Residences and Shops*

As urbanization proceeded apace in the Edo period, dozō-style buildings came to be used not only as storehouses, but as residential buildings and shops. Despite functional differences, however, dozō continued to be spoken of as kura, or some variation thereof, such as *sumai-kura* (住居蔵, residence kura), *zashiki-gura* (座敷蔵, parlor kura), or *mise-gura* (店蔵, shop kura). In effect, the fireproof qualities of the dozō led to the adaption of the building to purposes other than storage, and the meaning of the word kura was further expanded.

Dozō residences appeared in Kansai as well as in Kanto, although they were known by a different name there. The phenomenon was simple enough: people simply started building town houses in the same way they built the fire-resistant storehouses. Frequently a part of the dozō residence was used as a shop or a workshop, and it was rare that all the living areas in a residential compound were built in dozō style. For fireproofing, it was necessary that these buildings have small windows and doors, and they were consequently none too pleasant to live in. Furthermore, they were expensive to construct.

In many instances, only the parlor section, or zashiki, was in dozō style (pages 230–31 and diagram, overleaf). This was the best section of the house and the place where guests were entertained. As a rule it was two or three stories high, and often a part of it was used for storage, though this was not necessarily the case. The floors were covered with tatami, and in at least one room there were a tokonoma and the accompanying staggered shelves in traditional fashion. Closets were installed as needed, and there were interior posts and beams that would not normally be found in dozō used only for storage. There were usually from one to three entrances with double swinging doors.

This section of the house was as a rule used only on special occasions, including marriages and religious ceremonies, and it was not occupied by the family most of the time.

It is known from records that parlors of this type were built in some numbers in Kyoto during the Edo period, but practically no example has survived. In Tokyo, quite a few examples remained until the Great Kanto Earthquake of 1923, but they are all gone now. Dozō parlors are relatively numerous even today in Yamagata Prefecture and in the Izu Peninsula.

Shigure Hasegawa, the novelist (1879–1941), who as a young girl had lived in a dozō-style house, wrote as follows: "My grandmother's dressing room was on the second floor. Downstairs there was a beautiful parlor, but here there were wooden chests, and chests of drawers, and smaller containers with drawers all the way up to the ceiling. Near the window on the garden side of the second floor, there was a one-mat grille that admitted light to the first floor. A scarlet carpet was spread in the center of the room, and on this stood a mirror stand with a round gold mirror in the ancient style. On the third floor, attached to the column supporting the roof, was an inscription written by her husband saying, 'Hasegawa Ubei built this in 1856.' My grandmother would sit there surrounded by a six-panel screen with pictures near the bottom and, with a black lacquered pail in front of her, apply tooth blackener to her remaining teeth. I remember the day when my younger brother was born. It was the day of the Girl's Festival, and my grandmother told me to put away the dolls that were arranged in the parlor for the occasion, because that night we would have a new member in the family."

When a fire broke out, a barrel of water was placed in the dozō part of the house, and the doors and windows shut and sealed. Even if the other rooms burned down, the dozō section was safe, and it could be used as living quarters until the rest of the house was rebuilt. Closing the dozō and taking flight was the typical Edo period method of fire protection, but there were others. One Edo period source, *Mimibukuro* by Negishi Shizue mentions an apothecary in a populous section of Edo whose dozō survived four major fires because he had covered the whole building with a leather cover. Another source, dated 1855, recommends covering buildings with a sort of tarpaulin soaked in water. Such methods must have been used only very rarely.

Dozō construction was often used only in the section of a house that served as a shop, for which the usual name was *mise-gura*. This type originated in Edo and spread to the whole Kanto region and thence toward

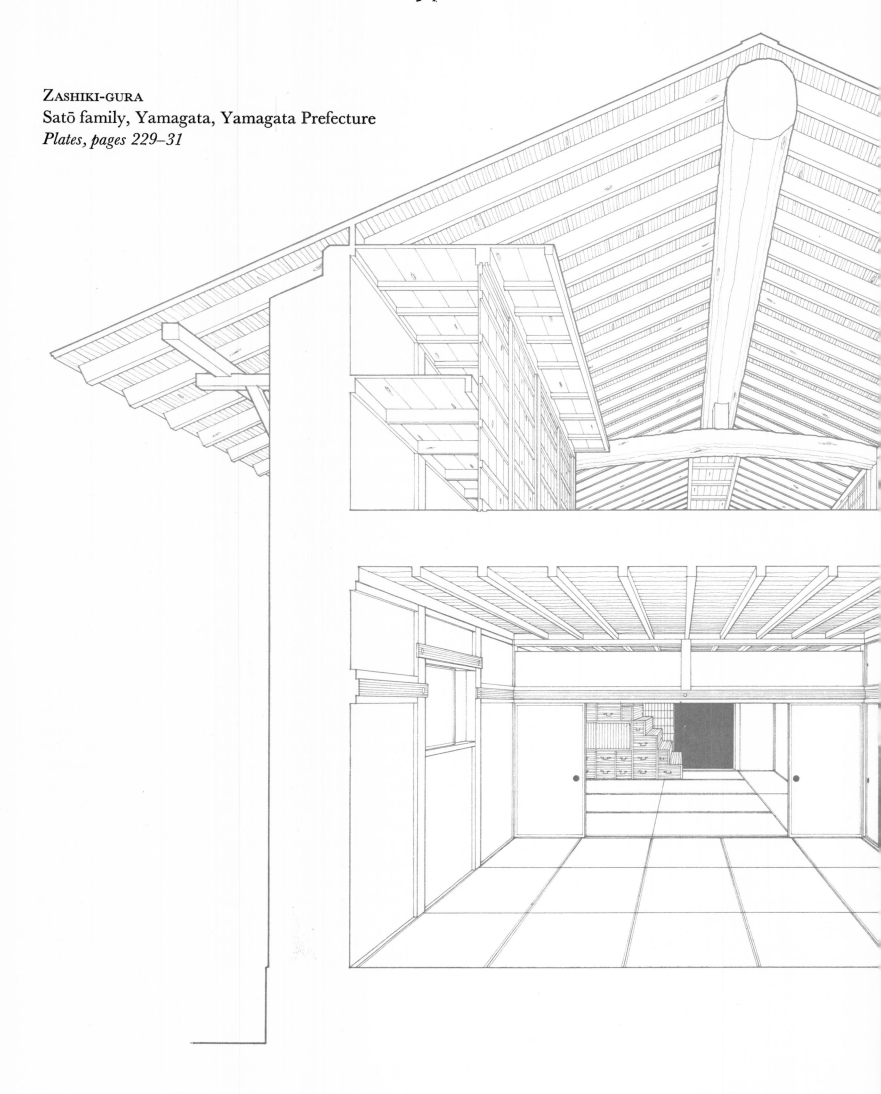

ZASHIKI-GURA
Satō family, Yamagata, Yamagata Prefecture
Plates, pages 229–31

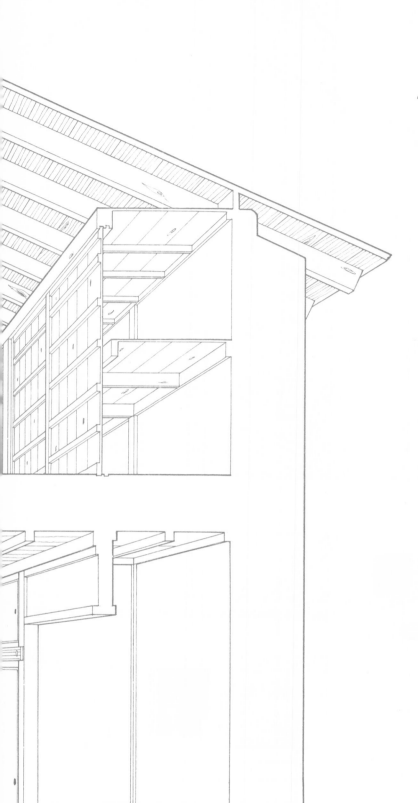

the northeast. Dozō shops do not seem to have spread to Kansai until around 1850.

Since people had to come in and out of the shops, the whole front of the first floor of the dozō was usually open. This was the main difference between dozō used for stores and those used for houses or parlors. To close this opening at night and during fires, there were special shutters made of wooden panels covered on both sides with plaster. Since these were heavy, they were made narrower than ordinary Japanese doors and were usually no more than 45 to 60 centimeters across, as opposed to 90 for ordinary doors. The door rabbets were deeper than for ordinary doors.

Dozō shops usually had two stories, with the shop on the first floor and a storage area, as well as quarters for apprentices and helpers, on the second. These quarters were usually gloomy and unpleasant, particularly in the summer, when they were also hot.

As a rule, there were no interior partitions in the shop proper, but at large stores such as Echigoya and Daimaru, which were located on corners, there was sometimes an L-shaped unfloored area adjacent to the two streets on which the building faced. Floors were almost always of wood, and in ordinary shops there was an unfloored entrance area on the front from 1.8 to 3.6 meters wide and 90 centimeters deep. This was where customers took off their footwear before entering the floored area. Often there was a hearth here, where the teakettle could be heated, and for this reason the area was sometimes called the "kettle area" (kamaba). In the ceiling there were usually several light windows covered with grilles, and in the floors there were openings for storage pits. As noted above, the large Daikoku-ya store in Edo was 11.7 meters wide by 29.3 meters long. It was a great open hall, and the floor plans show that there were counters for cash transactions, for accounts, for marking the prices on the articles, for calculating sums, and so on, in addition to nineteen sales counters.

Dozō shops are found today in considerable numbers in Kawagoe, Saitama Prefecture (pages 18–19, 220–25, and diagram, overleaf), and a few are scattered about in the towns of Kanto and eastern Japan, but not a single one has been preserved in Tokyo, those that existed in the Meiji period having been destroyed in the Great Kanto Earthquake of 1923. Shigure

Dozō shop
Kameya store, Kawagoe, Saitama Prefecture
Plates, pages 220–21

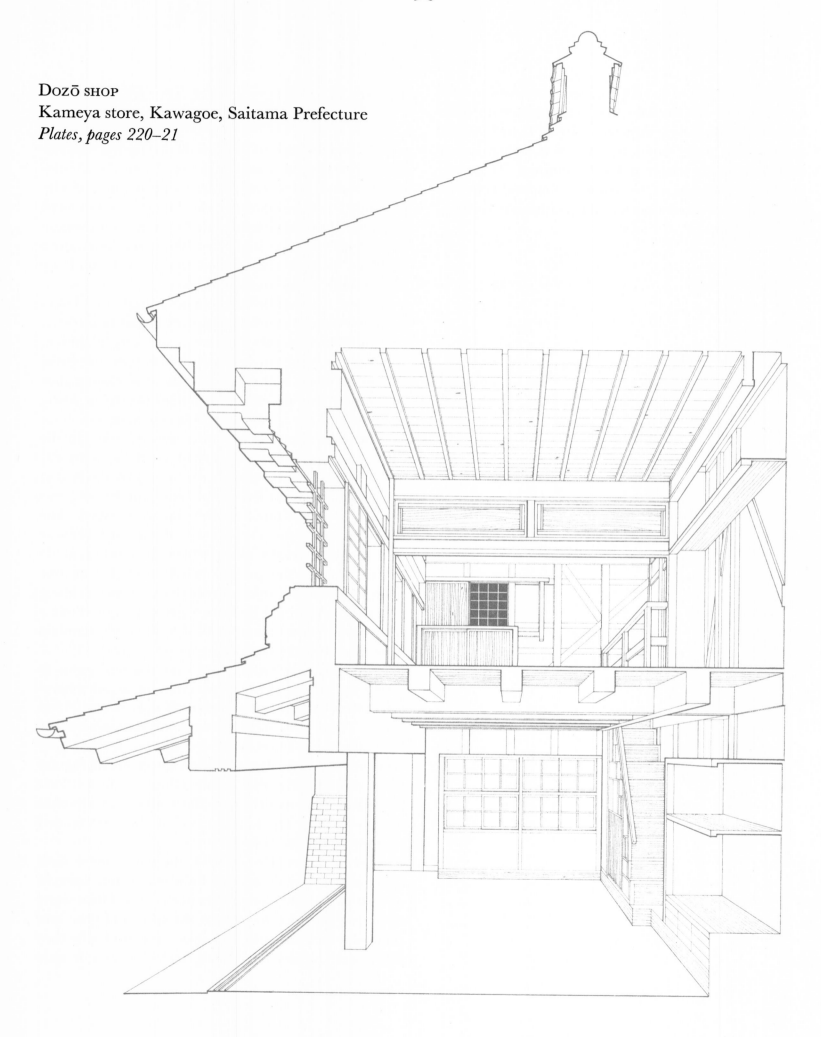

Hasegawa writes of a shop named Sanritsusha near her house in Nihombashi that was reputed to have withstood even the earthquake of 1691. It had started as a grocery store, but later turned to selling baked sweet potatoes in winter and ice in summer. To people like Shigure Hasegawa, the assorted shops of Tokyo in the Meiji period were poetic and picturesque remains from old Edo.

Dozō *Buildings and City Planning*

The first organized use of dozō construction for architectural groups was in the castles of the Momoyama period. In a way, castle construction was city planning on a miniature scale, but it was not until long after the Momoyama period that the construction of dozō on an urban scale was considered. Such dozō buildings as were constructed were usually built by private individuals and feudal lords.

Around the middle of the Edo period, the Tokugawa government and the daimyos began to incorporate dozō architecture into town and city planning. An example is the rows of dozō storehouses that came to line the rivers and canals of Edo. The eastern part of the city had an extensive system of canals, along which consumer goods and building materials were shipped from the outlying areas into the city. In the early part of the Edo period, such goods were usually unloaded on empty lots on the banks of rivers and canals. At first very few people had storehouses, and the goods were simply stacked up as received. The stacked goods, however, became a fire hazard, because they furnished paths along which fires could easily spread. In 1648 the government decreed that anyone piling tinder to a height of more than 1.8 meters along the riverbanks would be fined a string of cash. Similar regulations followed, and in 1651 lumber and bamboo were placed in the same category as tinder.

It appears that around 1665 storehouses began to spring up, and in 1670 the government issued a blanket permit for the construction of dozō along riverbanks. The reason for this permit was that most of the land along the riverbanks was not private but government property. In 1669 local government regulations encouraging the construction of dozō along riverbanks were issued, and the reason was given as fire prevention. The lines formed by the dozō tended to stop the spread of fires.

After the Great Fire of 1657, the government built stone embankments several hundred meters long in at least two places along rivers in the city. These were, of course, intended to prevent the spread of fires, and they may have done so, but they were gradually torn down and replaced by dozō, which were not only effective fire barriers but could also be used for storing goods unloaded by the riverbanks.

Around the middle of the Edo period, there appeared a number of scholars who promoted the construction of dozō-style buildings because of their effectiveness against the spread of fires. One was Muro Kyūsō (1658–1734), a Confucian in government employ, who argued in favor of dozō in *Kenkaroku* [Proposal for things to be done]. In the provinces, Japanese who had studied Western architecture with the Dutch at Dejima championed stone and brick buildings for fire prevention; prominent among these men were the ex-samurai Honda Toshiaki (1744–1821), who was a native of Echigo (Niigata Prefecture), and Hoashi Banri (1778–1852), an elder advisor in the feudal house of Hiji in Bungo Province (Oita Prefecture). The Western structures these men proposed were not constructed, however, and if they had been, their structures would have been unsuited to this country of earthquakes.

It was not until the end of the Edo period that organized placement of dozō-style buildings achieved any noteworthy degree of urban fire protection in the broad sense. The movement began in 1830, when Ikehara Yoshijirō presented the shogunate with a plan for construction of new dozō as a protective measure against great fires. Ikehara was what was known as a "man of Iga, a watchman," which means that he was a descendant of one of a group of low-ranking samurai from Iga Province who had assisted Tokugawa Ieyasu in battle and had for their reward been brought to Edo and installed in a number of minor official positions. How it happened that a plan for Edo by a man of such low rank reached the eyes of the government is not clear.

Ikehara's plan called for building dozō around each city block and having all the houses within the blocks roofed with tile. Considering that Edo's great fires always resulted from the spreading of a small fire, this method sounds most reasonable. In the 1830s, however, the shogunate was on the verge of collapse, and whether it adopted Ikehara's plan or not, it was in no position to carry out effectively a great program of urban construction.

A man who considered the possibility of construction on an urban scale of dozō buildings was Kamo no

Norikiyo (1789–1861), who started as a Shinto priest at the Kami-Kamo Shrine in Kyoto but later moved to Edo and set up a private academy called Zuiu-en. In his *Hinoyōjin shikata* [How to protect against fire], which was published in 1837, he first presented his ideas for dozō of a new type.

The aims for creating the new type were: (1) to protect against the great fires to which the city was so often subjected; (2) to create buildings that could withstand the cannons used by potential invaders from abroad; and (3) to hold down construction costs, and particularly carpenters' fees, which had a way of soaring after fires to a level three to ten times that prevailing in areas other than Edo.

He proposed that the new buildings have walls made by stacking, in log-cabin style, huge square timbers, 30 centimeters to the side and 6.3 meters long. The floor of the second story and the ceiling would be made of the same timbers. The roof would be made of tile and would be supported not by the traditional wooden framework but by a triangular mound of earth. According to Kamo's estimate, the cost of such a building as he proposed would be in line with the standards then prevailing. Actually, Kamo's proposal seems rather unrealistic, though it at least shows a strong humanistic concern for the protection of the city's people from fire.

In his next book *Yuniwa no inao* [Rice ears in a sacred place], Kamo proposed a fire prevention plan for Edo, based on the construction of the buildings described in the earlier work. His plan called for building a spirallike fire barrier composed of these structures and extending from the northeast part of Edo around by the north and west sides of the castle and back around the south to the eastern moat, a distance of some twenty-five kilometers. One reason for the spirallike line was that the principal sections of the inner and outer moats also formed a rough spiral, and the moats would also be useful in preventing the spread of fire.

Kamo's plan was ignored by the shogunate, but Kamo could hardly have been disappointed, because the shogunate never paid any attention to proposals by anyone outside its own bureaucracy. Far from being listened to, Kamo was arrested in 1847 and exiled to the island of Hachijō-jima, off the Izu Peninsula. The reason for his exile does not appear to be his architectural plans, but rather his criticism from the Shinto viewpoint of Confucianism, which was the philosophy of the samurai of the time.

Kamo's ideas blossomed out of season, and they were soon forgotten. Before many years had passed, the industrial revolution swept away dozō architecture itself, and his proposals became meaningless.

It was by no means only Kamo's dozō that underwent this fate. On the contrary, after the industrial revolution, the kura quickly became a thing of the past. Even the kura of the Edo period, the dozō, ceased, from the viewpoint of structure and materials, to be suited to the times. If we of today look upon the kura as a thing of beauty and regret its passing, it is because we see it as a symbol of the continuity of history from ancient times until only recently. Confined by the limits of premodern structure and materials, it could advance only so far in the architectural sense. And yet the traditional storehouse had a beauty of its own down through the ages. Indeed, perhaps we are better able to understand the value of this beauty now that history has put an end to the role of the storehouse and released it from utilitarian function.

Wooden Storehouses

105–7. *Sutra Repository and Treasure Storehouse*
    105. *Entrance of the Sutra Repository*
106–7. *Treasure Storehouse and Sutra Repository.* The Treasure Storehouse (*hōzō*) of the Tōshōdai-ji is at the left, the Sutra Repository (*kyōzō*), at the right. These two buildings, which date from the eighth century, are examples of the log-cabin storehouse, or *azekura*, which was widely used in the early Buddhist monasteries. The logs are triangular in section, but with the corners cut off, presumably to improve the fit at the points of contact and at the same time to make possible a smooth, straight interior wall. The stairways are an addition: originally there were no permanent stairways, and the buildings were entered when necessary by ladder. (See diagram, pages 62–63.)

Tōshōdai-ji, Nara

108–9. *Mike-no-mikura in the Inner Shrine*
This diminutive storehouse, which is of uncertain date, is one of the minor buildings at the Ise Shrine. Like the main building of the shrine, it has a raised floor, a post-and-beam structure, heavy board walls, separate ridge support posts outside the wall plane, and the ornamental extended bargeboards (*chigi*) and cross-logs (*katsuogi*) on the ridge. Buildings of this type are probably descended from the raised-floor storehouses of the Yayoi period. (See plate, pages 122–23.) The roof here is made of boards rather than thatch.

Ise Shrine, Ise, Mie Prefecture

110–11. *Treasure Storehouse*
This is an example of the log-cabin, or azekura, style. Though this type is today preserved only at temples and shrines, in ancient times it was used for secular buildings, storehouses included.

Itsukushima Shrine, Miyajima, Hiroshima Prefecture

112–13. *Sutra Repository*
    112. *Exterior.* This building is in the style of Buddhist halls of worship.
    113. *Interior.* The sutra case is known as *rintenzō*. (See plate, page 5).

Onjō-ji, Ōtsu, Shiga Prefecture

114–15. *Treasure Storehouse and Sutra Repository*
    114. *The Kōfūzō, a treasure storehouse*
    115. *Detail of the Sutra Repository.* In these two storehouses, which were built in the eighth century, the wooden walls were covered on the outside with plaster as a fire precaution. (See diagram, page 33.)

Hōryū-ji, Ikaruga, Nara Prefecture

116–21. *Storehouse and treasure-houses*
    116–17. *Storehouse for the Miniature Shrine*
    118. *Detail of the Lower Treasure-House*
    119. *Detail of the Upper Treasure-House*
    120–21. *Detail of the Lower Treasure-House.* Important Shinto shrines such as the famous Tōshōgū require considerable storage space for their treasures and paraphernalia. At Nikko, the storehouses, like the other buildings in the shrine, are very colorful and ornate. The Upper, Middle, and Lower treasure-houses, which stand in the compound before the Yōmei Gate, are in a highly decorative version of the azekura style, which dropped out of general use nearly ten centuries ago.

Tōshōgū, Nikko, Tochigi Prefecture

122–23. *Raised-floor storehouse*
This is a reconstruction at the Toro site, one of the most important archaeological remains from the Yayoi period. Storehouses of this type were the most advanced structures of their time. Similar raised-floor buildings were later used as shrines or houses.

Shizuoka, Shizuoka Prefecture

124–27. *Raised-floor storehouses*
These thatched-roof structures have a post-and-beam structure, and the space underneath them can be used as a work area in rainy weather. (See diagram, pages 66–67, and plate, page 8–9.)

Yamatohama, Amami-Ōshima, Kagoshima Prefecture

128–29. *Houses and storehouses*
    128. *Thatched-roof houses*
    129. *Board-wall storehouses.* The area around Shirakawa is famous for its huge thatched-roof farmhouses, which were made so big because they housed large patriarchal families. Their heavy gabled roofs have given them the name *gasshō-zukuri*, or "clasped hands style." Often their storehouses were reduced versions of the houses themselves. The example on page 129 is a typical *itagura*, belonging to the Wada family. (See diagram, page 60.)

Shirakawa, Gifu Prefecture

130. *Board-wall storehouse*
This is a typical itagura with a board roof. Similar buildings are found in farming areas all over Japan.

Matsuba family, Kamioka, Gifu Prefecture

131. *Detail of board-wall storehouse*
In itagura, the posts were placed at intervals of from 30 to

45 centimeters and linked with horizontal braces, also set at intervals of from 30 to 45 centimeters.

Asahi, Yamagata Prefecture

132–33. *Board-wall storehouse*

Most Japanese storehouses have no fixed interior partitions, but in those in Shirakawa and Shōkawa in Gifu Prefecture, the first floor was sometimes divided into two rooms with a hallway in front of them. Shown here is an example, which on the outside is a typical itagura. The stairway to the second floor, which is one large room, is in the hallway. As a rule, farmers in this area keep grain in one of the downstairs rooms and tools and farming implements in the other. Household goods are kept on the second floor. (See diagram, pages 58–59.)

Ōsawa family, Shōkawa, Gifu Prefecture

134. *Rice storehouse*

Small granaries of this type, called *kokubitsu*, are found in the Musashino and Chichibu regions (western Tokyo and Saitama prefectures). They are a developed form of a type of rice bin that was built in the *doma* (dirt-floored rooms) of farmhouses.

Kodera family, Kiyose, Tokyo Prefecture

135. *Board-wall storehouse*

Asahi, Yamagata Prefecture

136–38. *Wooden storehouses and stone roof*

136–37. Wooden storehouses. One traditional method of guarding storehouses from fire was simply to place them at a safe distance from the living quarters. In the Shiine district, as in farming communities in various other regions, the storehouses were all grouped together outside the village proper.

138. Stone roof. The building itself, along with the roof support structure, was of wood, but a stone-slab roof provided a certain amount of protection from fire.

Izuhara, Nagasaki Prefecture

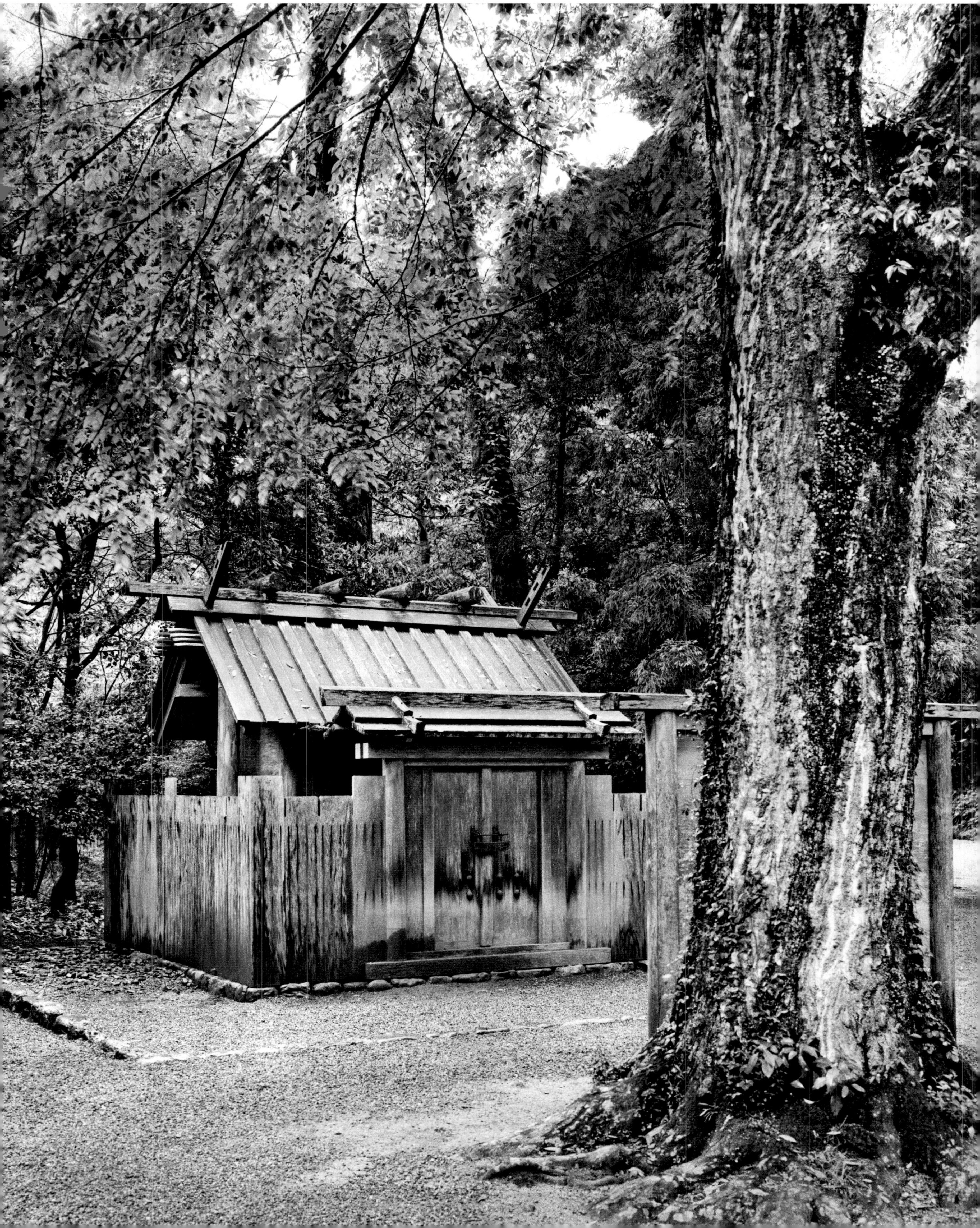

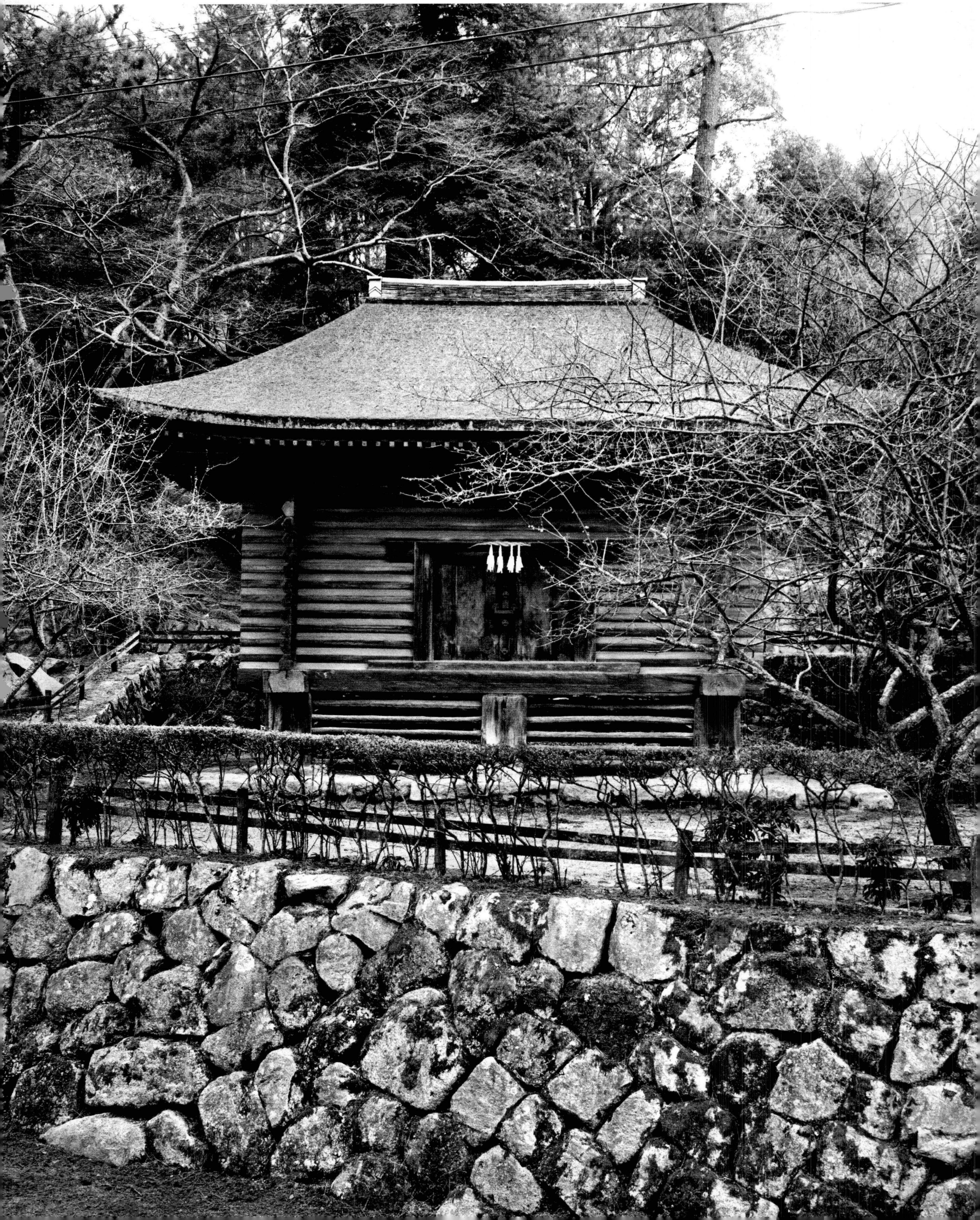

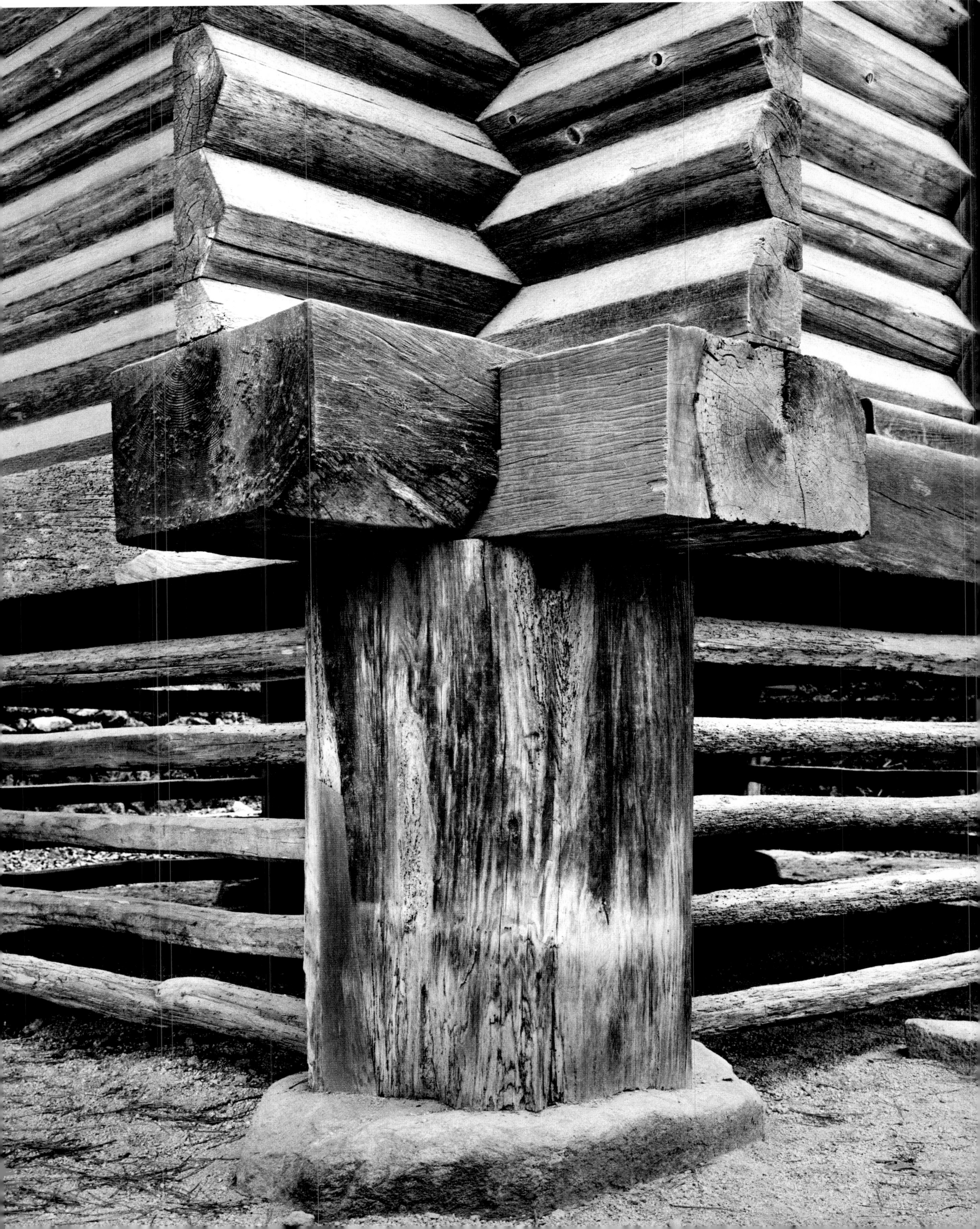

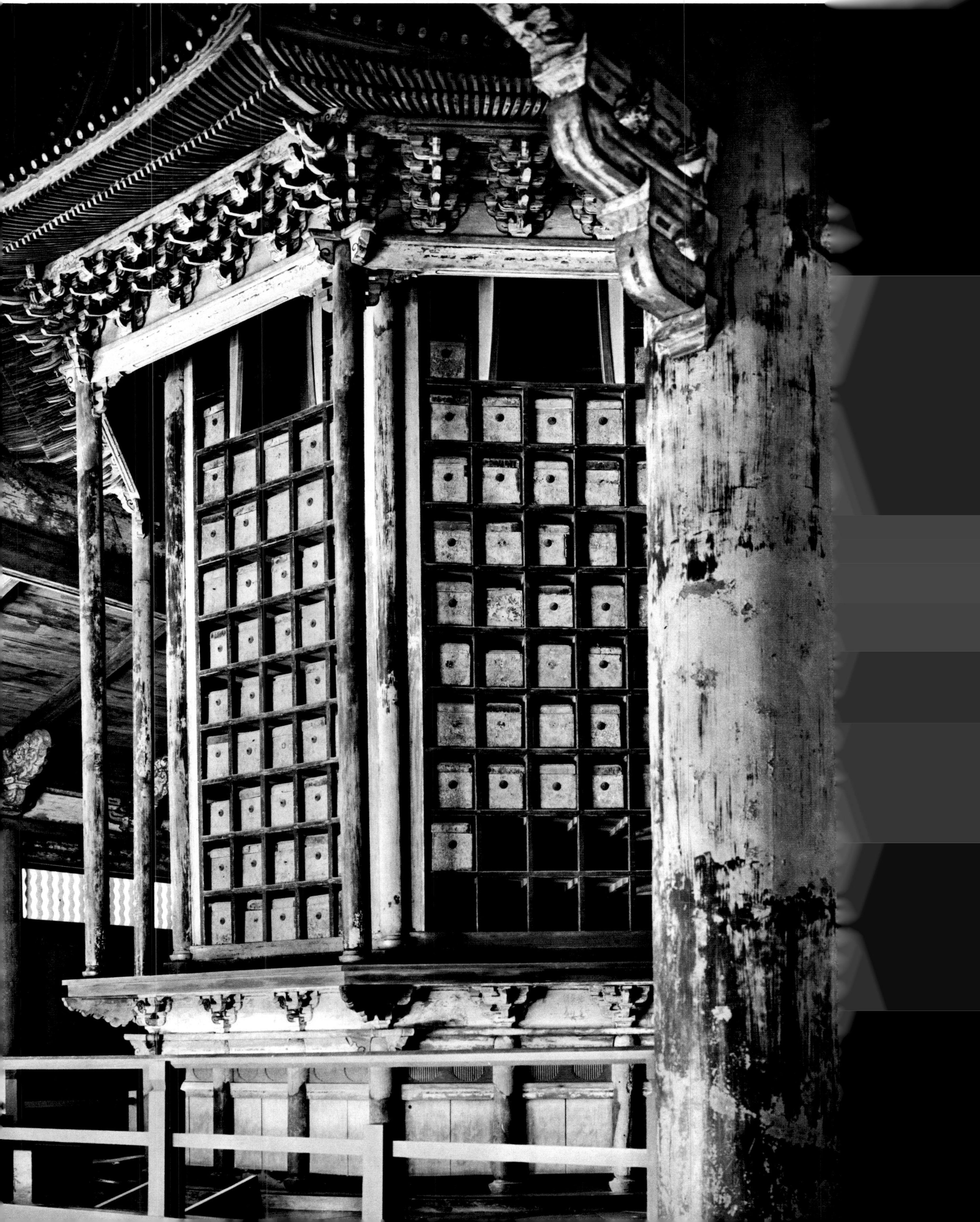

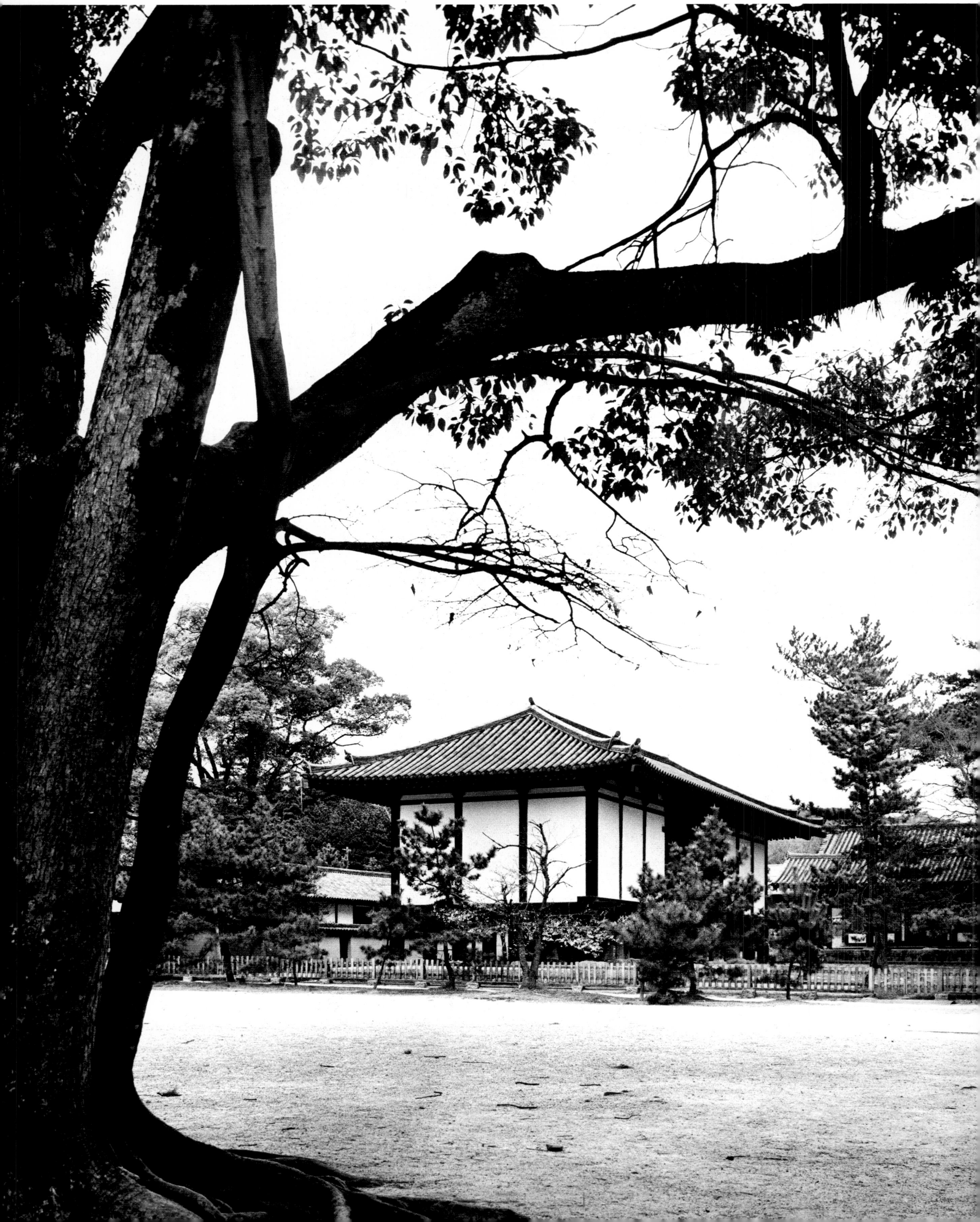

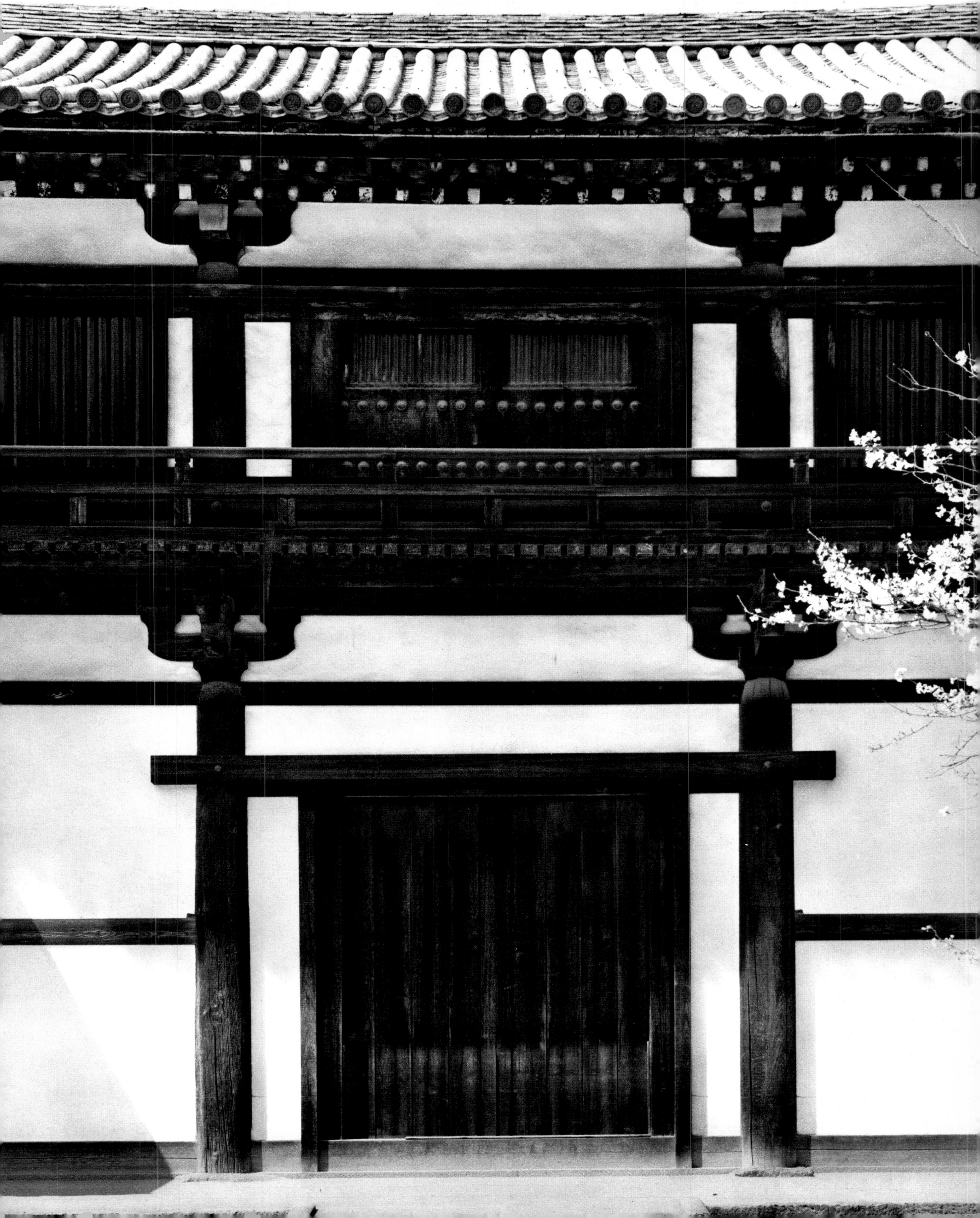

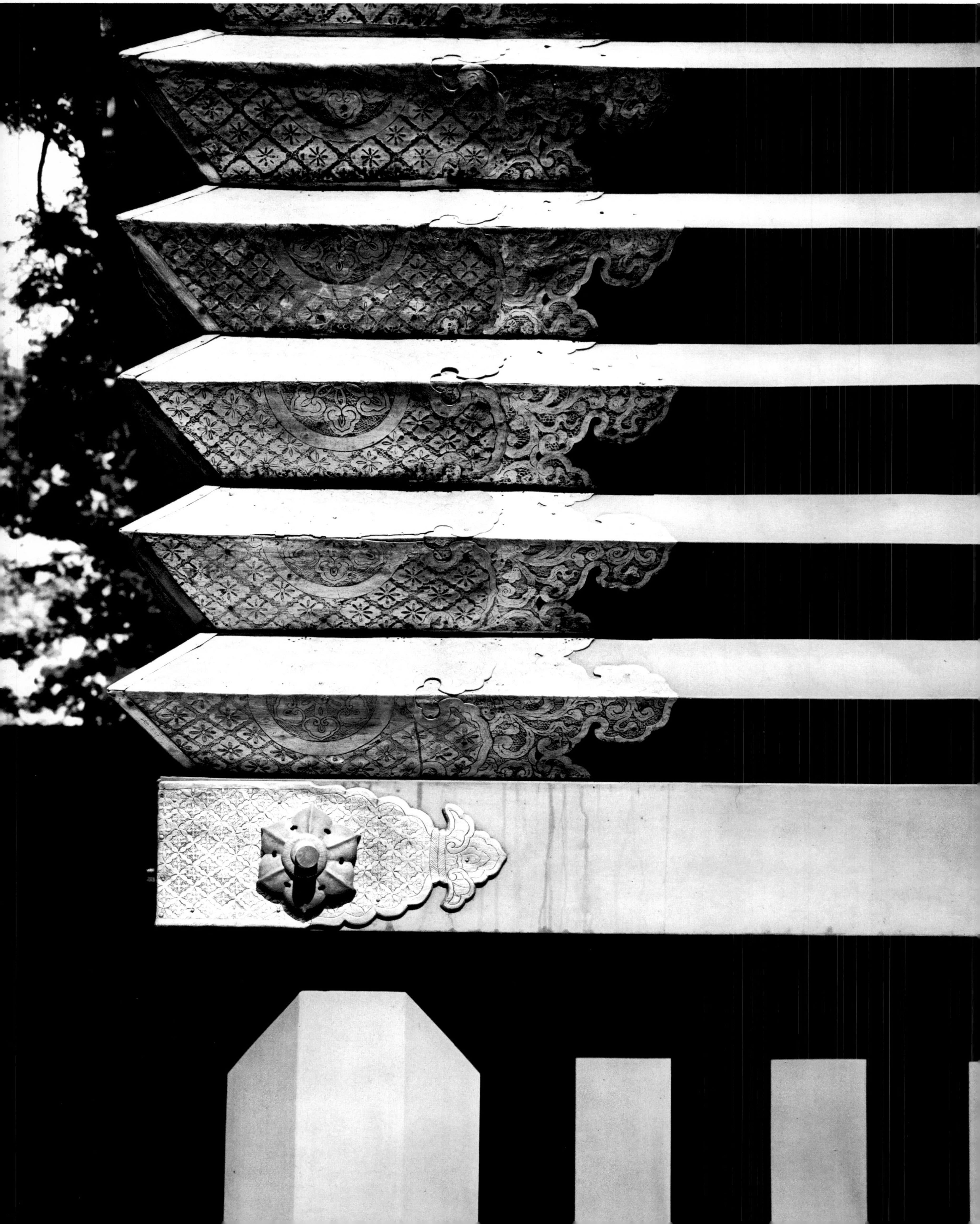

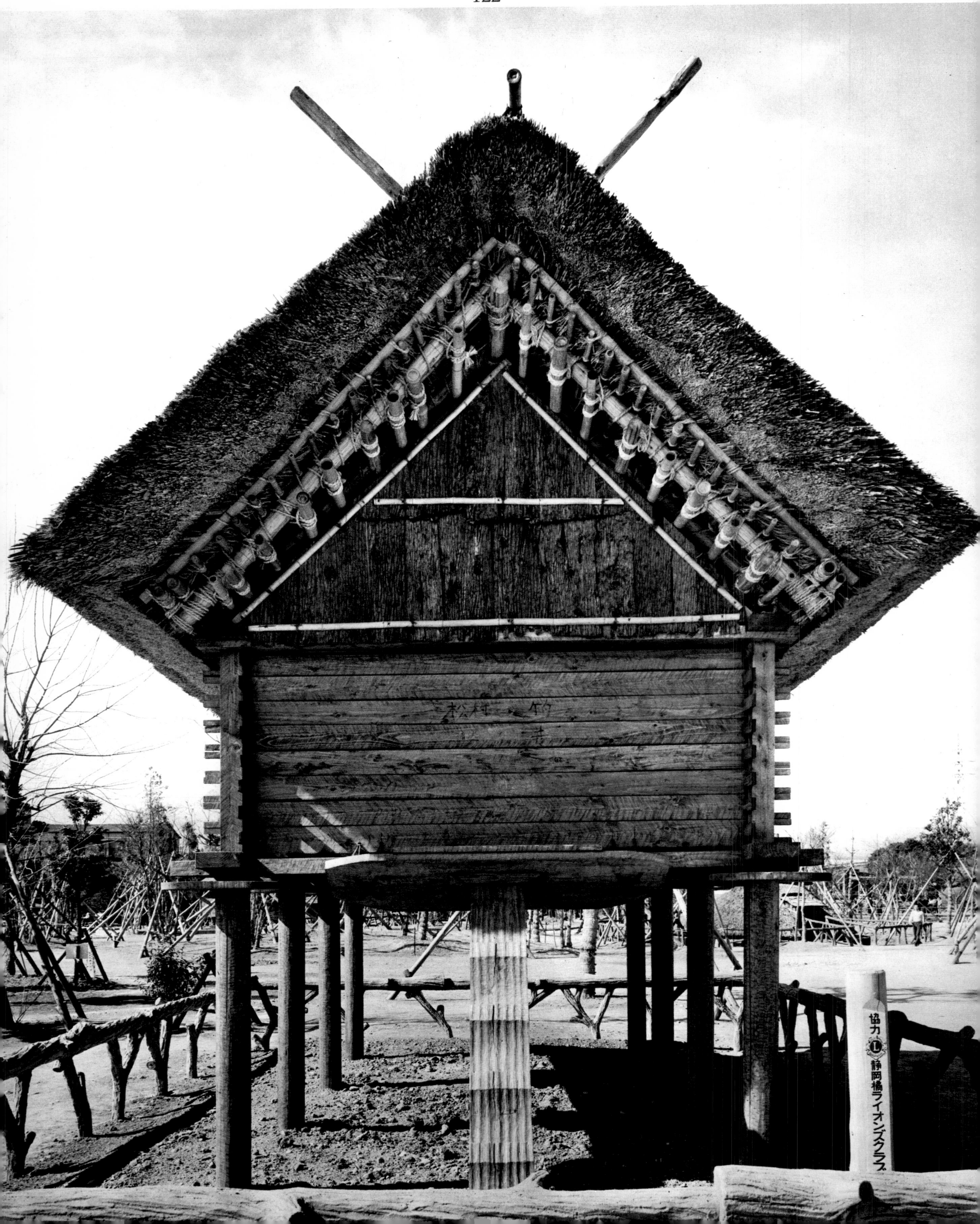
協力
静岡橋ライオンズクラブ

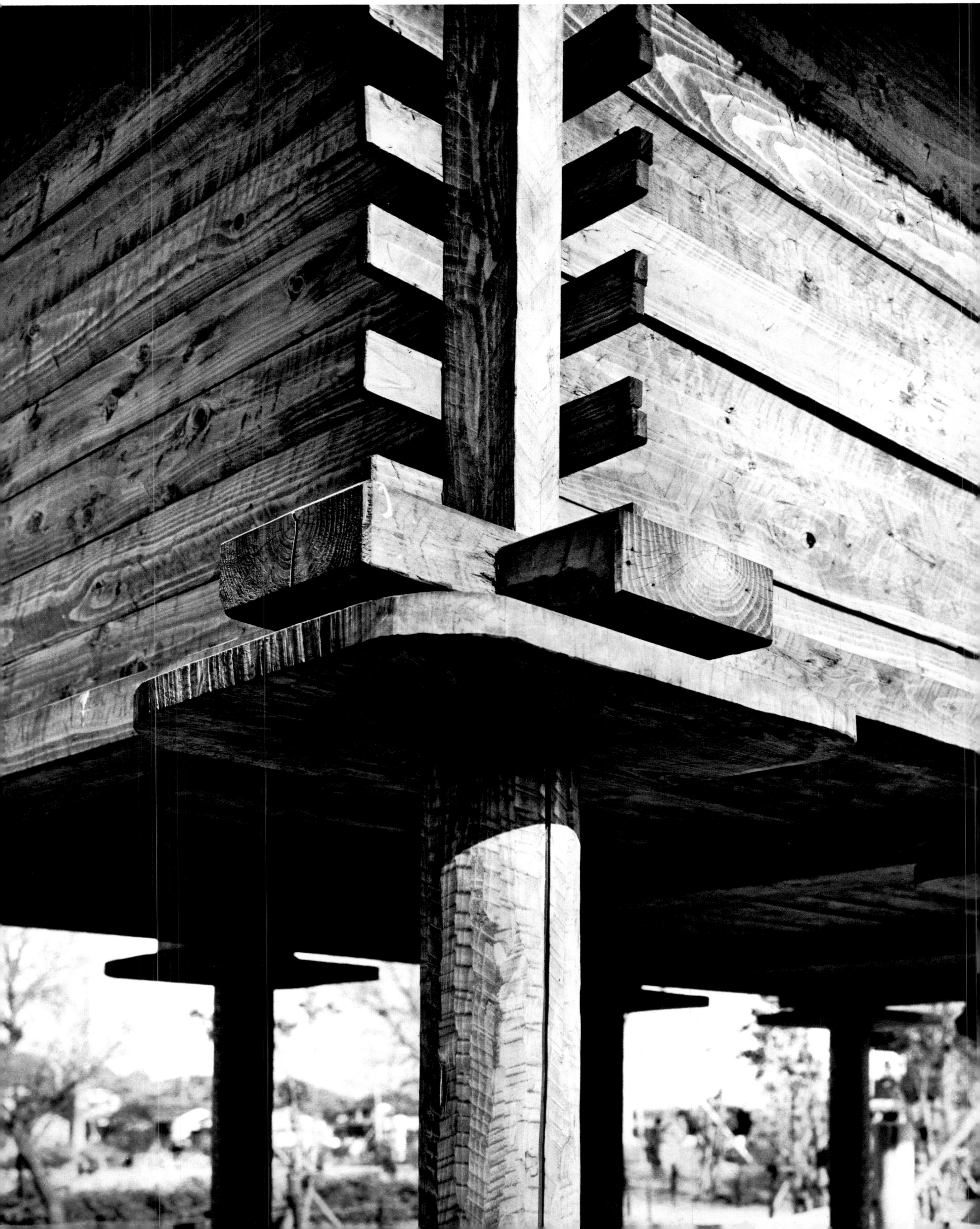

Stone Storehouses

143–45. *Stone ammunition storehouse*

    143. Interior

    144–45. Front. This arsenal is the only existing storehouse in Japan of its kind. The beams and ceiling are of stone, and the tile roof is supported by dirt and sand piled on the ceiling. Built in the Edo period, the storehouse has an area of 2.7 by 14.4 meters, and its walls are 1.8 meters thick. Though very few storehouses with stone bearing walls were ever constructed, a similar effect was achieved by using the interiors of the stone foundations of castles as storage areas. (See diagram, page 76–77.)

                                    Osaka Castle, Osaka

146–51. *Stone storehouses, window and entrance*

    146–47. Stone storehouses. Stone storehouses are rare in Japan, and buildings known as *ishigura* are usually not stone buildings in the Western sense, because they have wooden frames. The buildings shown here are basically board-wall storehouses, *itagura*, with a stone sheathing, though they appear to be built entirely of stone. It would seem that Europeans who came to Japan in the sixteenth and seventeenth centuries introduced the idea of stone warehouses of Western style, but no example remains. For that matter, no example of the Japanese stone and wood storehouse is to be found until the late Edo period. Since there has been a relatively high degree of urbanization since very early times, it seems likely that people tried from time to time to build with stone rather than wood so as to achieve protection from fires, but presumably such efforts were brought to grief by frequent earthquakes.

    148. Window of stone storehouse. The subjects chosen by the anonymous sculptors were rarely imaginative. As a rule, they were confined to family crests (for example, the leaves under the gable), images of Daikoku and Ebisu (on the shutters), and various propitious motifs such as flying cranes, pine trees, and plum trees. This storehouse is in the village of Tokujirō.

    149. Entrance of stone storehouse. In the general vicinity of Utsunomiya, there are several quarries where a soft tufa called Ōya stone or Nikko stone is available. As stone goes in Japan, these are relatively cheap, and the people of the area used them for building storehouses. They are soft and easy to carve, a feature that led builders of storehouses to ornament their buildings with relief sculpture such as that shown here. The same qualities led Frank Lloyd Wright to make extensive use of Ōya stone in his Imperial Hotel in Tokyo. Though Ōya and Nikko are fundamentally the same kind of stone, the Nikko stone, which is quarried at the village of Tokujirō, is whiter and less grainy than Ōya stone,

as can be seen from the photographs, and as a result, carvings in Nikko stone usually have finer detail than those in Ōya stone. This storehouse in the village of Ōya belongs to the Yuzawa family.

    150–51. Side and back of stone storehouse. Stone storehouses were usually modeled on *dozō*: details such as windows and the cornicelike underside of the eaves were almost exactly the same as in the plaster buildings. The stone sheathing was anchored to the wooden structure with large broad-headed nails, visible in the picture on page 150. After the opening of Japan to the West, some builders adopted such outward trappings as arched windows. Even though these had no structural function, their Occidental shape added a prestigious touch of the exotic. This storehouse belongs to the Watanabe family of the village of Ōya. (See diagram, page 78, and plate, pages 10–11.)

                Utsunomiya, Tochigi Prefecture

152–53. *Dutch Trading Center*

    152. Dutch Trading Center

    153. Window of stone storehouse. After the Tokugawa government adopted a policy of isolationism in the early seventeenth century, Dutch traders were allowed to maintain a trading office on the island of Dejima in Nagasaki. Their stone warehouse was Western in appearance, but the structure was of wood, in the Japanese tradition. Interestingly enough, no effort was made to duplicate the features of the dozō.

                Nagasaki, Nagasaki Prefecture

154–58. *Stone storehouses*

                Otaru, Hokkaido Prefecture

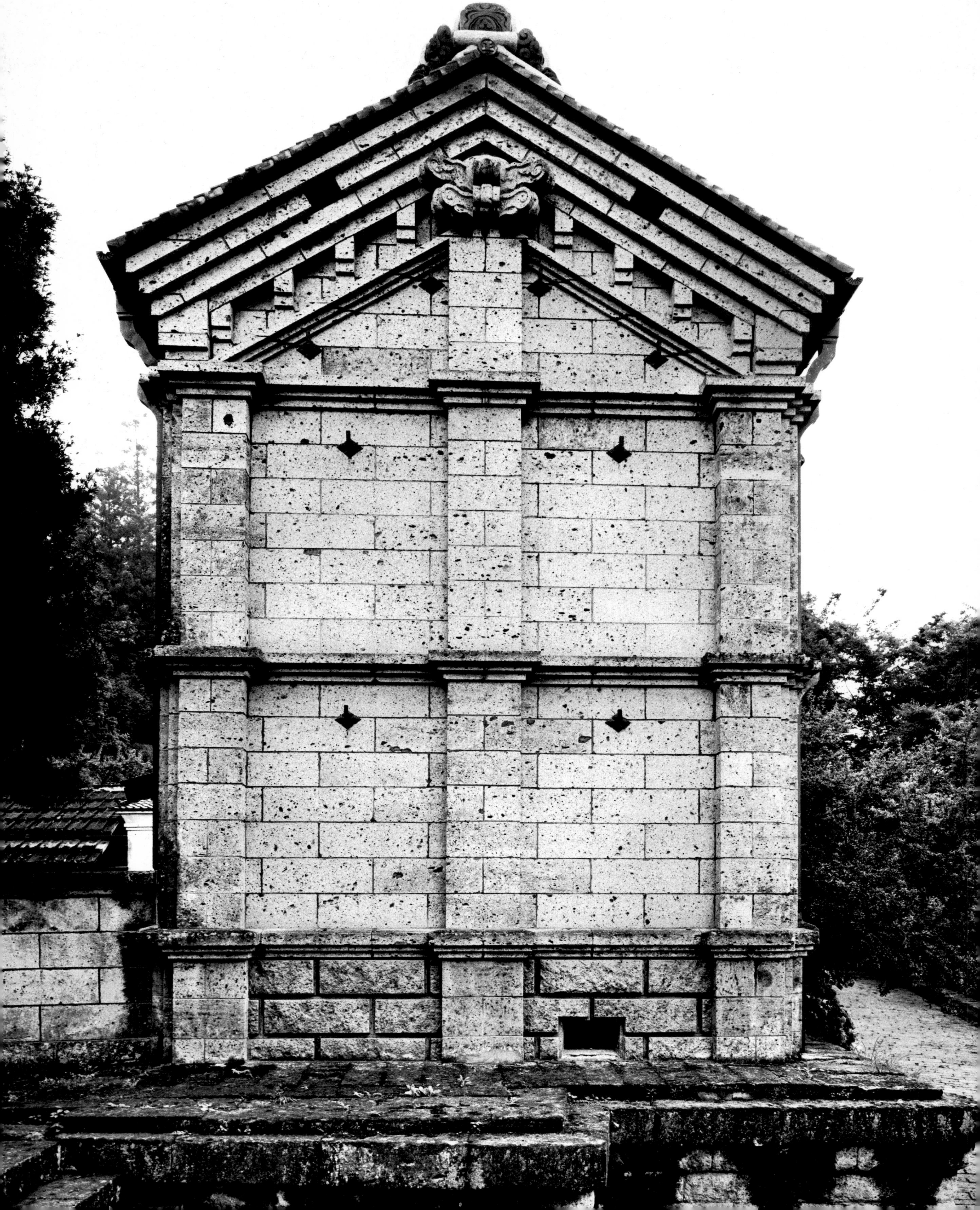

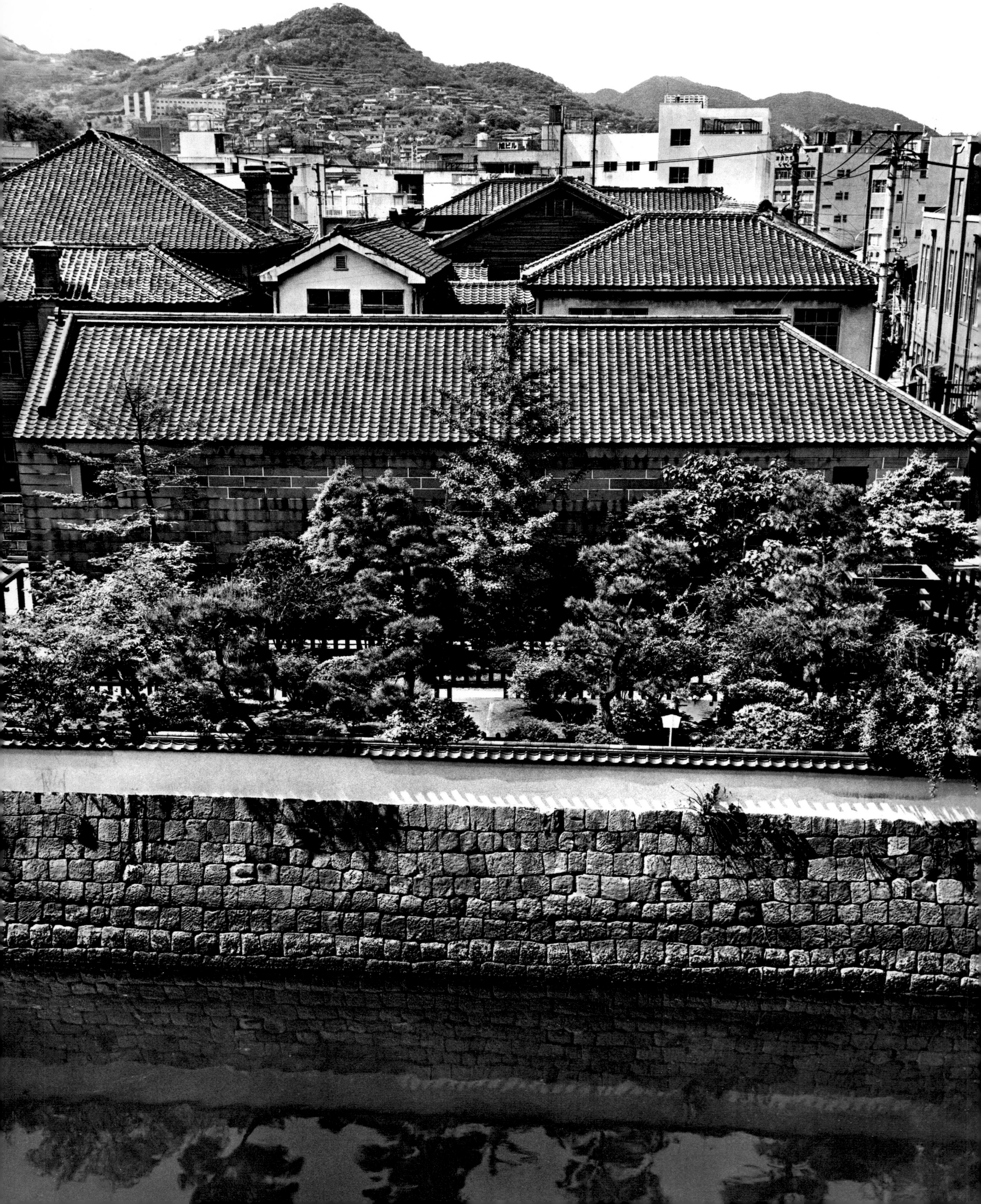
旭ビル

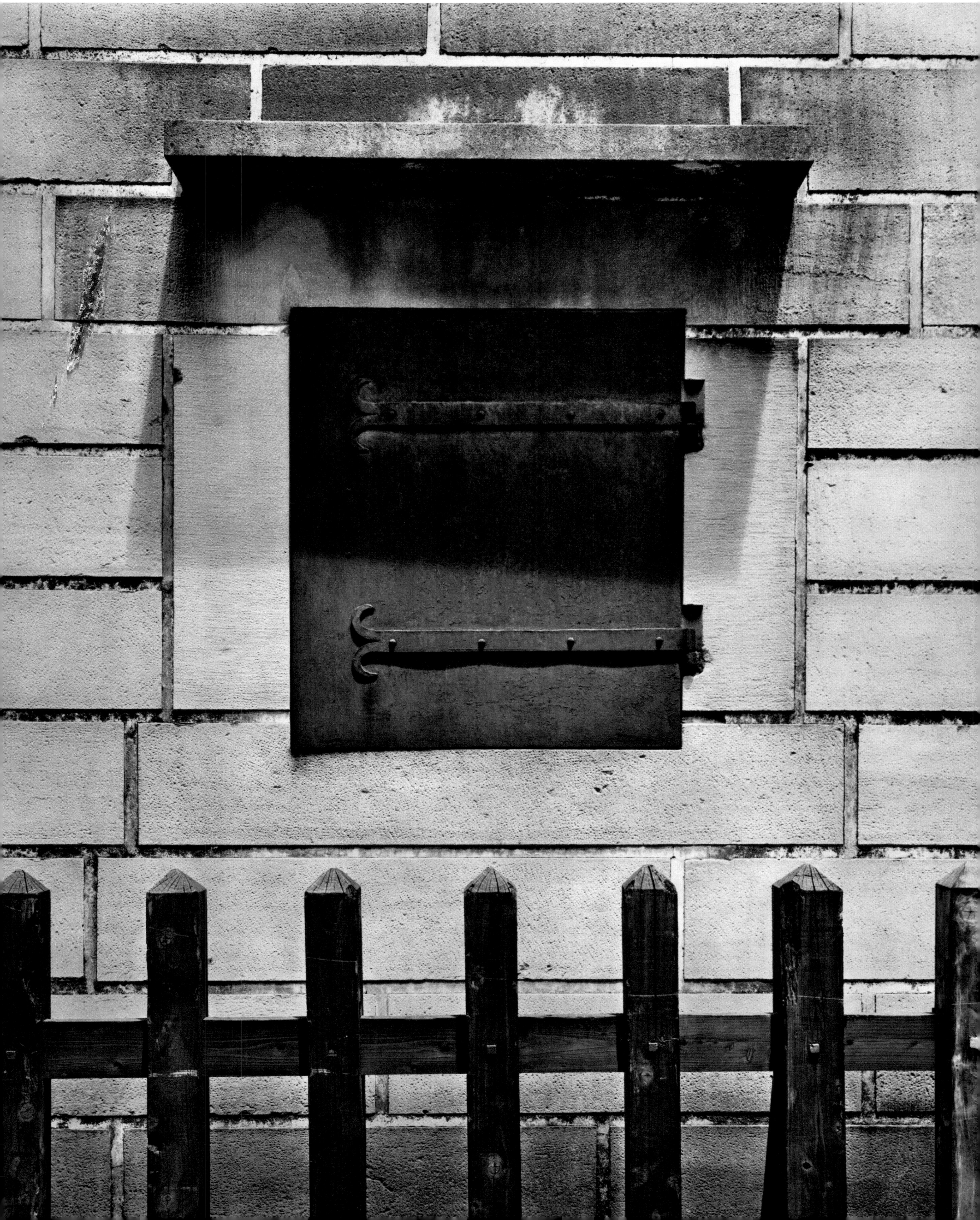

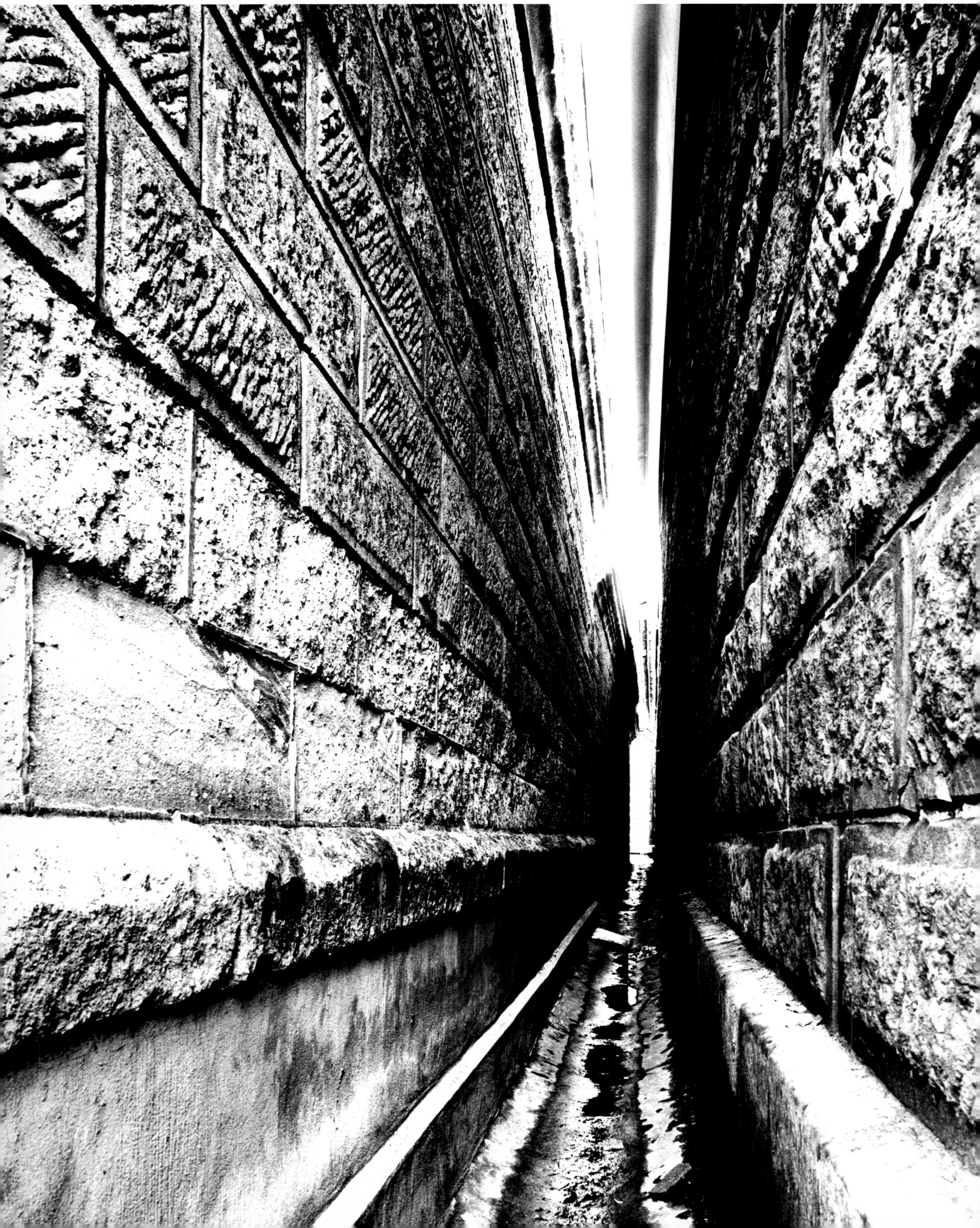

Clay Storehouses

163. *The village of Niisu*
The white walls of a *dozō*-style storehouse stand out among the other buildings. The *dozō* marks the house to which it is attached as being one of the more affluent in the community.
Aizumi, Tokushima Prefecture

164–65. *Plaster walled storehouse*
The view is through the blinds of the main house.
Kamigyō, Kyoto

166. *Group of storehouses*
Monzen, Ishikawa Prefecture

167. *White plaster storehouses*
Travelers in premodern Japan judged the wealth of communities they passed through by the number of storehouses they saw.
Yamaguchi, Nagano Prefecture

168–69. *Indigo storehouse*
The Yoshino River valley in Tokushima Prefecture has long been a center of production of indigo dye. Indigo storehouses (*aigura*) were used not only as storehouses but as factories for producing the dye. They were consequently relatively large, and their floors were made to provide good drainage, because the production of the dye entailed the use of a good deal of water.
Okumura family, Aizumi, Tokushima Prefecture

170–71. *House and storehouses*
The white plaster storehouses surround the main house.
Nagatomi family, Ibokawa, Hyogo Prefecture

172–73. *House and storehouses*
The main house, which is the building with the highest roof, is barely visible because of the impressive storehouses around it.
Inubuse family, Aizumi, Tokushima Prefecture

174–75. *Soy sauce storehouses*
174. *Exterior.* Like the indigo storehouses, soy sauce storehouses have traditionally doubled as factories. These handsome white plaster storehouses are used to produce soy sauce for the imperial household.
175. *Interior.* Dozō-style buildings were well suited to the manufacture of sake, soy sauce, yeast, and indigo because all of these products were made by fermentation, which required the stable interior temperatures that dozō provided.
Kikkōman Soy Sauce Company, Noda, Chiba Prefecture

176–77. *Soy sauce storehouse*
Marukin Soy Sauce Company, Shōdoshima, Kagawa Prefecture

178–80. *Sake storehouses*
Sake storehouses, like indigo and soy sauce storehouses, have been and are used as factories. In this example, the plaster walls of the dozō have been covered on the outside with planks.
Fushimi, Kyoto

181. *Sake storehouses*
Aramasa Sake Company, Akita, Akita Prefecture

182–83. *Silk storehouse*
Suwa, Nagano Prefecture

184. *House with enclosed storehouse*
(See diagram of similar storehouse, pages 72–73.)
Suwa, Nagano Prefecture

185. *Storehouses*
The Inubuse family has for generations been dealing in traditional Chinese medicines. This group of storehouses is used for drying and storing herbs from which the medicines are made.
Aizumi, Tokushima Prefecture

186–87. *Rice storehouse*
The Suga family are landowners of long standing, and this storehouse was used in the past for storing the rice that their tenants paid to them each year. The building is of the *sayagura* type, that is, the building proper is of fire-resistant plaster construction, but the roof is flammable. The scaffoldlike grid under the gable supports the roof. This type of construction was employed to reduce costs.
Ichinomiya, Kumamoto Prefecture

188–89. *Dozō with namako walls*
The Izu Peninsula is subject to frequent typhoons, and the plaster walls of dozō there are often covered with *namako* walls, which are made of flat square tiles and a diagonal plaster ribbing. Here the seams between the roof tiles have also been sealed with plaster to prevent rain from seeping in. The mark in the circular tile at the end of the ridge is the owner's trademark.
Shimoda, Shizuoka Prefecture

190–92. *Castle walls and fortifications*
Most of Kumamoto Castle was destroyed at the time of the Satsuma Rebellion in 1877, but a portion of the walls and some of the outer fortifications survived. The buildings are of typical dozō construction. The lower parts of the walls were covered with wood to protect the plaster underneath from rain. They were used for storing supplies and ammunition, but since they also were part of the defense ramparts, they have small openings for guns. The projections at the corners of the buildings were designed so that defenders could throw stones down on attackers attempting to climb the walls. There was another building to the left of the one shown on page 192, but it burned down. This one was constructed between 1601 and 1607.

Kumamoto, Kumamoto Prefecture

193–95. *Gold storehouse*
This building was constructed in 1837 by the Tokugawa shogunate as a storehouse for gold coins. It is of classic dozō construction, with a *hongawara* tile roof and namako walls around the lower half of the exterior.

194–95. Side view. The entrance is under the separate eaves on the right. In the Edo period there were many storehouses in this part of Osaka Castle, but only this one and one other have been preserved. The rest were torn down in the Meiji period. (See diagram, pages 48–49.)

Osaka Castle, Osaka

196. *Storehouse for festival float*
This is a special type of storehouse found in the mountainous town of Takayama. Here, as in many other towns, there is an annual festival at which each district of the town parades its own float. During the rest of the year, the floats are kept in community storehouses such as that shown here. The storehouses usually have an upper and a lower door on the front. The design on the lower door is the district's mark.

Gifu Prefecture

197. *Storehouse for festival float*
This storehouse is similar in construction to the example on page 196, but here there is a miniature shrine in the rock outside the door. The shrine is dedicated to the god who protects from fire. More than half of Furukawa was destroyed by fire in 1904, and the townspeople are especially careful about fire prevention. (See diagram of similar storehouse, page 53.)

Furukawa, Gifu Prefecture

198. *Dozō with namako walls*
Minami-izu, Shizuoka Prefecture

199. *Dozō with wooden outer walls*
This storehouse is in a fishing village on the coast of the Sea of Japan. The winters are severe, and there is apt to be much snow. Many of the storehouses are consequently given added protection in the form of wooden walls over the plaster.

Izumozaki, Niigata Prefecture

200–201. *Dozō storehouse*
The area in Gifu Prefecture where this storehouse is located was in the past subject to floods, and many of the local storehouses, as well as the houses themselves, were built on stone platforms. This storehouse is used for household articles and family treasures. It is connected to the main house by a covered stairway, visible at the right, and it is also linked to a separate apartment, seen on the left. In front of the wall in the foreground there is a moat that surrounds the whole compound.

Ōhashi family, Ōgaki, Gifu Prefecture

202. *Sake storehouse*
Fushimi, along with Nada in Hyogo Prefecture, has since the seventeenth century been one of the most famous sake-producing districts in Japan, and it still has a number of large traditional sake storehouses. (See plate, page 14–15.)

Fushimi, Kyoto

203. *Sake storehouse*
In the Edo period, the Yamada family of Kyoto were important merchants dealing in silk thread, silk cloth, and sake. Until recently they had seven storehouses in their compound, but now they have stopped dealing in products other than sake, and there remain only the two storehouses shown here, which, though used for storing sake, are more important as symbols of the family tradition.

Nakagyō, Kyoto

204–5. *Drainage eaves on dozō wall*
This is the wall of a sake storehouse in the town of Saijō. This part of Japan is more subject to heavy rains than the eastern part of the country, and storehouse windows are often protected from rain by eaves of this sort.

Hiroshima Prefecture

206. *Drainage eaves of sake storehouse*
Here there are only two horizontal rows of drainage eaves, as opposed to the customary four or more, and the pattern of economy is also seen in the walls, which have no plaster finishing, as well as in the shutterless windows and *sangawara* tile roof.

Takahari, Okayama Prefecture

(continued on page 245)

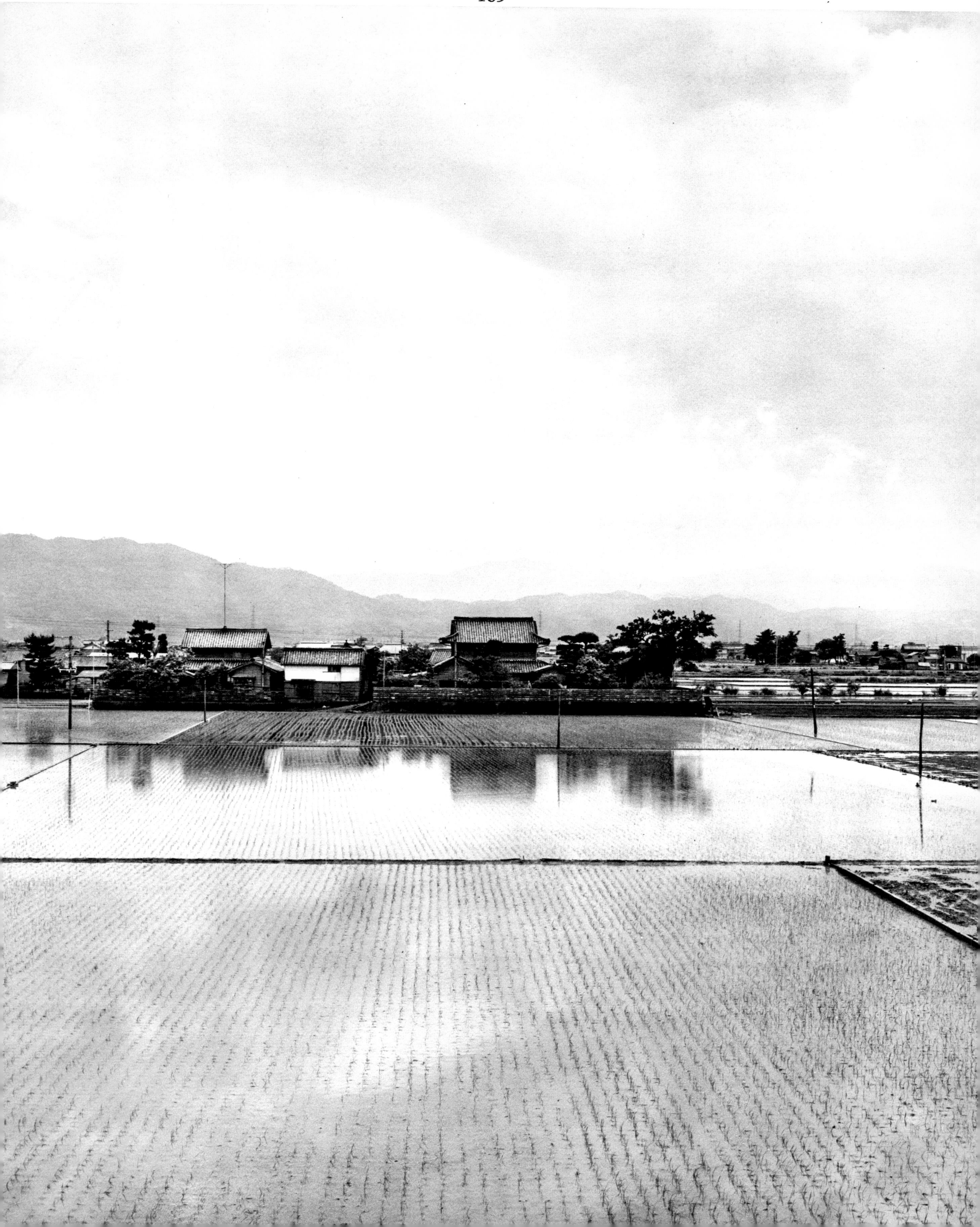

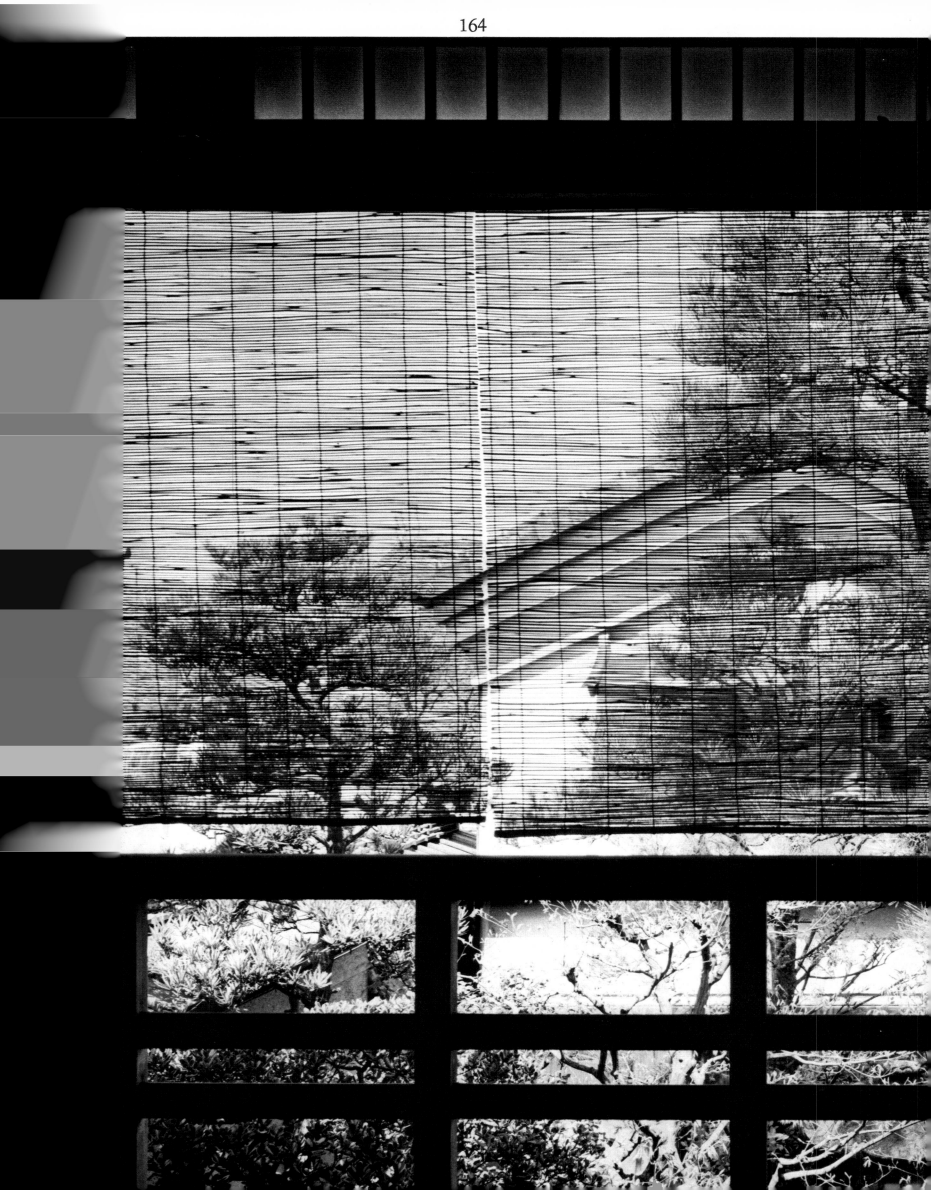

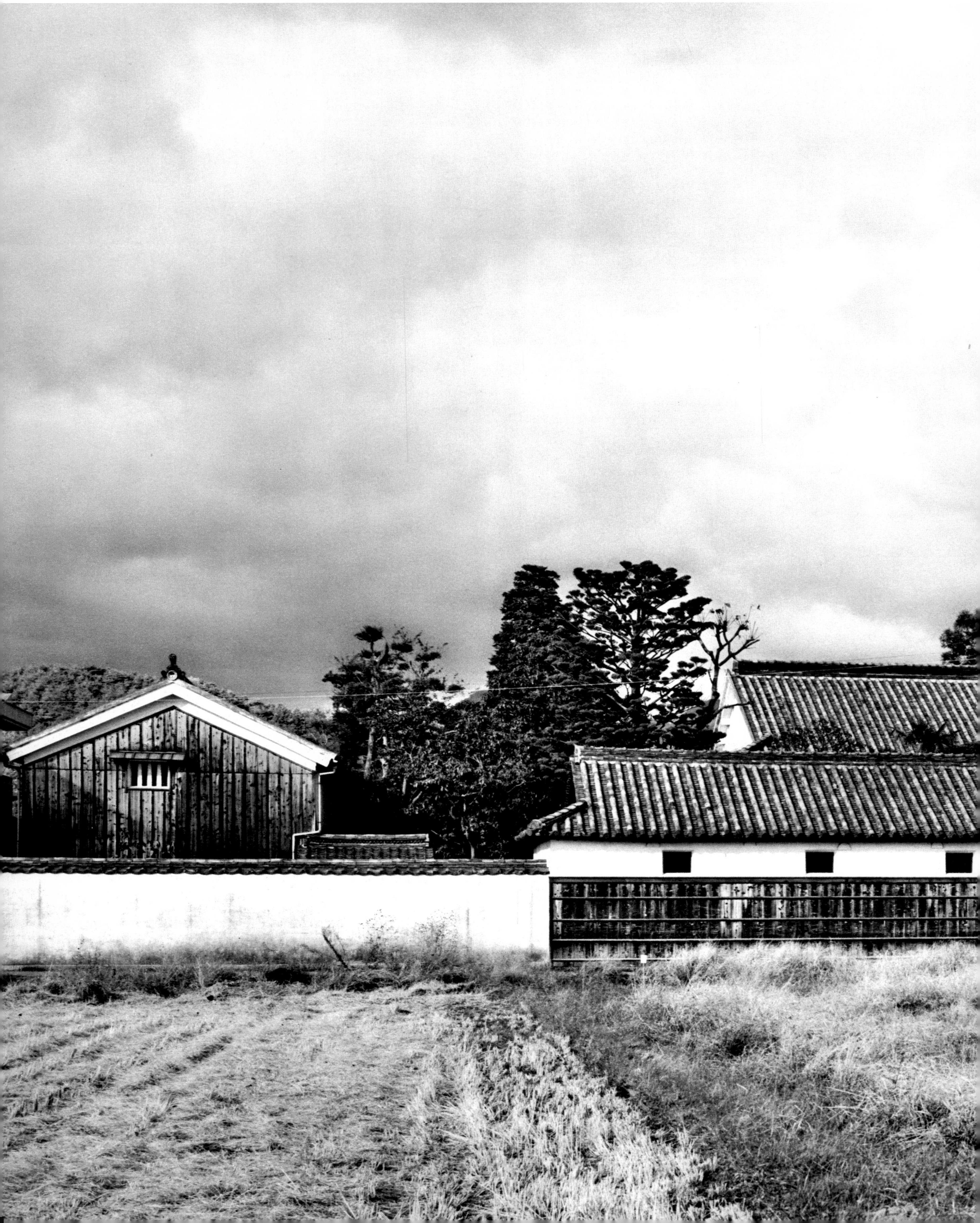

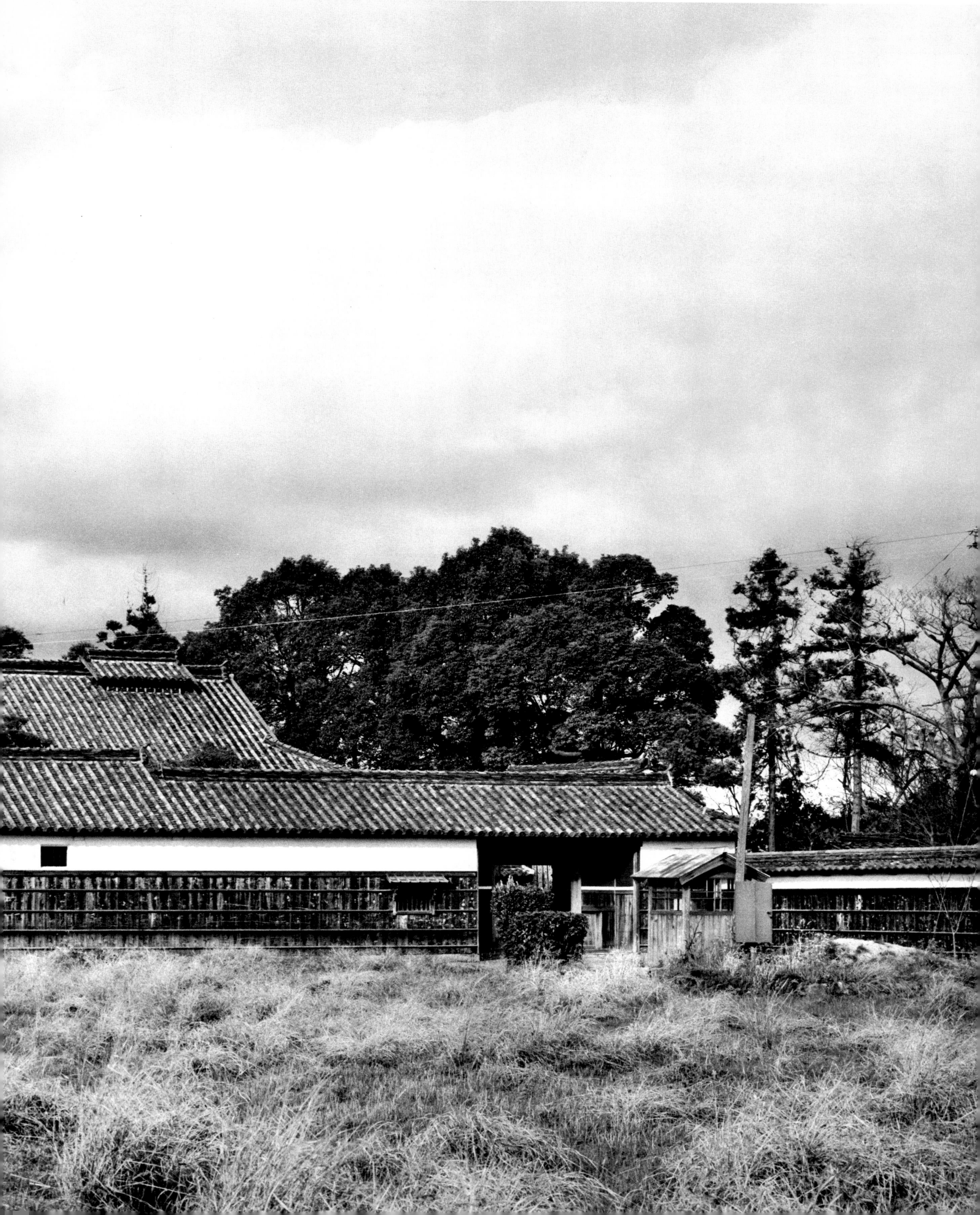

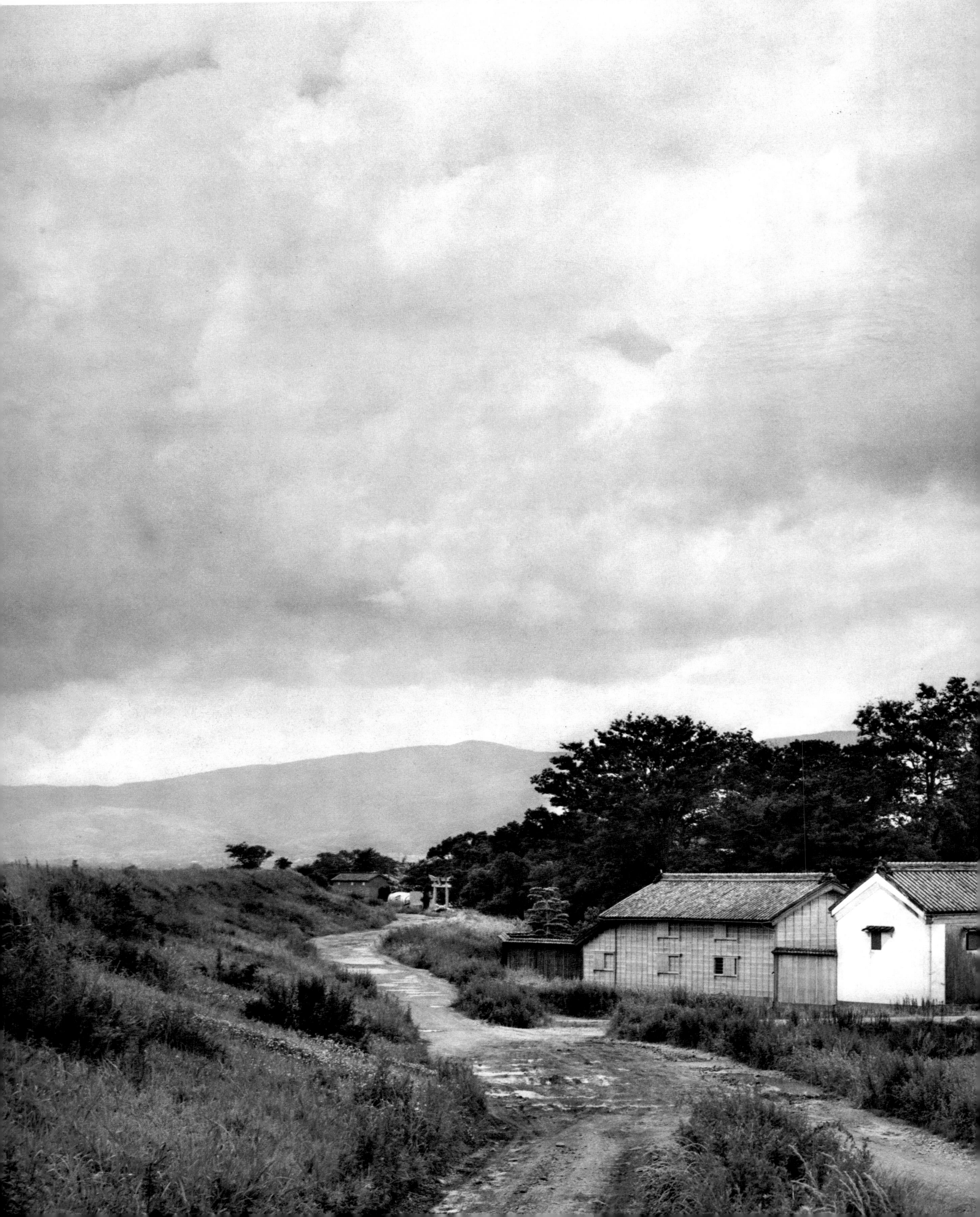

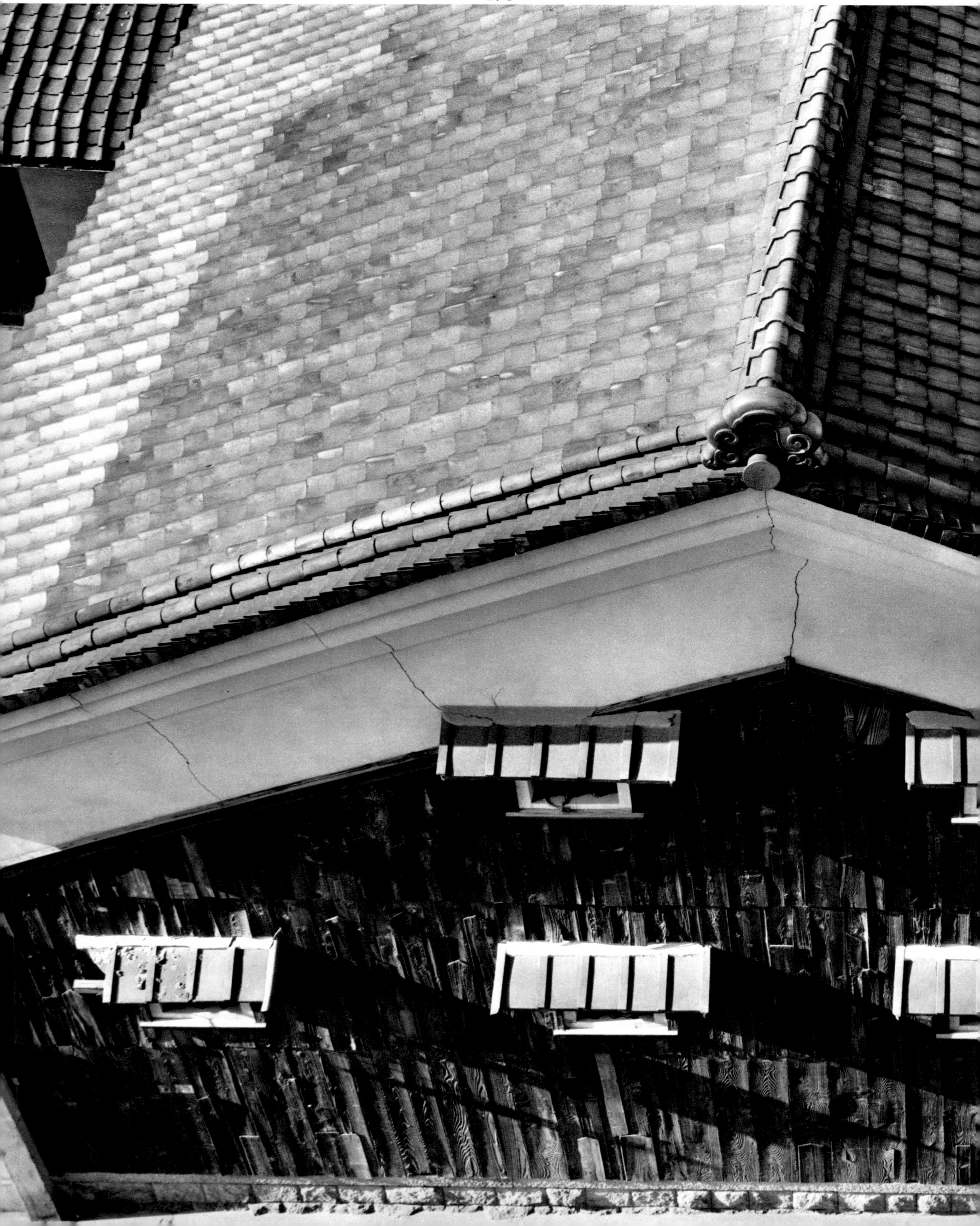

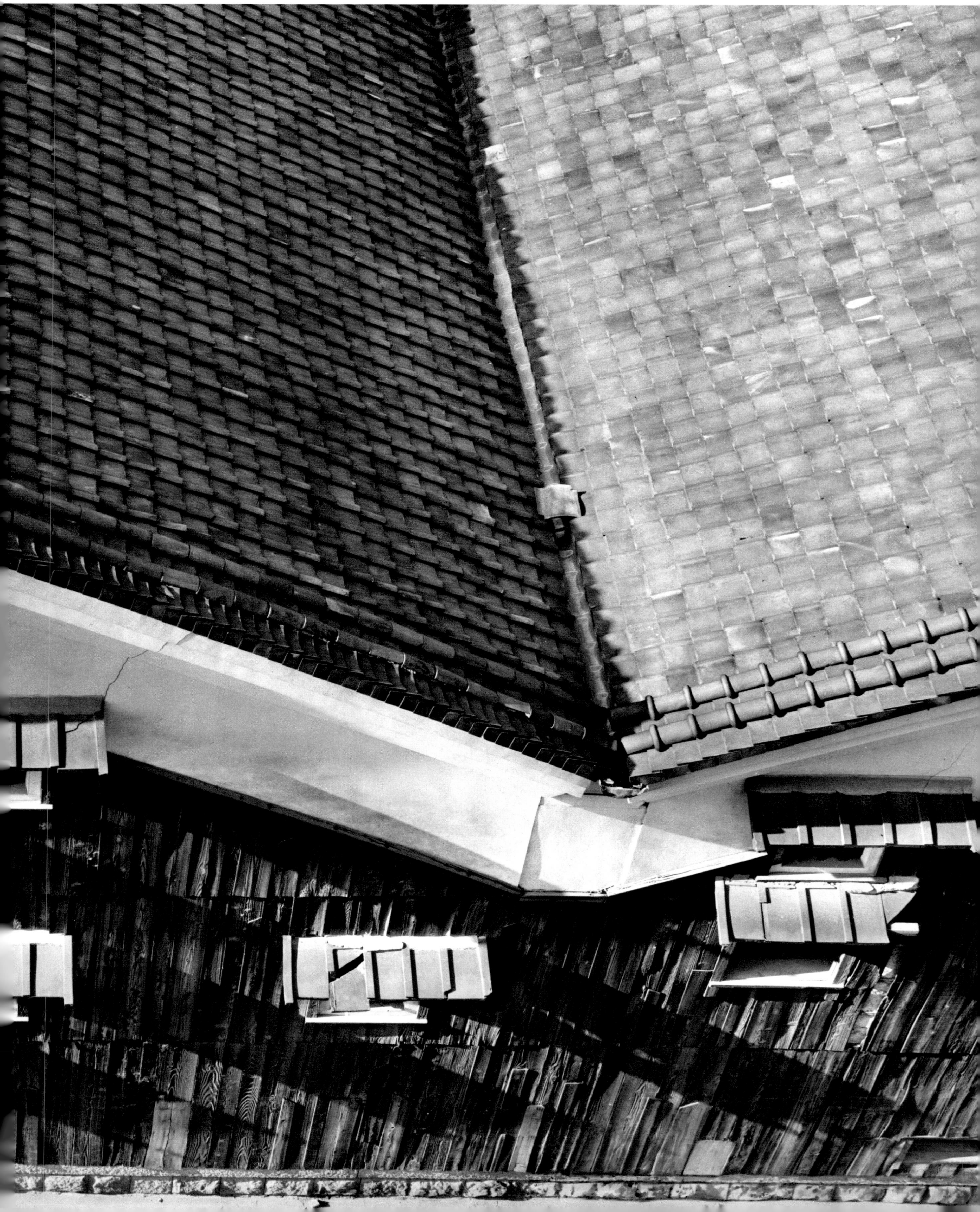

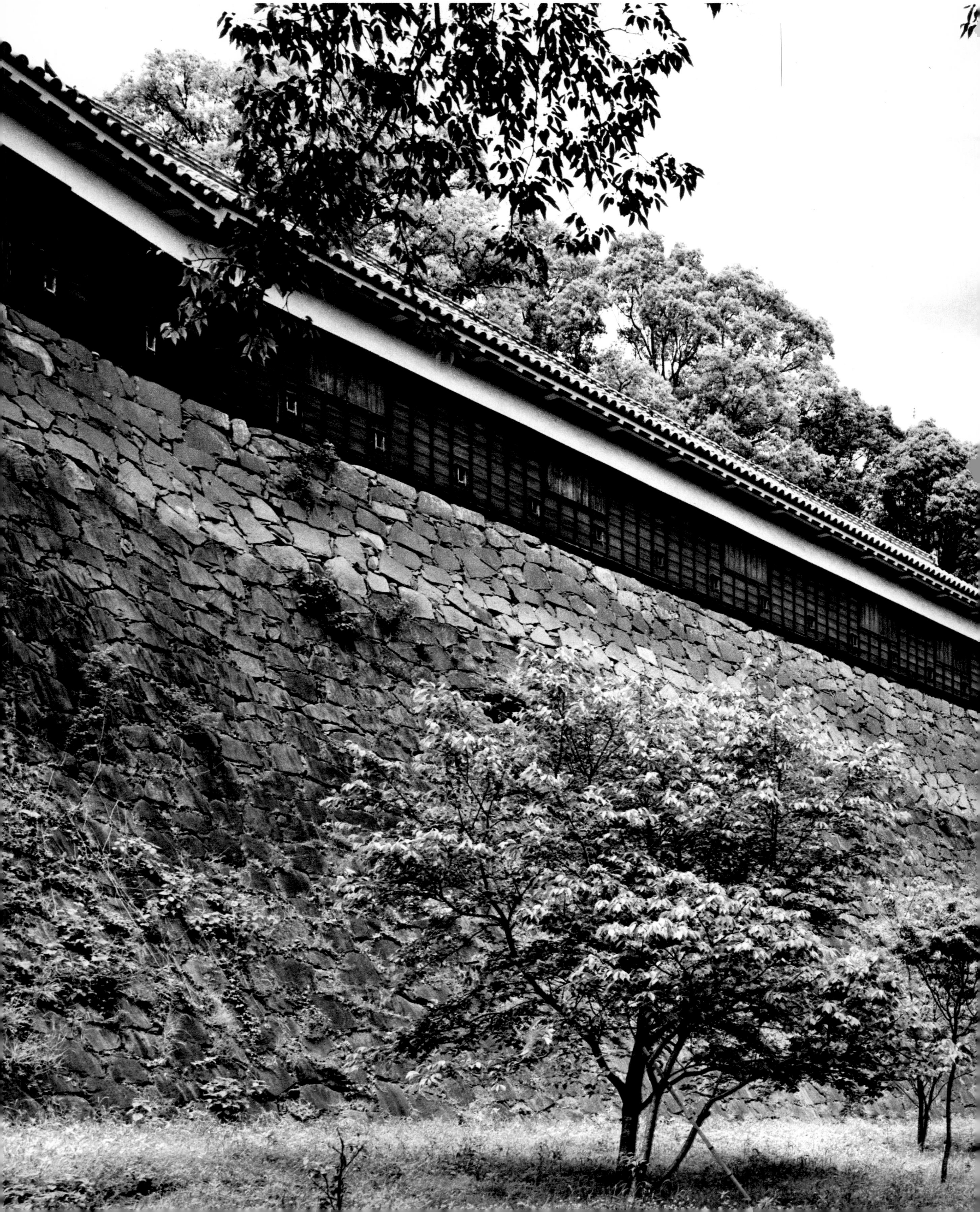

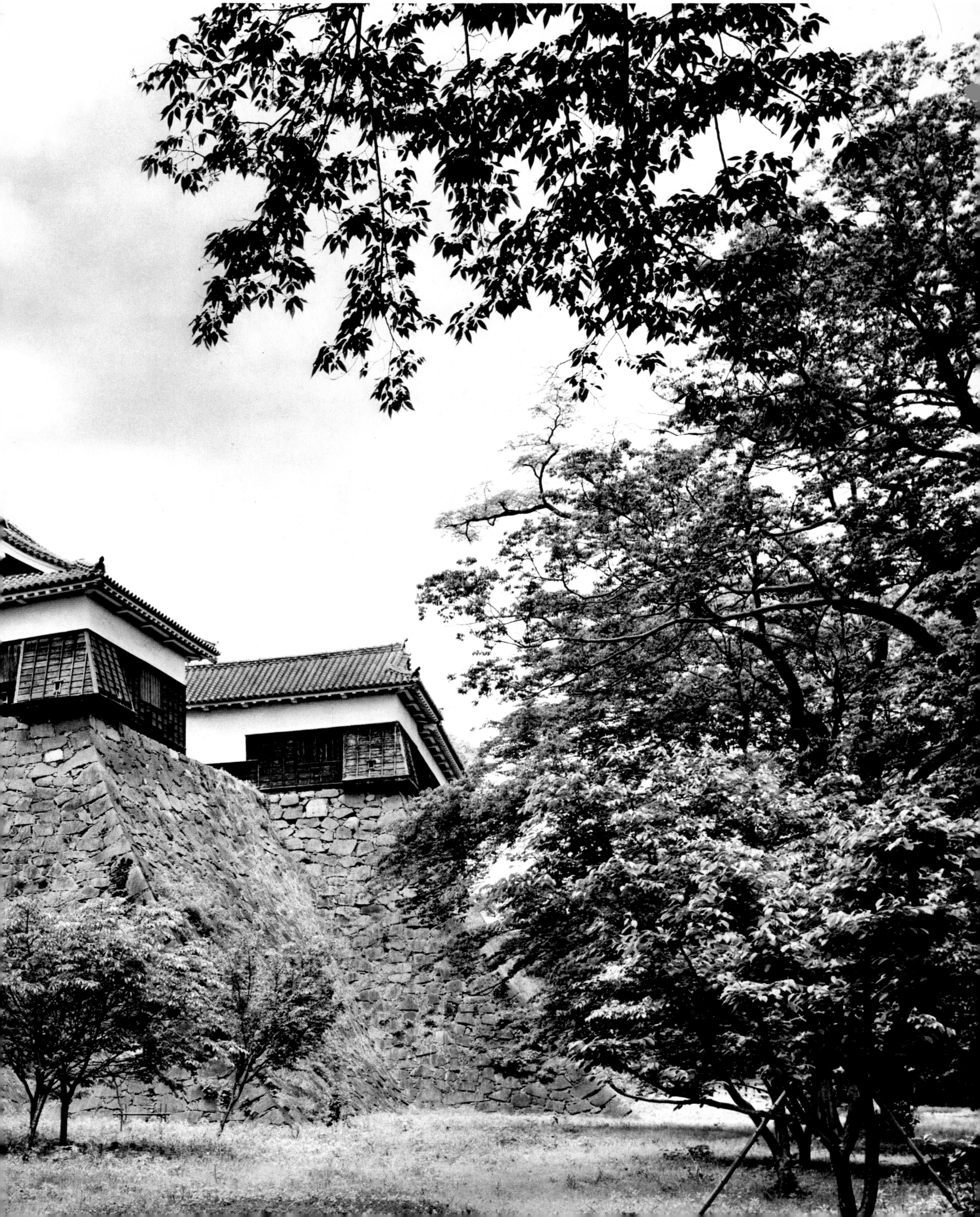

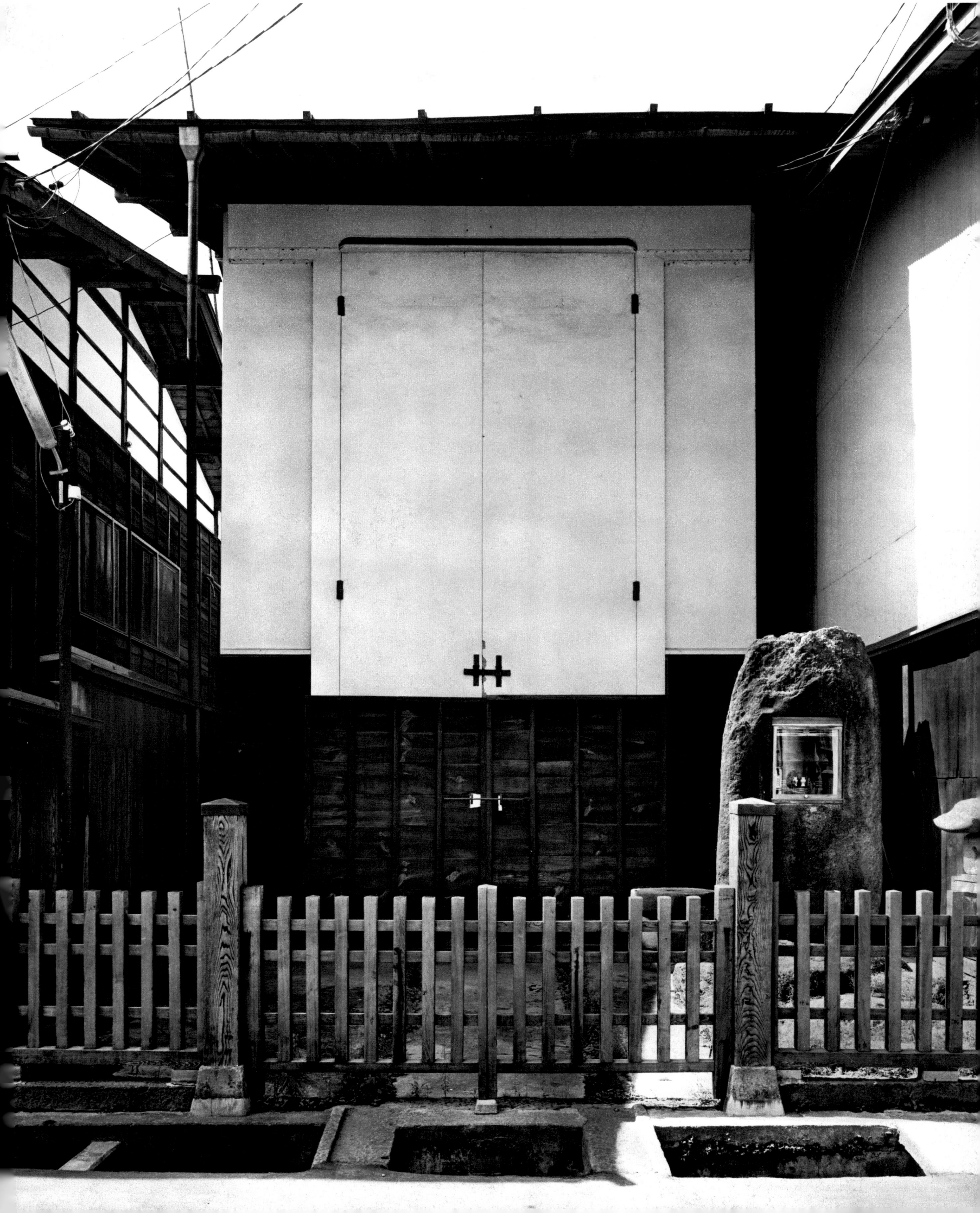

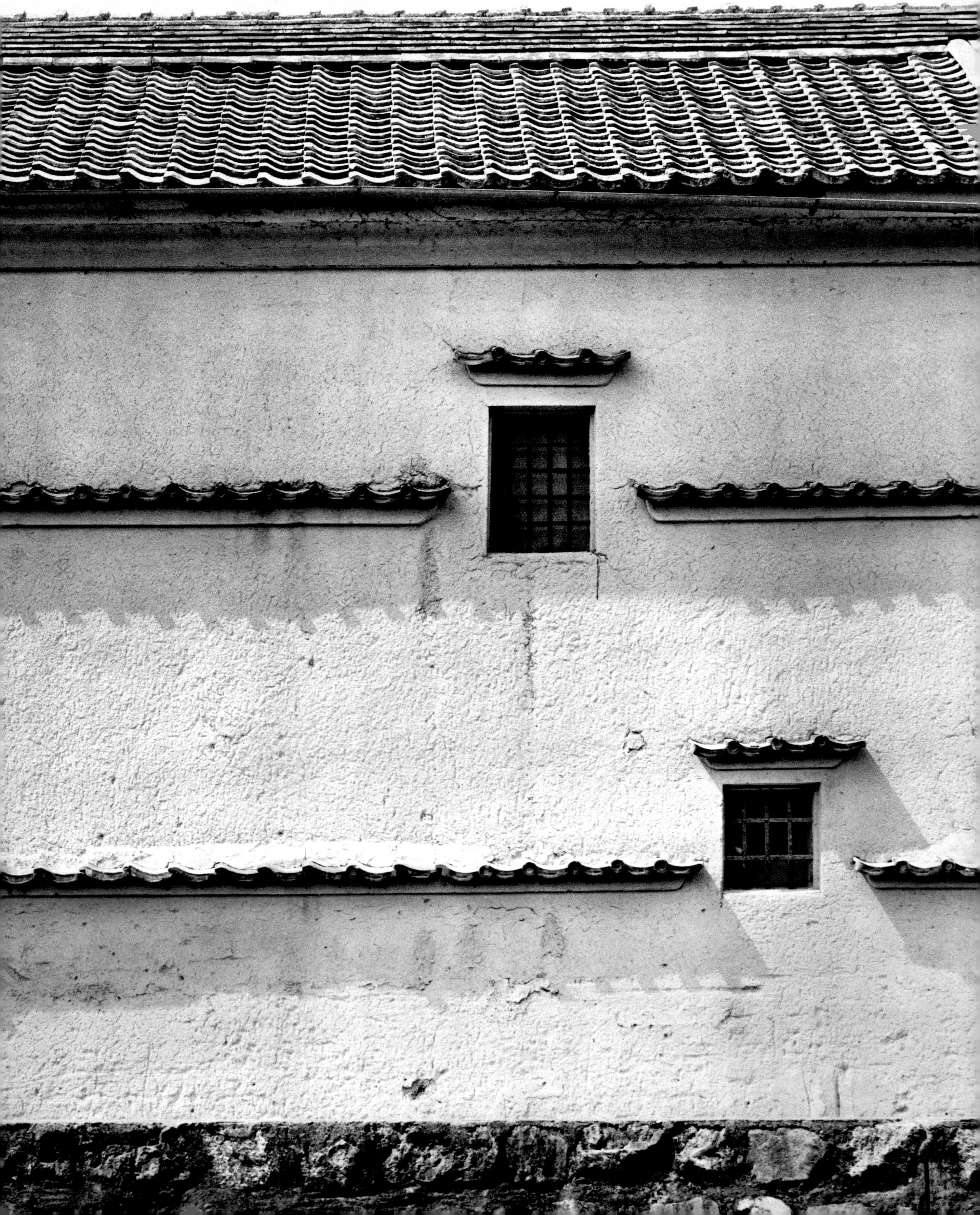

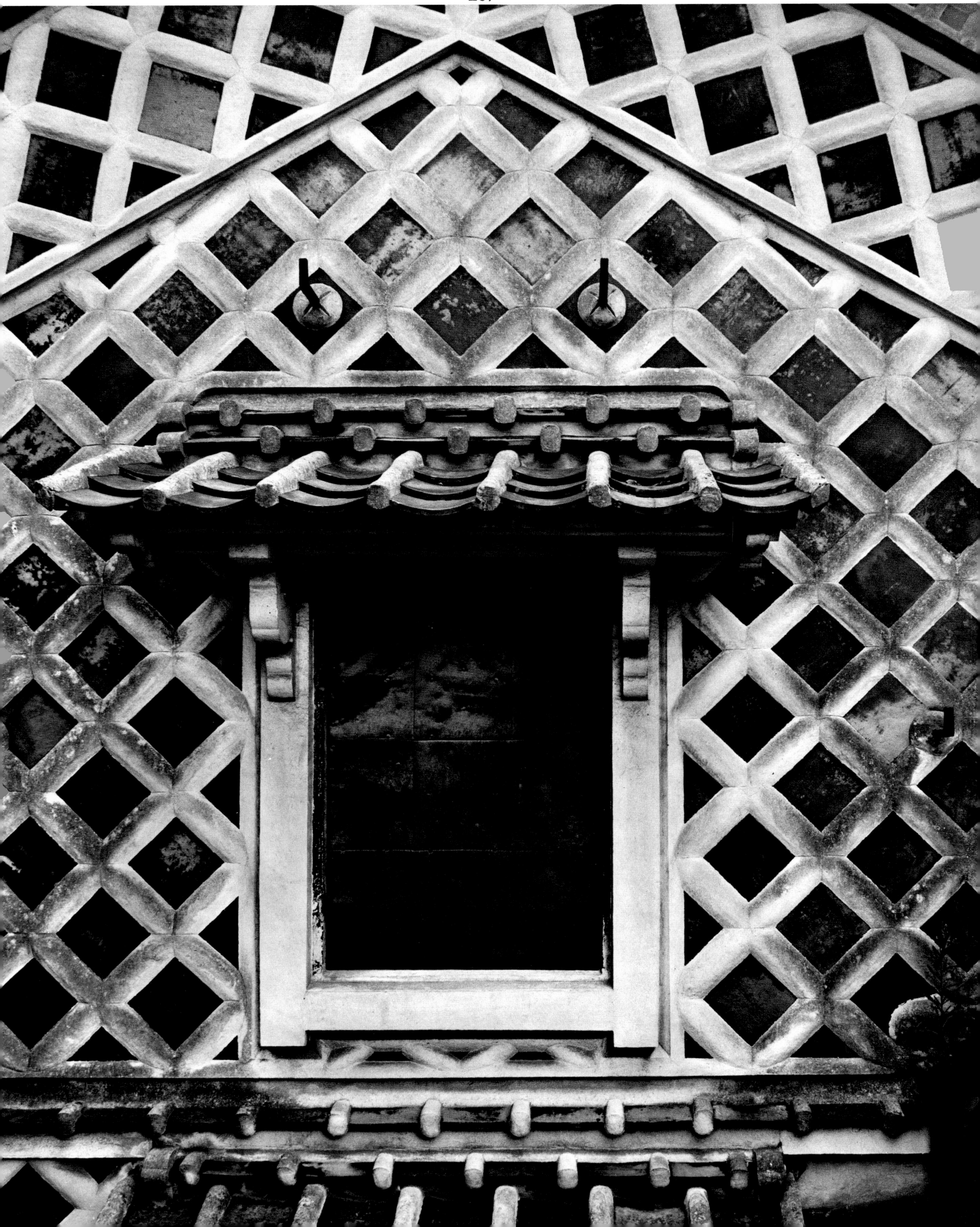

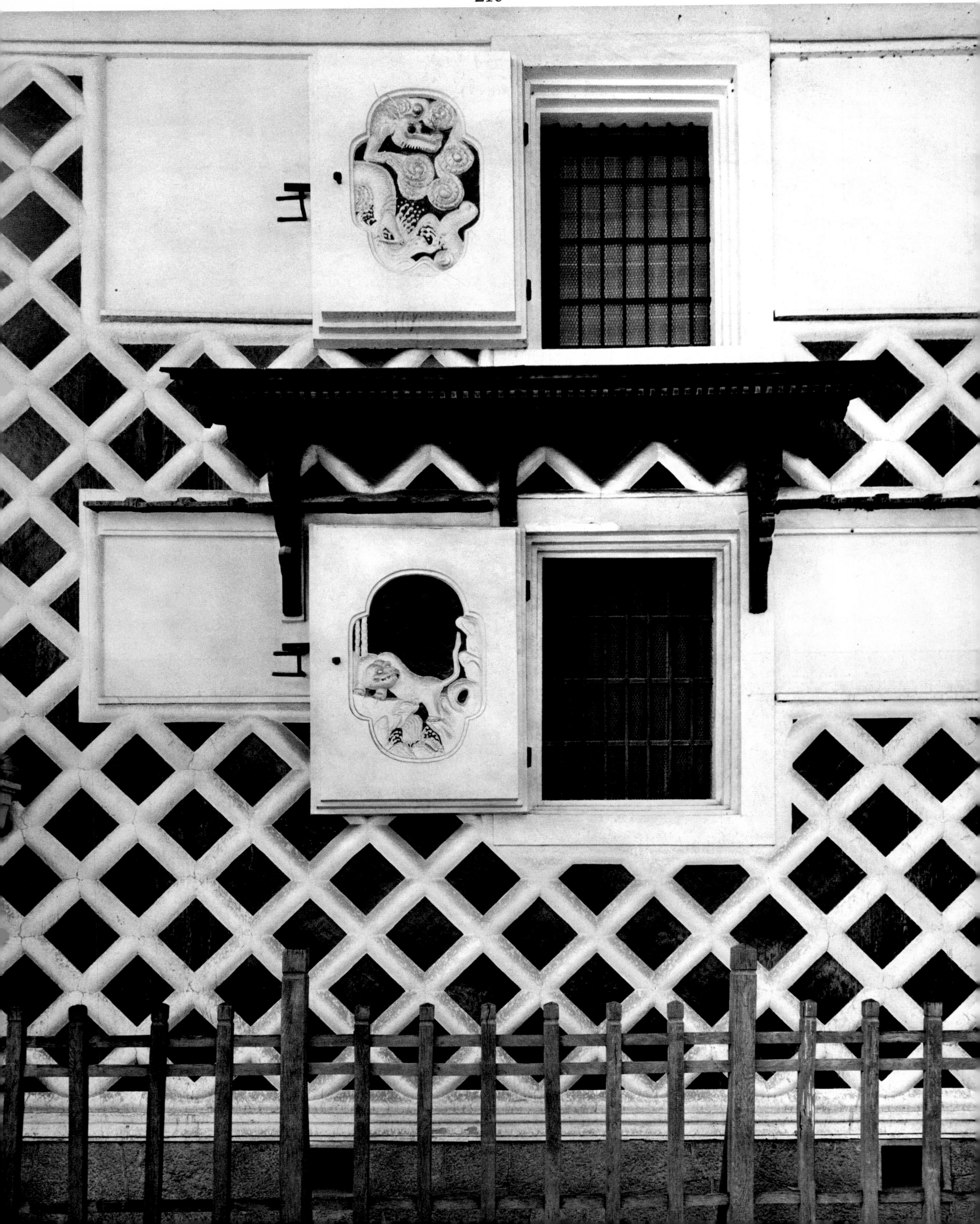

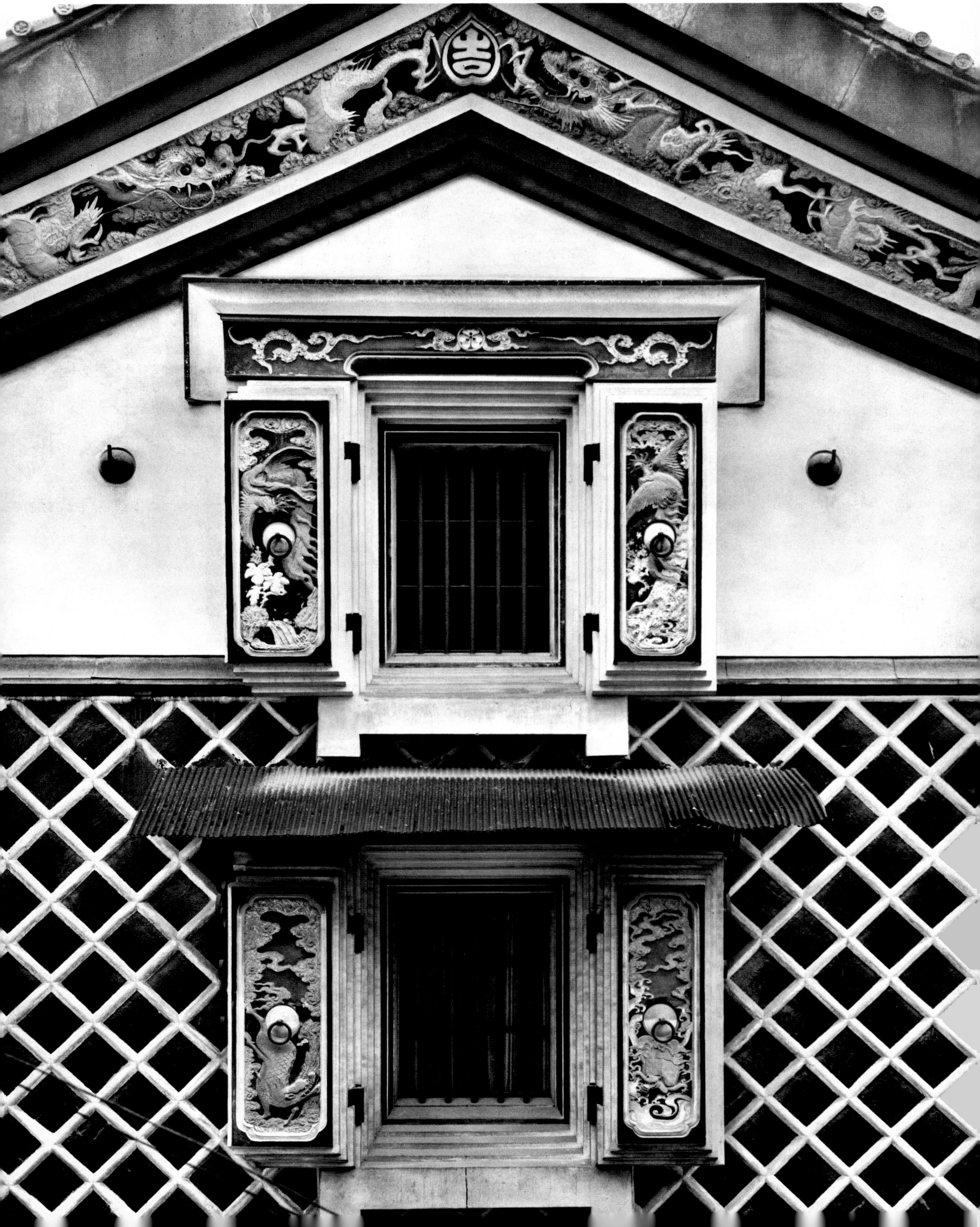
吉

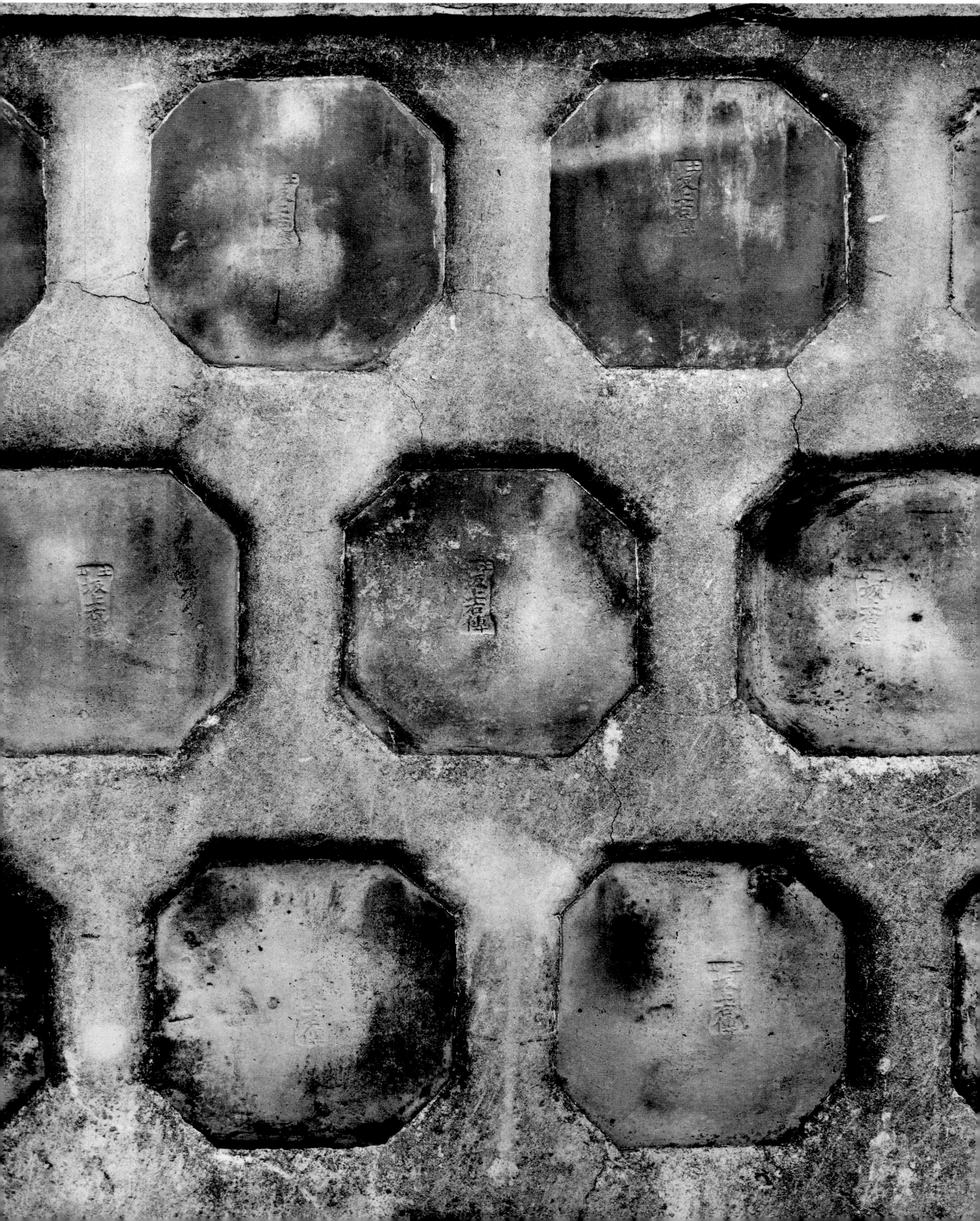

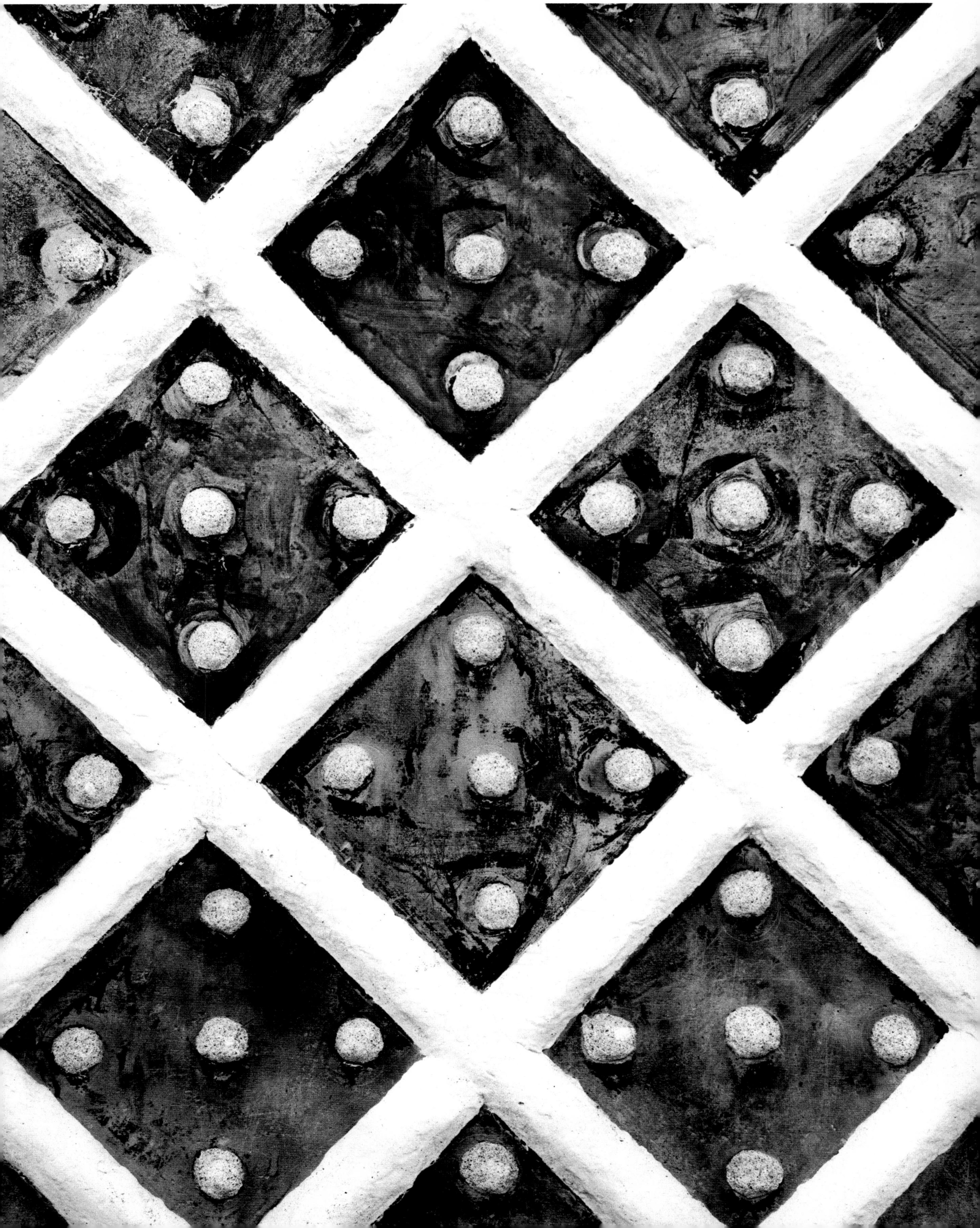

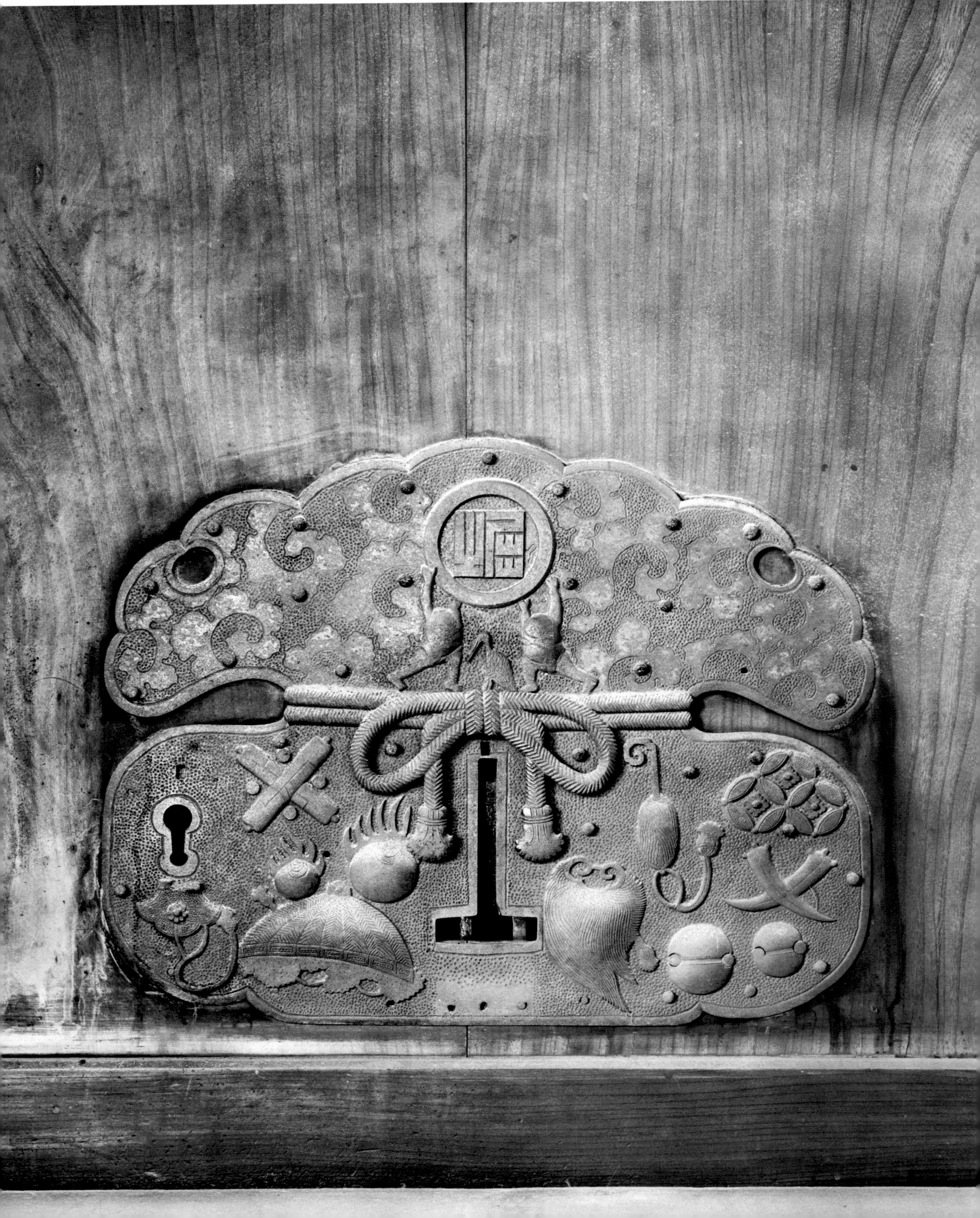

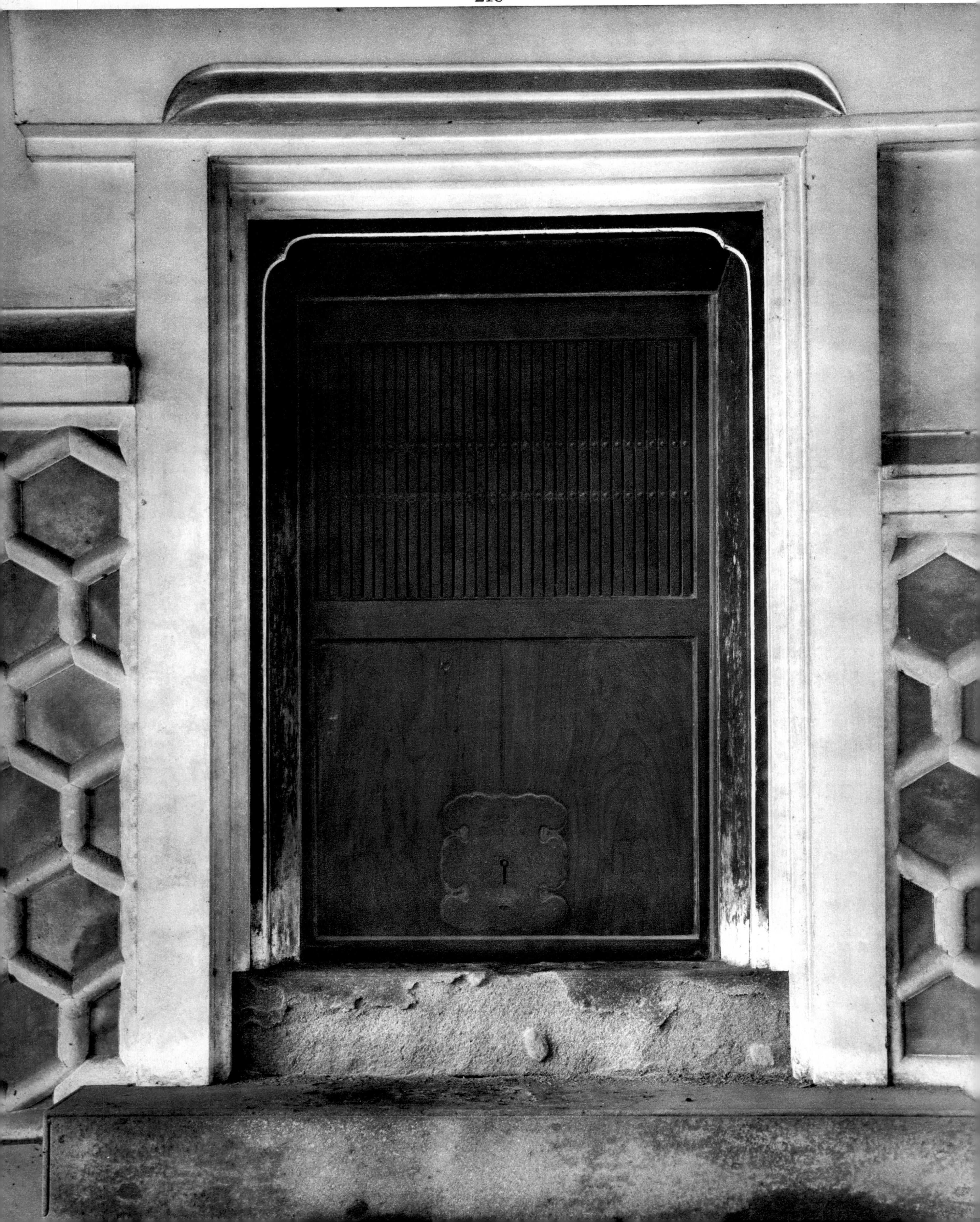

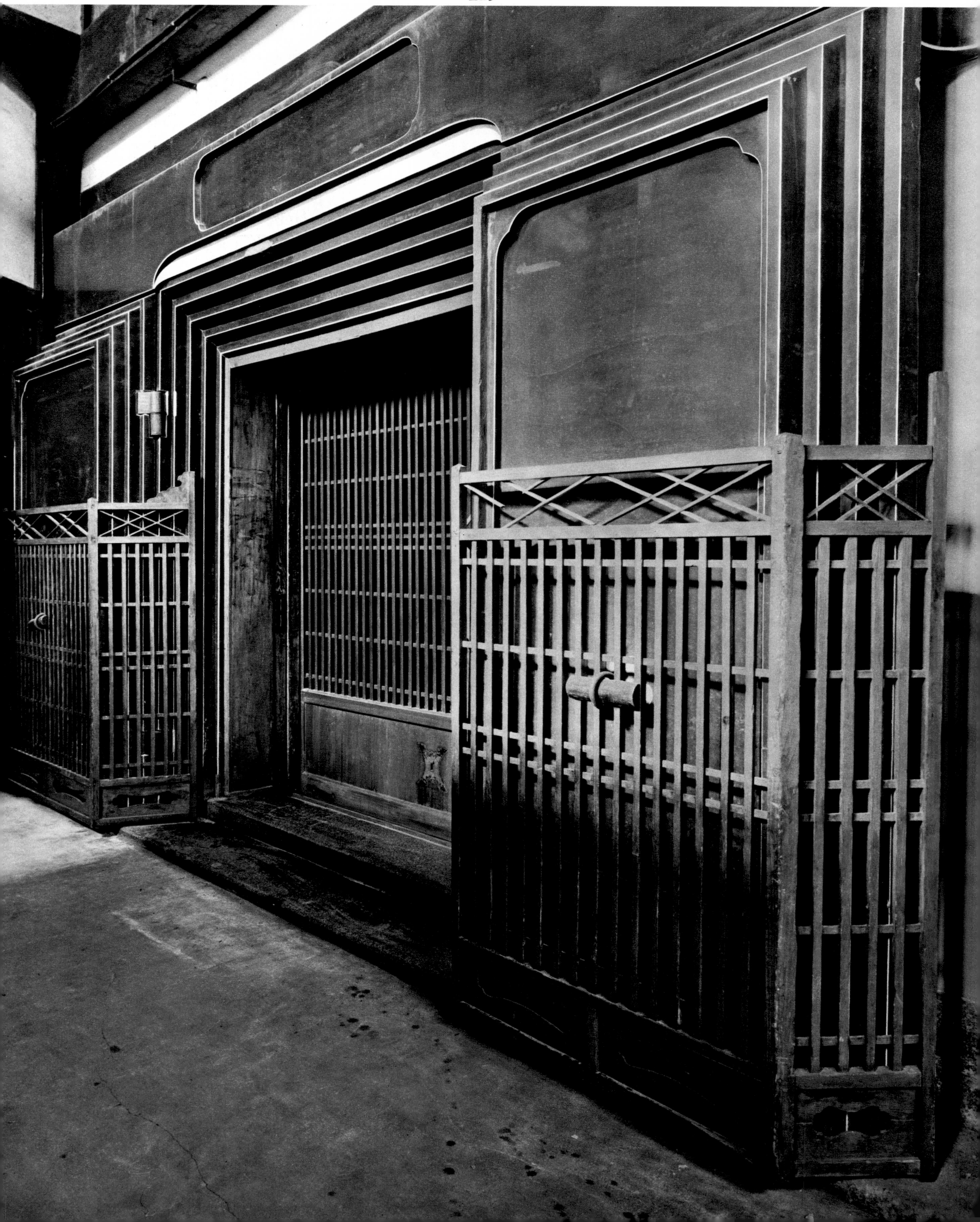

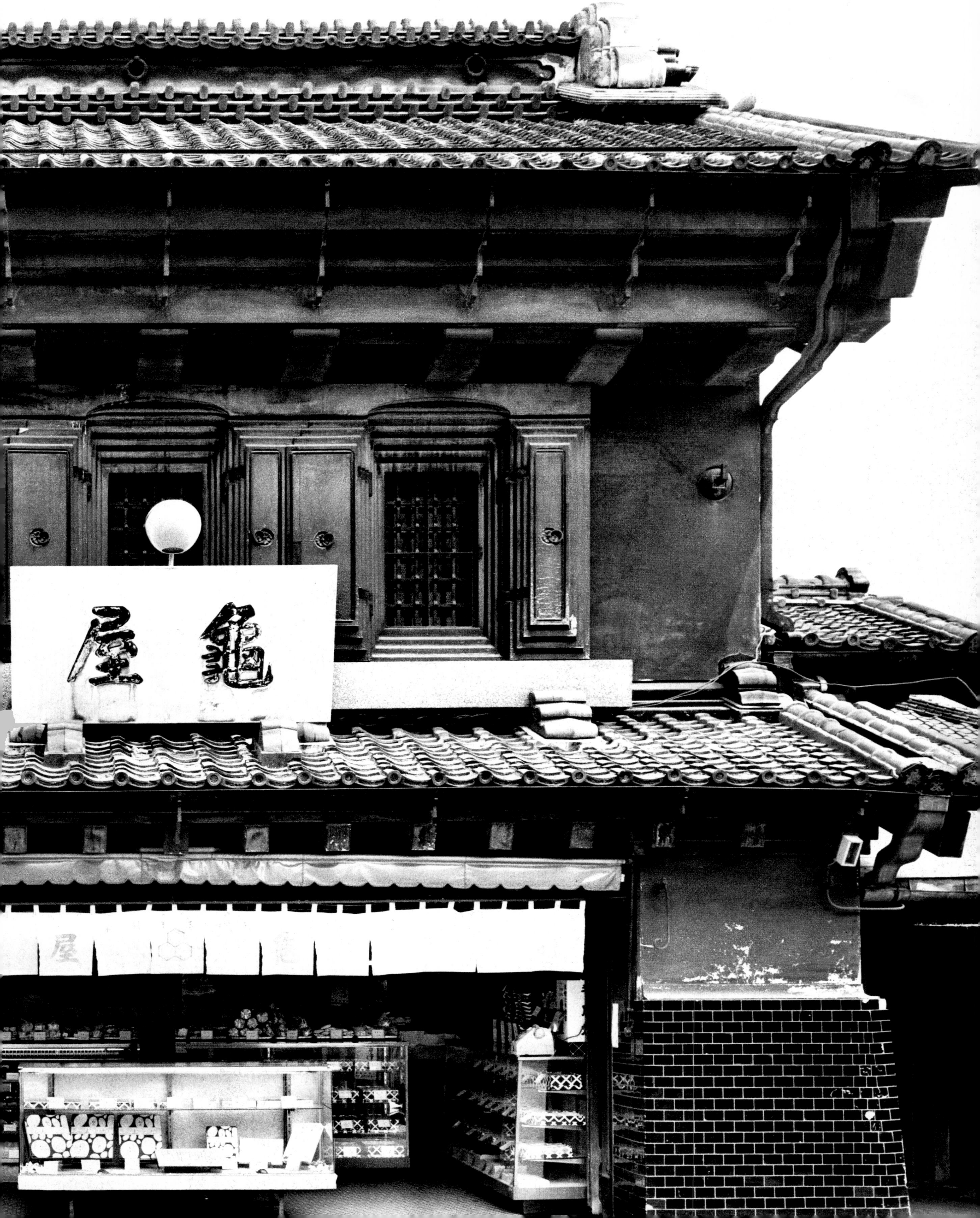
龜屋

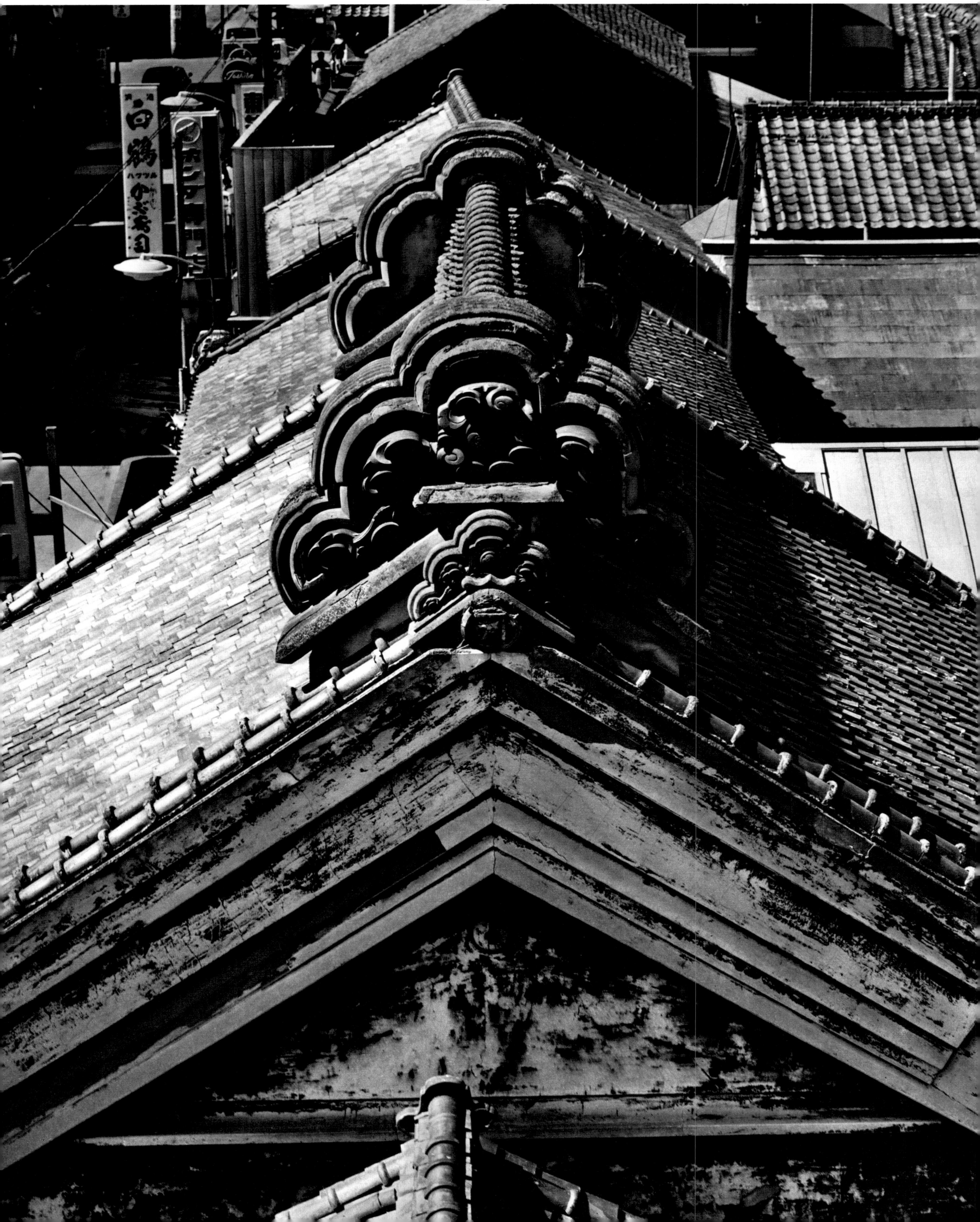
白鶴
ハクツル
Toshiba

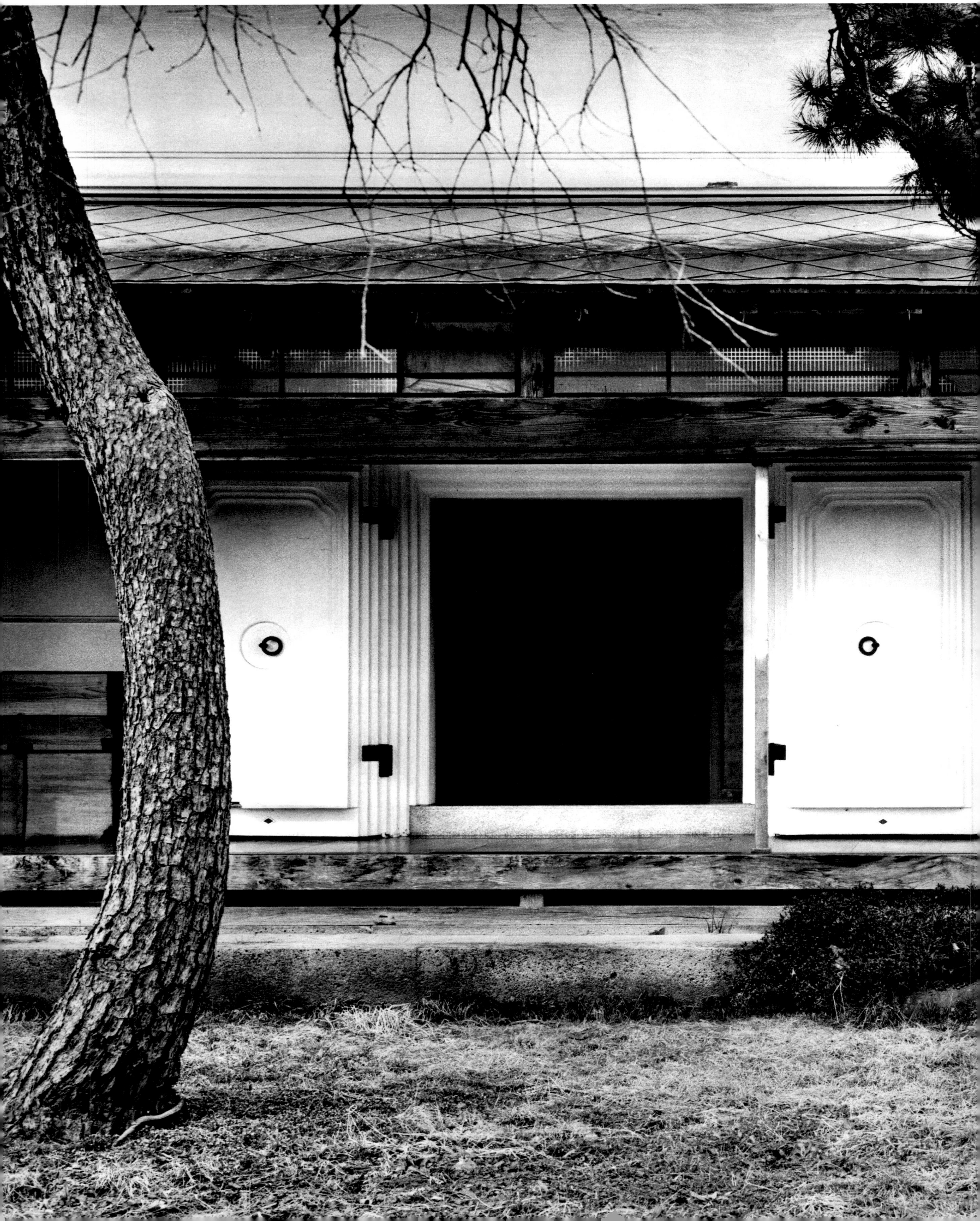

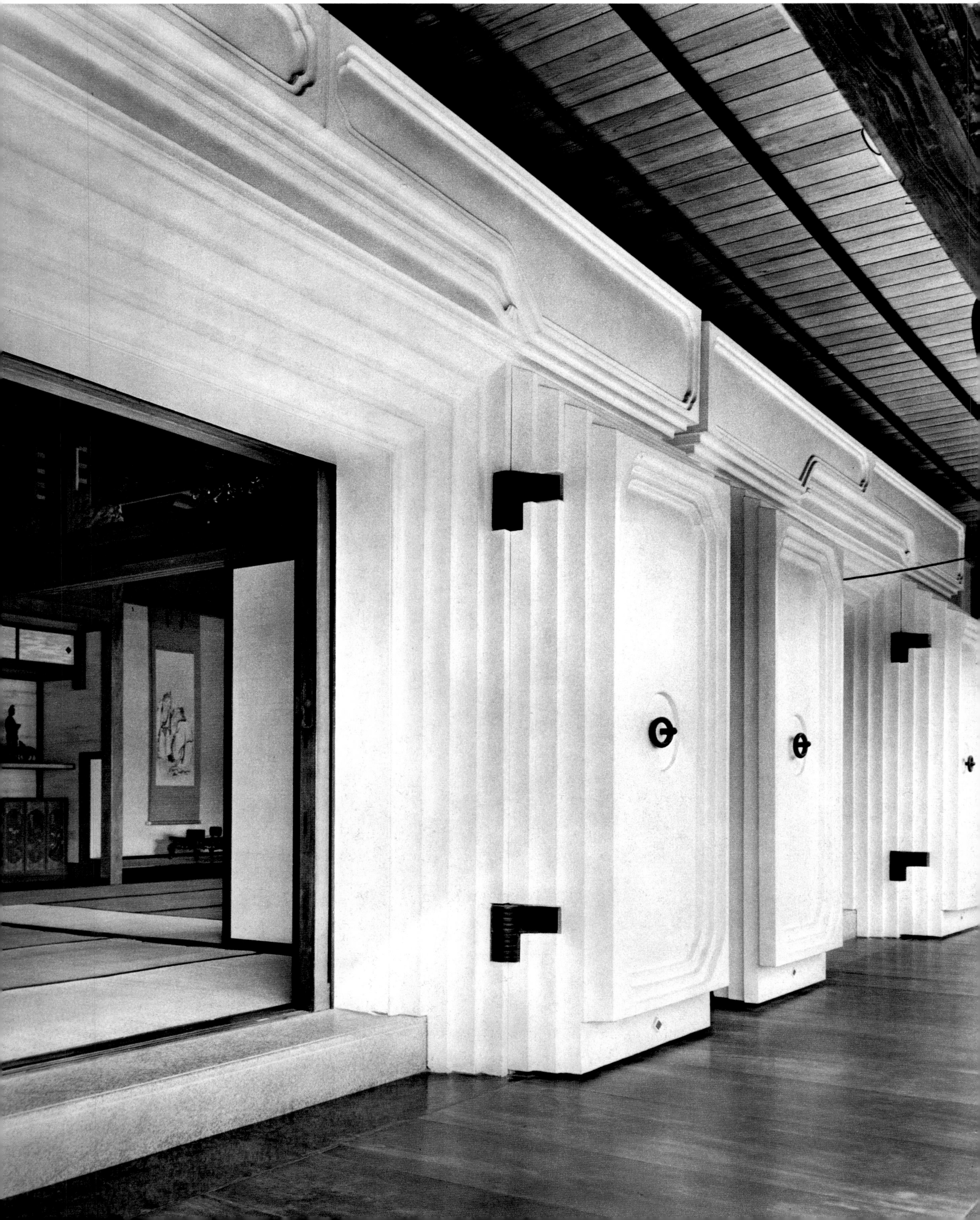

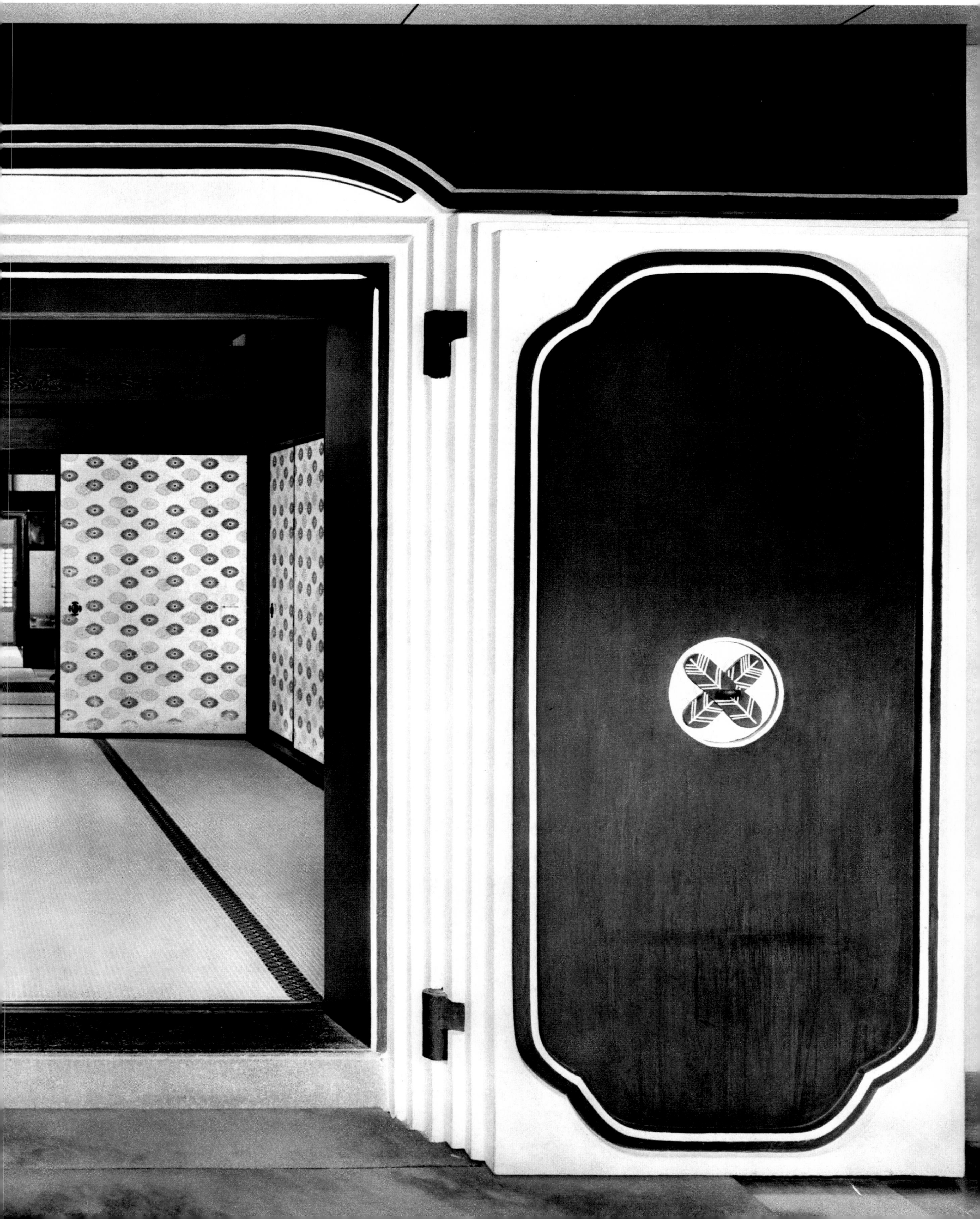

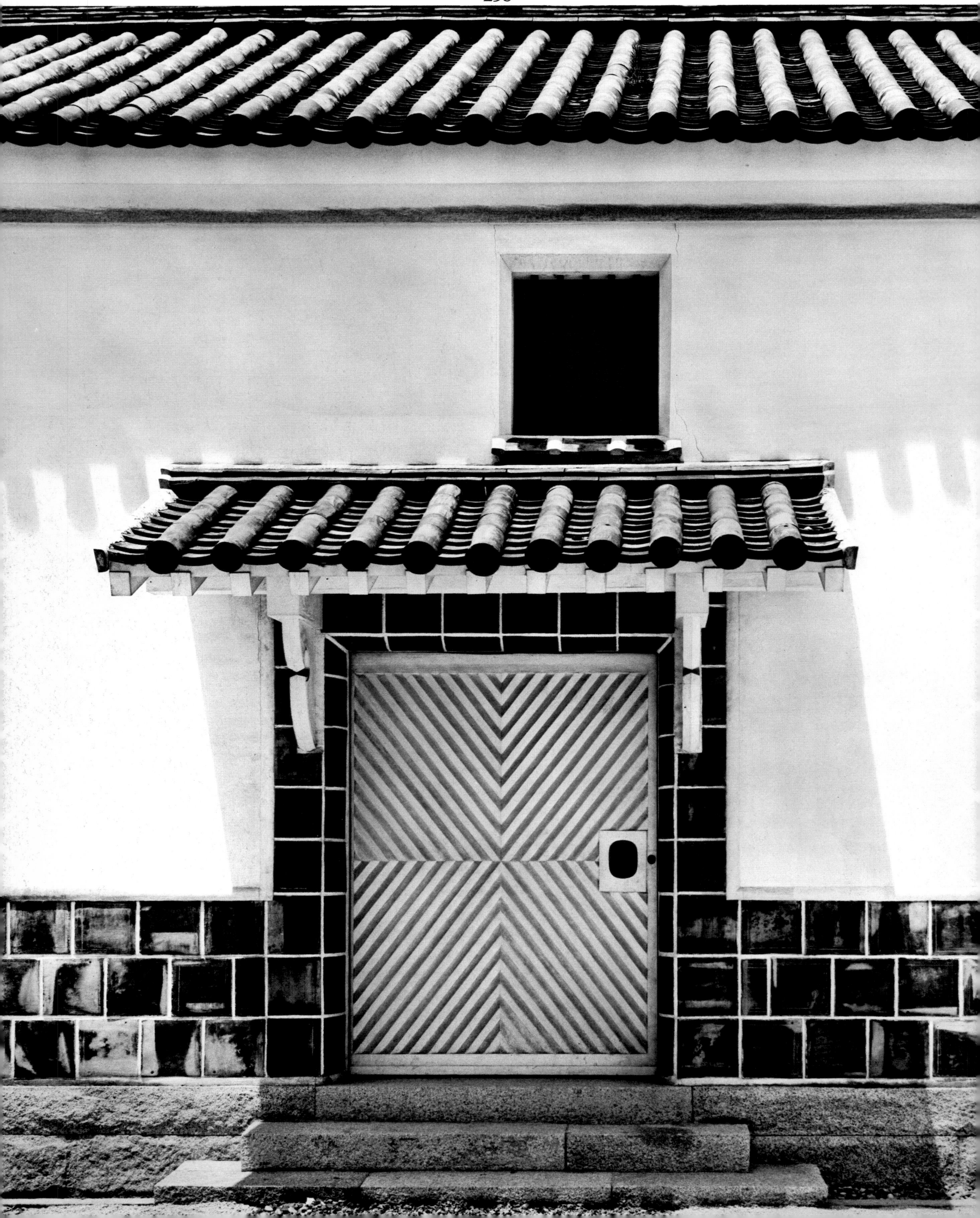

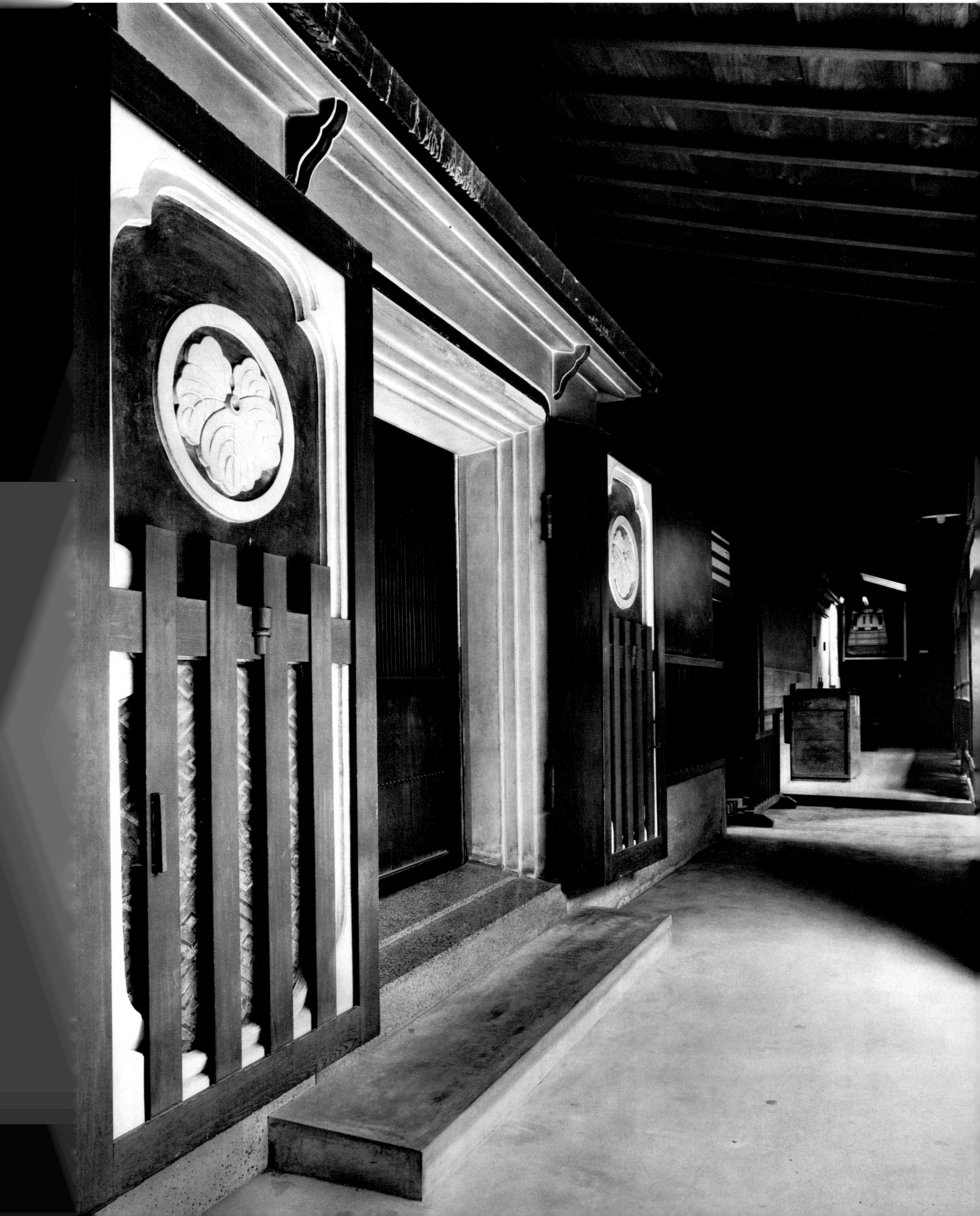

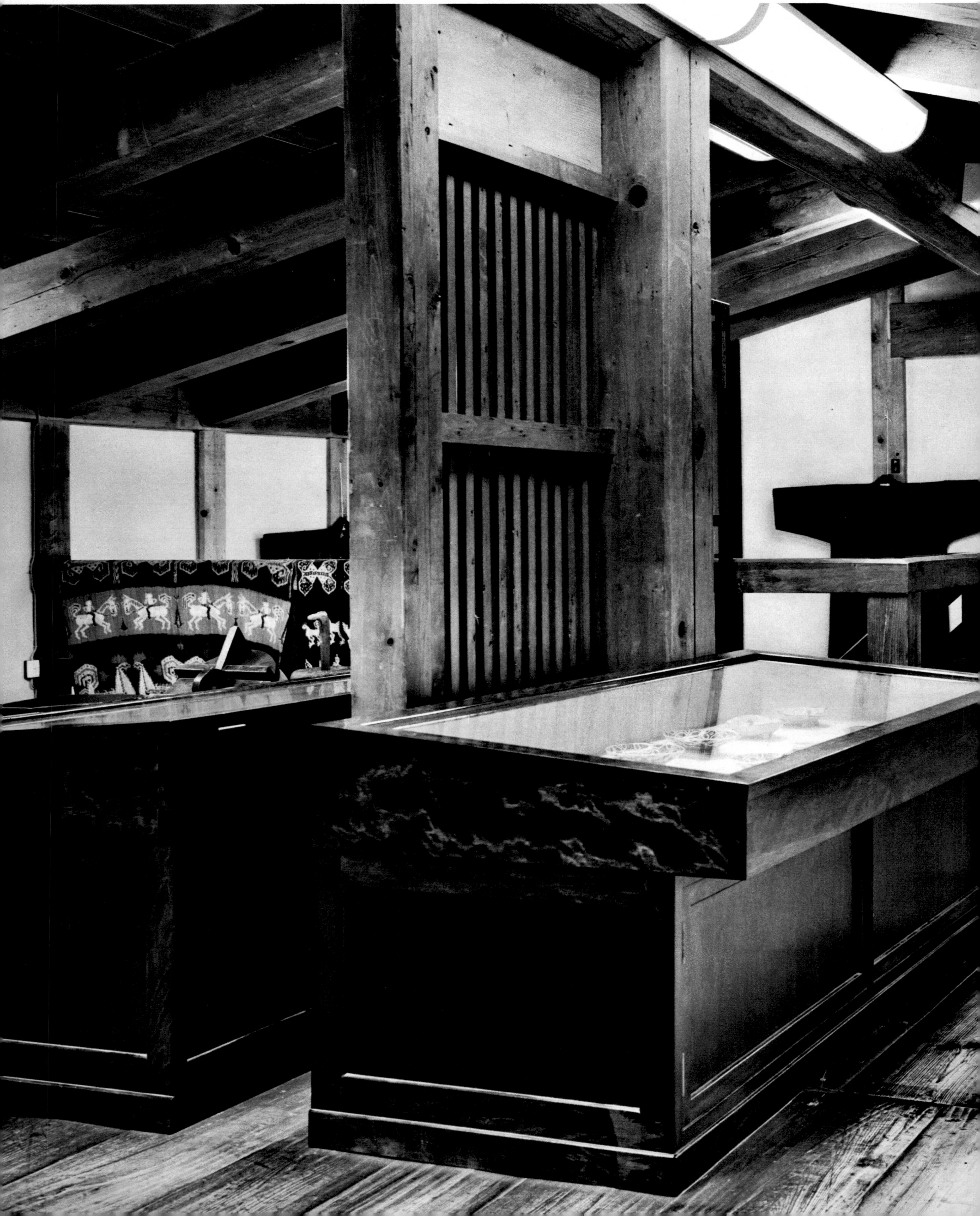

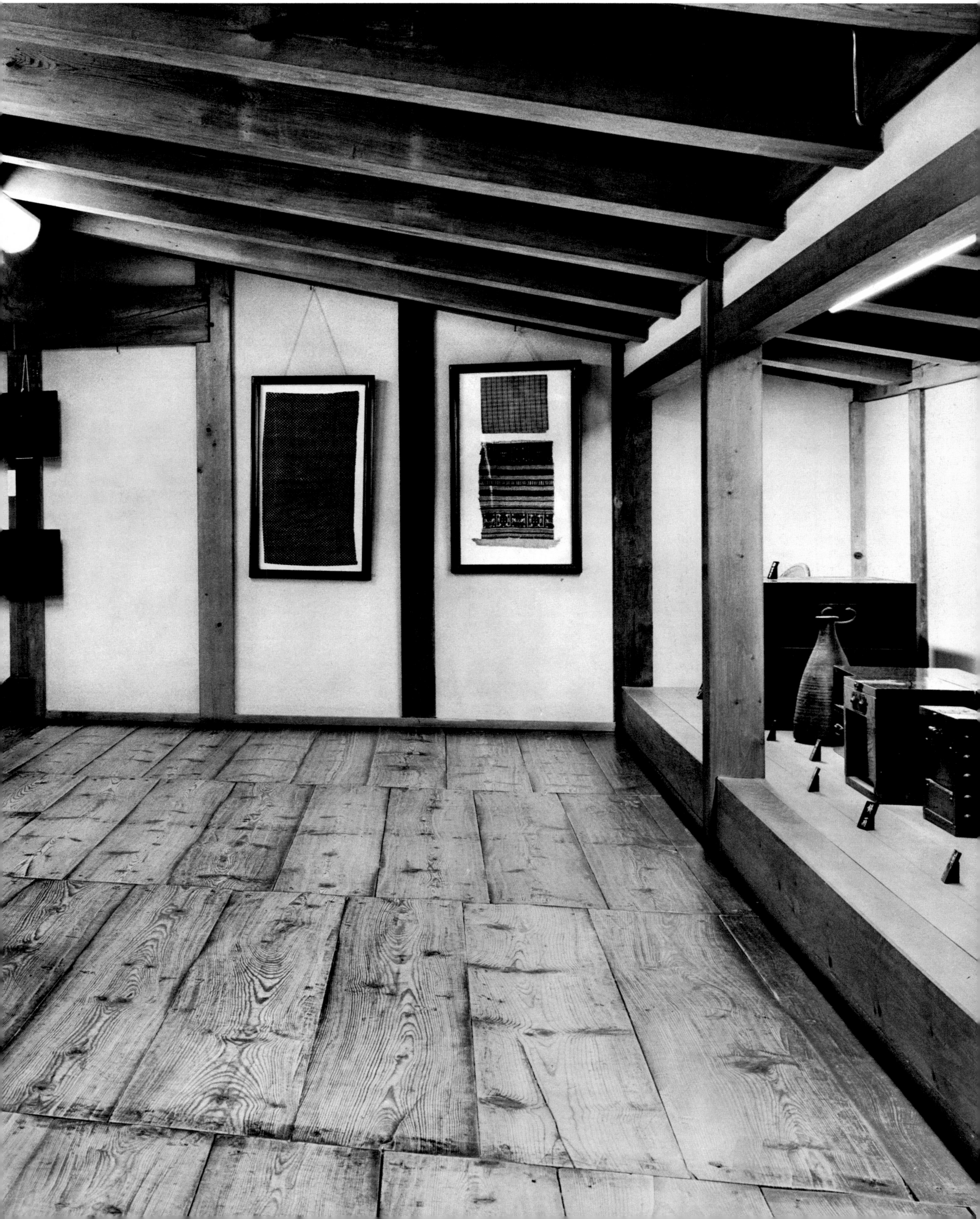

207. *Namako wall of dozō*
The two hooks above the window support a simple scaffolding used when the wall is being repaired. Such hooks are often found in the storehouses of eastern Japan, but only rarely in those of western Japan.

Shimoda, Shizuoka Prefecture

208–9. *Dozō storehouse*
This storehouse is used for household articles and family valuables. The metal-covered sliding door is unusual. Buildings of this kind usually have a wooden door covered with white plaster. Inside the metal door is a wooden door with grille that can be locked. Some hotel keepers in this vicinity have remodeled old storehouses of this kind and use them as rooms for guests. (See plate, pages 16–17.)

Yoda family, Matsuzaki, Shizuoka Prefecture

210. *Windows of dozō*
The reliefs on the shutters are called "trowel pictures," *kote-e*, and were made by the plasterers. The upper one shows a dragon and waves; the lower, a mythical lion and waves. The dragon and mythical lions are considered to be symbols of strength, and they are carved on the shutters to protect the storehouse from harm.

Tsuji family, Katsuyama, Okayama Prefecture

211. *Windows of dozō*
The painted reliefs of dragons, phoenixes, and other mythical animals that captured the public imagination were often cleanly executed, but trite and in questionable taste. (See plate, pages 12–13.)

Saffron Sake Company, Nagaoka, Niigata Prefecture

212. *Detail of dozō wall*
The name of the tile maker has been impressed into the flat tiles of the namako wall. The characters say "Uden of Tsuchiyama."

Suga family, Ichinomiya, Kumamoto Prefecture

213. *Detail of dozō wall*
This namako wall is unusual in that there are five circular lumps of white plaster on the surface of each tile. These cover the heads of the nails with which the tiles were attached to the wall and were intended to prevent water from seeping into the nail holes. Ordinarily the nail holes were in the four corners of the tiles and were concealed by the diagonal strips of plaster.

Mitsu, Hyogo Prefecture

214. *Lock on door of dozō*
The Horiuchi family had this lock made by a blacksmith in the Edo period. The overall shape represents a type of moneybag used in the Edo period for storing gold and silver coins. There are two keyholes, and two keys had to be inserted simultaneously to open the lock.

Shiojiri, Nagano Prefecture

215. *Iron latch on door of dozō*
The typical dozō had three doors in the entranceway: an inner grille door, an intermediate white sliding door, and an outer double swinging door. The only strong lock was on the innermost door. The outer fireproof doors were fastened only with a simple latch of the type shown here. The inscription on the latch indicates that it was forged by a blacksmith named Isaburō, who lived in the Semba district of Osaka.

Ikaruga, Nara Prefecture

216. *Lock on door of dozō*
This lock is on the grille door of a storehouse used for household articles. It bears a design of two plum blossoms and the heads of two good luck mallets. The belief was that by waving one of these mallets around one could obtain anything one wished. The mallet on the left concealed the keyhole, but since the lock is somewhat in disrepair, part of the keyhole can be seen.

Kita family, Nonoichi, Ishikawa Prefecture

217. *Storehouse keys*
The Kadomi family were shipping agents in the Edo period, and they still have storehouses for household articles, commercial goods, soy sauce, and other items. As the six keys suggest, there are six storehouses in all. The round bells were attached to the keys to give warning when someone was tampering with them and to enable people to tell by the sound which key they were selecting.

Monzen, Ishikawa Prefecture

218. *Entrance of dozō*
Here the double swinging doors usually employed as the outermost doors of the storehouse have been omitted. The plaster-covered "white door" is slid out of view, and what is seen is the innermost door, the upper half of which is a grille.

Horiuchi family, Shiojiri, Nagano Prefecture

219. *Entrance of dozō*
The entrance to a typical dozō usually looks like this in the daytime. The grille door admits air into the interior during the daylight hours, which is necessary because of the damp

climate. The white-plastered middle door is customarily closed at night and when fires occur, but the heavy outer doors are normally closed only when fires break out. The outer doors are protected by movable grilles.

Ryōzeki Sake Company, Yuzawa, Akita Prefecture

220–21. *Dozō shop*

This building was built after the Kawagoe fire of 1893 and is consequently among the last Edo-style dozō constructed. The first floor is one large room that forms the shop proper. The second floor is a warehouse. The building to the left of the store is another warehouse. Not visible are a house and two other storehouses located behind the store. (See diagram, page 96.)

Kameya store, Kawagoe, Saitama Prefecture

222. *Ridge of dozō shop*

The fundamental purpose of the large end tile was to protect the ridge from fire, but the exaggerated example seen here was also intended to symbolize the store's solidity and dependability. The varying forms of these tiles were marks of identity.

Fukazen store, Kawagoe, Saitama Prefecture

223. *Ridge of dozō shop*

In the Kansai district, end tiles of storehouses, like those of Buddhist temples, were usually in the form of gargoyles, but in Kanto they were usually of some abstract form, such as that seen here, and they were often decorated with the family crest or a trademark. (See plate, pages 18–19.)

Harada Rice Store, Kawagoe, Saitama Prefecture

224–25. *Windows of a dozō shop*

The typical dozō of the Kanto region had a final outside coating of black plaster, but in the example shown here the black has worn off to a large extent, exposing the white plaster underneath. Inside the iron grids in the windows are sliding panels, which are used to close the openings in ordinary times. Like the outer doors, the thick shutters are closed only when there is a fire.

Machikan Hardware Store, Kawagoe, Saitama Prefecture

226–28. *Zashiki-gura*

226–27. Front. A *zashiki* is the best room of a traditional Japanese house and consequently the room in which guests are entertained and ceremonies held. When the zashiki is built in dozō style, it is called a *zashiki-gura*. This was a fairly common type in the Edo period, but the best surviving examples are found in Yamagata Prefecture. This zashiki-gura now has a galvanized

sheet-iron roof, but the roof was originally made of thick shingles. Tile roofs, which are apt to be damaged in freezing weather, are not often used in this area because of the severe winters.

228. Entrance. The building's exterior is the same as that of the typical dozō storehouse, but the interior is a zashiki with the traditional tokonoma and staggered shelves.

Suzuki family, Asahi, Yamagata Prefecture

229–31. *Zashiki-gura*

229. Staircase. This building has two stories, of which the first is a living room and the second a storage place for household articles. Here the space underneath the stairs is converted into a large chest of drawers.

230–31. Interior. The zashiki is composed of the two rooms in the foreground, the closer one being an anteroom that can be combined with the other room by removing the sliding doors. The room in the distance connects the zashiki-gura with the family store, which is also a dozō. The Satō family's crest, a stylized hawk-wing design, is painted on the doors. (See diagram, pages 94–95.)

Satō family, Yamagata, Yamagata Prefecture

232–33. *Dozō museum*

This dozō is now the Kurashiki Archaeological Museum, but it formerly belonged to the Koyama family and was used as a place to hang dried fish.

Kurashiki, Okayama Prefecture

234. *Dozō used as guest room*

This two-story room was formerly a warehouse belonging to a wholesale sugar dealer. Unless a dozō was designed as a zashiki-gura, it had no ceiling, and the beams were exposed.

Kurashiki Inn, Kurashiki, Okayama Prefecture

235. *Dozō used as living quarters*

This dozō was formerly a storehouse for rice, but it has been modified to serve as living quarters for the grandfather of the present head of the Kusudo family.

Kurashiki, Okayama Prefecture

236–40. *Dozō art museum*

236–37. Group of dozō. These buildings were formerly storehouses for rice, but their interiors have been modified to serve as display rooms in the Ohara Museum of Art.

238. Entrance to display room. As was often the case with rice storehouses, the heavy outer doors of the dozō were omitted. Here the sliding plaster-covered door known as the "white door" is visible.

239. Namako wall and grille window. In the Kurashiki district the flat tiles of namako walls are not usually placed on the diagonal. The wall shown here is a modification made when the storehouse was converted into a museum.

240. Display room. The major changes are the replacement of the original wooden floor with a tile floor and the installation of modern lighting. The poles half sunk into the walls were to protect the walls from damage when rice sacks were stacked against them.

Ōhara Museum of Art, Kurashiki, Okayama Prefecture

241–43. *Dozō folk art museum*

241. Entrance. The building was formerly a library and storehouse for household articles.

242–43. Interior. The storehouse has been redecorated to some extent and is now used as a display room for various household articles and implements passed down over the generation in the Kusakabe family. (See diagrams, pages 86–87 and 88–89.)

Takayama, Gifu Prefecture

244. *Dozō atelier*

This residential complex formerly belonged to the Irie family of Marugame on the island of Shikoku, but the well-known sculptor Isamu Noguchi bought it and moved it to the suburbs of Takamatsu. Noguchi converted the dozō at the left into an atelier. The building with the higher roof is the main house. The Iries are descended from the samurai class, but, possibly because they lived in a small country town, the house is virtually the same in style as the houses of the tradesmen of Marugame.

Mure, Kagawa Prefecture

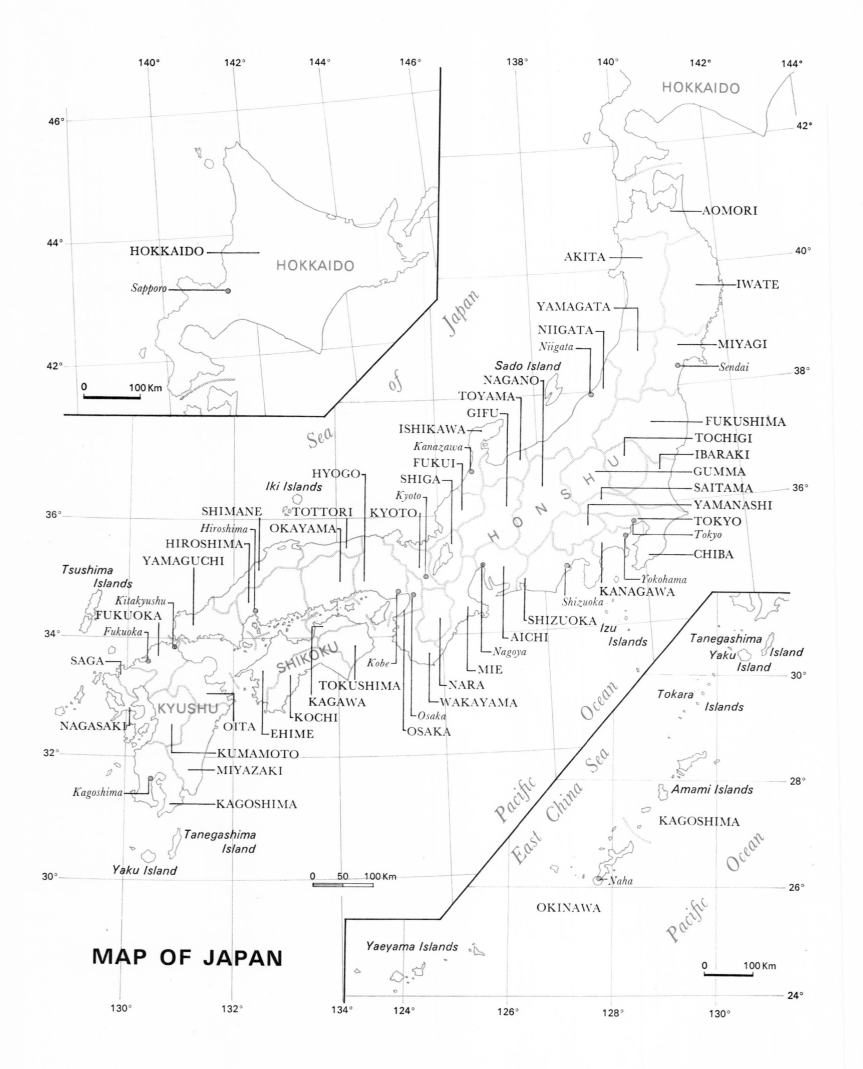

140° 142° 144° 146° 138° 140° 142° 144°

HOKKAIDO

46° 42°

44° HOKKAIDO 40°

HOKKAIDO AOMORI

AKITA

Sapporo IWATE

YAMAGATA

42° NIIGATA MIYAGI 38°

Niigata

Sado Island *Sendai*

NAGANO

TOYAMA FUKUSHIMA

GIFU TOCHIGI

ISHIKAWA IBARAKI

Kanazawa GUMMA

FUKUI SAITAMA

HYOGO SHIGA YAMANASHI 36°

Iki Islands *Kyoto* TOKYO

36° SHIMANE TOTTORI KYOTO *Tokyo*

Hiroshima OKAYAMA CHIBA

HIROSHIMA

YAMAGUCHI

Tsushima KANAGAWA

Islands *Yokohama*

Kitakyushu SHIZUOKA *Shizuoka*

FUKUOKA *Izu* *Tanegashima*

34° *Fukuoka* AICHI *Islands* *Yaku* *Island*

SAGA *Nagoya* *Tokara* 30°

Kobe MIE *Islands*

SHIKOKU

KYUSHU TOKUSHIMA NARA

KAGAWA WAKAYAMA

NAGASAKI KOCHI *Osaka* *Amami Islands* 28°

OITA EHIME OSAKA

32° KUMAMOTO KAGOSHIMA

MIYAZAKI

Kagoshima KAGOSHIMA

30° Tanegashima *Naha* 26°

Island

Yaku Island OKINAWA

Yaeyama Islands Pacific

MAP OF JAPAN Ocean

24°

130° 132° 134° 124° 126° 128° 130°

0 100 Km

0 50 100 Km

0 100 Km

HONSHU

Sea of Japan

Pacific Ocean

East China Sea

Index-Glossary

187/3000.-